HOSPITAL AND CLINICAL PHARMACY

HOSPITAL AND CLINICAL PHARMACY

Sanjive Aggarwal

ANMOL PUBLICATIONS PVT. LTD.
NEW DELHI-110 002 (INDIA)

ANMOL PUBLICATIONS PVT. LTD.
Regd. Office: 4360/4, Ansari Road, Daryaganj,
New Delhi-110002 (India)
Tel.: 23278000, 23261597, 23286875, 23255577
Fax: 91-11-23280289
Email: anmolpub@gmail.com
Visit us at: www.anmolpublications.com

Branch Office: No. 1015, Ist Main Road, BSK IIIrd Stage
IIIrd Phase, IIIrd Block, Bangalore-560 085 (India)
Tel.: 080-41723429 • Fax: 080-26723604
Email: anmolpublicationsbangalore@gmail.com

Hospital and Clinical Pharmacy

First Edition, 2010

PRINTED IN INDIA

Printed at Mehra Offset Press, Delhi.

Contents

	Preface	*vii*
1.	Anatomy and Physiology	1
2.	Skin Function	30
3.	The Process of Respiration	49
4.	The Digestive System	77
5.	First Aid and Emergency Procedures	95
6.	Soft Tissue Injuries	132
7.	Special Wounds	160
8.	Injuries	190
9.	Poisons	216
10.	Drug Abuse	235
11.	Burns	241
12.	Cold Exposure Injury	255
13.	Rescue and Transportation Procedures	275
	Index	302

Preface

Clinical pharmacy is the branch of Pharmacy where pharmacists and pharmaconomists provide patient care that optimizes the use of medication and promotes health, wellness and disease prevention. Clinical pharmacists and clinical pharmaconomists care for patients in all health care settings but the clinical pharmacy movement initially began inside hospitals and clinics. Clinical pharmacists/pharmaconomists often collaborate with physicians and other healthcare professionals.

The systems of health care, clinical pharmacists are experts in the therapeutic use of medications. They routinely provide medication therapy evaluations and recommendations to patients and other health care professionals. Clinical pharmacists are a primary source of scientifically valid information and advice regarding the safe, appropriate, and cost-effective use of medications.

Hospital pharmacies can usually be found within the premises of the hospital. Hospital pharmacies usually stock a larger range of medications, including more specialized and investigational medications (medicines that are being studied, but have not yet been approved), than would be feasible in the community setting. Hospital pharmacies typically provide medications for the hospitalized patients only, and are not retail establishments.

A more appropriate definition for clinical pharmacy is, "Clinical pharmacy is the branch of pharmacy which deals with various aspect of patient care, dispensing of drugs and advising patient on the safe and rational use of drug." In some states, clinical pharmacists are given prescriptive authority.

Author

Chapter 1

Anatomy and Physiology

Knowledge of how the human body is constructed and how it works is an important part of the training of everyone concerned with healing the sick or managing emergency conditions following injury. This chapter will provide you with a general knowledge of the structures and functions of the body. The human body is a combination of organ systems with a supporting framework of muscles and bones and an external covering of skin.

The study of the body is divided into the three following sciences: Anatomy—the study of body structures and the relation of one part to another Physiology—the study of the processes and functions of the body tissue and organs. Basically, it is the study of how the body works—how the various parts function individually and in relation to each other. Embryology—the study of the development of the body from a fertilized egg, or ovum.

TERMS OF POSITION AND DIRECTION

The planes of the body are imaginary lines dividing it into sections. They are used as reference points in locating anatomical structures. The Median, or Midsagittal, Plane divides the body into right and left halves on its vertical axis. This plane passes through the sagittal suture of the cranium; therefore, any plane parallel to it is called a Sagittal Plane. Frontal planes are drawn perpendicular to the sagittal lines and divide the body into anterior and posterior sections. Since this line passes through the coronalsuture of the cranium, frontal planes are also called coronal planes.

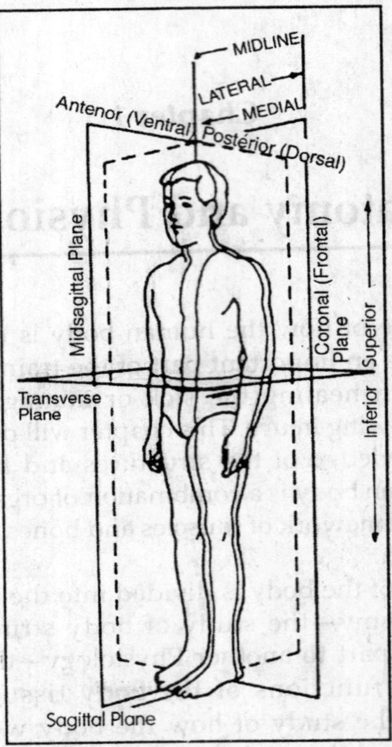

Fig. Planes of the Body.

The Horizontal or Transverse, Plane, which is drawn at right angles to both sagittal and frontal planes, divides the body into superior and inferior sections. To avoid misunderstanding in describing the location of anatomical structures, a standard body position, called the Anatomical Position, is used as a point of reference. This anatomical position is assumed when the body stands erect, with arms hanging at the sides, and palms of the hands turned forward.

Other commonly used anatomical terms include the following: Anterior or ventral—toward the front, or ventral (pertaining to the belly; abdomen), side of the body. Posterior or dorsal—toward the back, or dorsal, side of the body.

Medial—near or toward the midline of the body. Lateral—farther away from the midline of the body. Internal—inside.

External—outside. Proximal—nearer the point of origin or closer to the body. Distal—away from the point of origin or away from the body.

Superior—higher than or above. Cranial—toward the head. Caudal—toward the lower end of the body. Inferior—lower than or below. Erect—normal standing position of the body. Supine—lying position of the body, face up. Prone—lying position of the body, face down. Lateral recumbent—lying position of the body on either side. Peripheral—The outward part or surface of a structure.

CHARACTERISTICS OF LIVING MATTER

All living things, animals and plants, are Organisms that undergo chemical processes by which they sustain life and regenerate cells. The difference between them is that animals have sensations and the power of voluntary movement and require oxygen and organic food. Plants require only carbon dioxide and inorganic matter for food and have neither voluntary movement nor special sensory organs.

In man, some of the characteristic functions necessary for survival include digestion, metabolism, and homeostasis. Digestion involves the physical and chemical breakdown of the food we eat into its simplest forms. Metabolism is the process of absorption, storage, and use of these foods for body growth, maintenance, and repair.

Fiomeostasis is the body's self-regulated control of its internal environment. It allows the organism to maintain a state of constancy or equilibrium, in spite of vast changes in the external environment.

THE CELL

The smallest unit of life, the cell, is the basic structural unit of all living things and a functional unit all by itself. It is composed of a viscid, jellylike substance, called Protoplasm, upon which depend all the vital functions of nutrition, secretion, growth, circulation, reproduction, excitability, and movement. As such, protoplasm has been called "the secret of life."

A typical cell is made up of the plasma membrane, a nucleus, and the cytoplasm. The Plasma Membrane is a selectively permeable membrane surrounding the cell. In addition to holding the cell together, the membrane selectively controls the exchange of materials between the cell and its environment by physical and chemical means.

Solids and gases, such as oxygen, proteins, carbohydrates, and mineral salts, pass through the plasma membrane by a process known as Diffusion. The Nucleus is a small, dense, usually spherical body that controls the chemical reactions occurring in the cell. The substance contained in the nucleus is called Nucleoplasm.

It is also important in the cell's reproduction, since genetic information for the cell is stored there. Every human cell contains 46 chromosomes, and each chromosome has thousands of genes that determine the cell's function.

The Cytoplasm is a water-to-gelatinous substance surrounding the nucleus and is contained by the plasma membrane. The cytoplasm is all of the cell protoplasm except the nucleus.

The simplest living organism consists of a single cell. The amoeba is a unicellular animal. The single cell of such a one-celled organism must be able to carry on all processes necessary for life. This cell is called a Simple or Undifferentiated Cell. In multicellular organisms, cells vary in size, shape, and number of nuclei.

When stained, the various cell structures can be more readily recognized under a microscope. Other differences such as the number and type of cells can be seen with the aid of a microscope. Many cells are highly specialized. Specialized Cells perform special functions, such as muscle, which contracts, or epithelial cells of the skin, which protect.

TISSUES

Tissues are groups of specialized cells similar in structure and function. They are classified into five main groups: epithelial, connective, muscular, liquid, and nervous.

- *Epithelial*: The lining tissue of the body is called

epitheliums. It forms the outer covering of the body known as the free surface of the skin. It also forms the lining of the digestive, respiratory, and urinary tracts; blood and lymph vessels; serous cavities; and tubules of certain secretory glands, such as the liver and kidneys. This tissue has little intercellular fluid and may be further subdivided into three types:

- *Columnar*: The chief functions of this tissue are to secrete digestive fluids and absorb digested foods and fluids. It consists of long narrow cells set close together,resemb-ling a palisade-type fence. In certain areas, such as the nostrils, bronchial tubes, and trachea, this tissue has a crown of microscopic hairlike processes known as cilia. These cilia provide motion to move secretions and other matter along the surfaces from which they extend. They also act as a barrier, preventing foreign matter from entering these cavities.
- *Squamous:* This is the main protective tissue of the body. It is composed of thin platelike or scalelike cells forming a mosaic pattern. This tissue is found in the tympanic membrane (eardrum) as a single layer of cells or in the free skin surface in multiple layers.

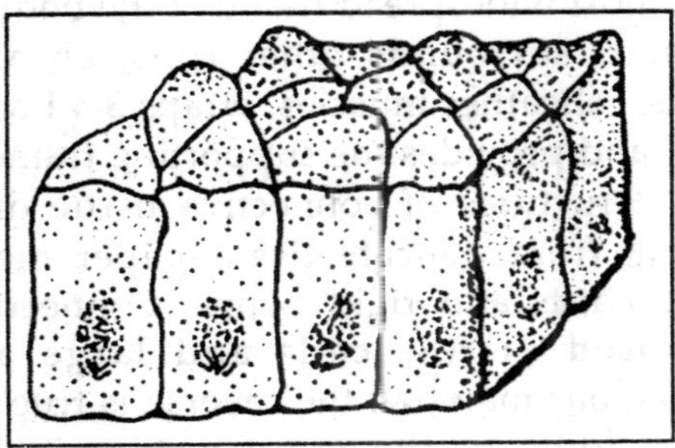

Fig. Columnar Epithelial Tissue

- *Cuboidal:* This is both a secretory and protective tissue whose cells are cubical. It is found in the more highly specialized organs of the body, such as the ovary and the kidney.

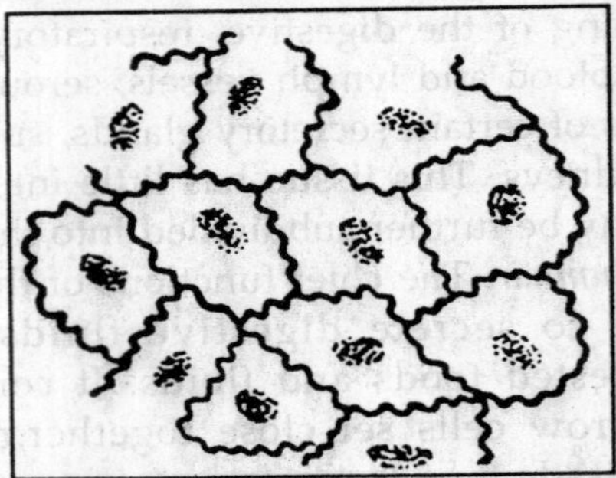

Fig. Squamous Epithelial Tissue

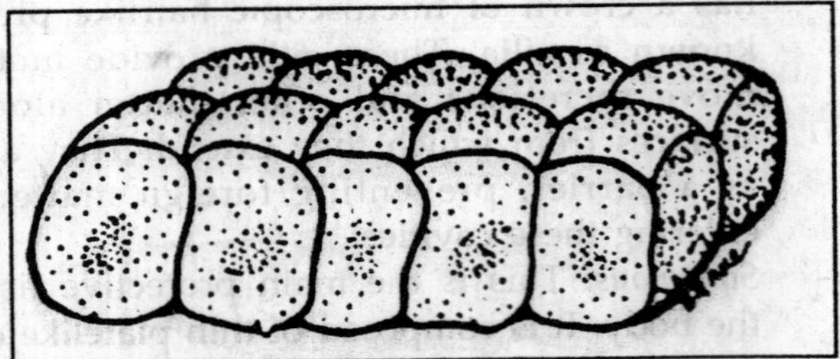

Fig. Cuboidal Epithelial Tissue.

- *Connective:* This is the supporting tissue of the various structures of the body. It has many variations and is the most widespread tissue of the body. It is highly vascular, surrounds other cells, encases internal organs, sheathes muscles, wraps 3-4 bones, encloses joints, and provides the supporting framework of the body. Structures of connective tissue differ widely, ranging from delicate tissue-paper membranes to strong cords and rigid bones. Connective tissue is composed of few cells and large amounts of intracellular material; the reverse is true of epithelial tissue. Some of the more predominant types of connective tissues are:
  - *Areolar*: This tissue connects the various tissues of the organs. It is continuous throughout the

body. Nerves, blood, and lymph vessels are found in this tissue.

Fig. Areolar Connective Tissue.

- *Adipose*: This tissue is generally called "fatty tissue." It acts as a reservoir for energy-producing foods; helps to reduce body heat loss because of its poor heat conductivity; and serves as support for various organs and fragile structures, such as the kidneys, blood vessels, and nerves.
- *Osseous*: This type is a dense fibrous connective tissue that forms tendons, ligaments, cartilage, and bone. These tissues form the supporting framework of the body.

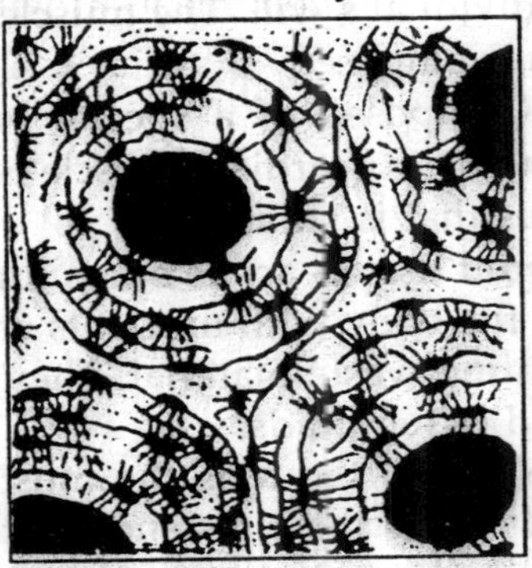

Fig. Osseous (Bone) Tissue.

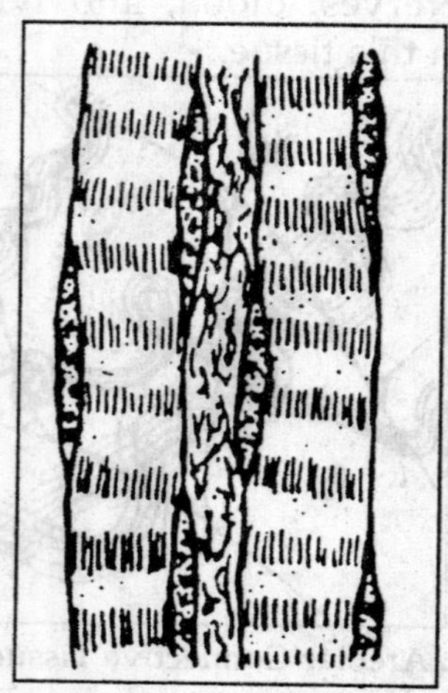

Fig. Striated (Voluntary) Muscle.

- *Muscular:* Muscular tissue provides for all body movement. There are two types, voluntary and involuntary.
  - Voluntary muscle fibers are striated, or striped, and are under the control of the individual's will. Muscles that attach to bone are voluntary muscles.
  - Involuntary muscle fibers are smooth, or nonstriated, and are not under the control of the individual's will. The muscles of the stomach are an example.

    Note: Composed of a special branched type of cell, the heart (cardiac) muscle is an involuntary muscles that is striated.
- *Liquid:* Liquid tissues act as a medium for supplying the body with nutrients and as a vehicle for eliminating waste material. They form the blood, lymph, and tissue fluids.
- *Nervous*: Nervous tissue is the most complex tissue in the body. It is the substance of the brain, spinal cord, and nerves. Nervous tissue requires more oxygen and nutrients than any other body tissue.

Fig. Non-striated (Involuntary) Muscle.

Fig. Cardiac Muscle

The basic cell of the nervous tissue is the neuron. This highly specialized cell receives stimuli from, and conducts impulses to, all parts of the body.

Organs

As a group of similar cells form tissues, similar tissues form organs such as the heart, liver, and kidneys. These organs are grouped together to form systems, such as the urinary system that is composed of the kidneys, ureters, bladder, and urethra.

The Skeletal System

The skeleton is the bony framework of the body, composed of 206 bones. It supports and gives shape to the body; protects vital organs; and provides sites of attachment for tendons, muscles, and ligaments.

The skeletal bones are joined members that make muscle movement possible.

ANATOMY OF BONES

Osteology is the study of the structure of bone. Bone is made up of inorganic mineral salts, calcium and phosphorus being the most prevalent, and an organic substance called ossein.

When human bone is soaked in dilute acid until all inorganic mineral salts are washed out, all that remains is a flexible piece of tissue that can easily be bent and twisted.

The inorganic mineral salts give bone its strength and hardness. Bone consists of a hard outer shell, called compact tissue, and an inner spongy, porous portion, called cancellous tissue. In the centre of the bone is the Medullary Canal, which contains marrow.

There are two types of marrow, red and yellow. Yellow marrow is ordinary bone marrow in which fat cells predominate. It is found in the medullary canals and cancellous tissue of long bones. Red marrow is one of the manufacturing centers of red blood cells and is found in the articular ends of long bones and in cancellous tissue.

At the ends of the long bones is a smooth, glossy tissue that forms the joint surfaces. This tissue is called articular cartilage because it articulates (joins) with, fits into, or moves in contact with similar surfaces of other bones.

The thin outer membrane surrounding the bone is called the Periosteum.

An important function of the periosteum is to supply nourishment to the bone. Capillaries and blood vessels run through the periosteum and dip into the bone surface, supplying it with blood and nourishment. The periosteum is the pain centre of the bone.

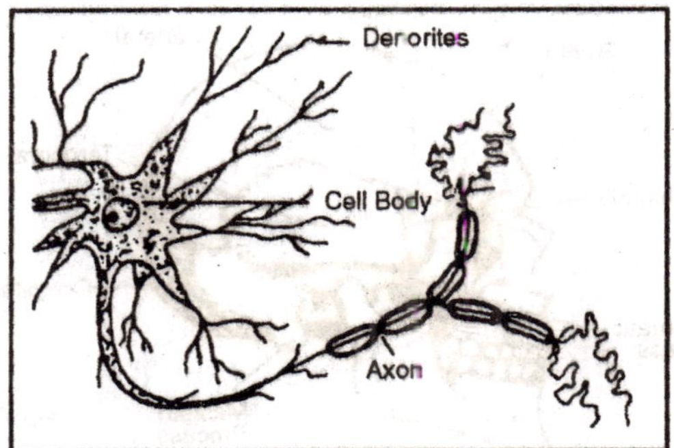

Fig. Neuron

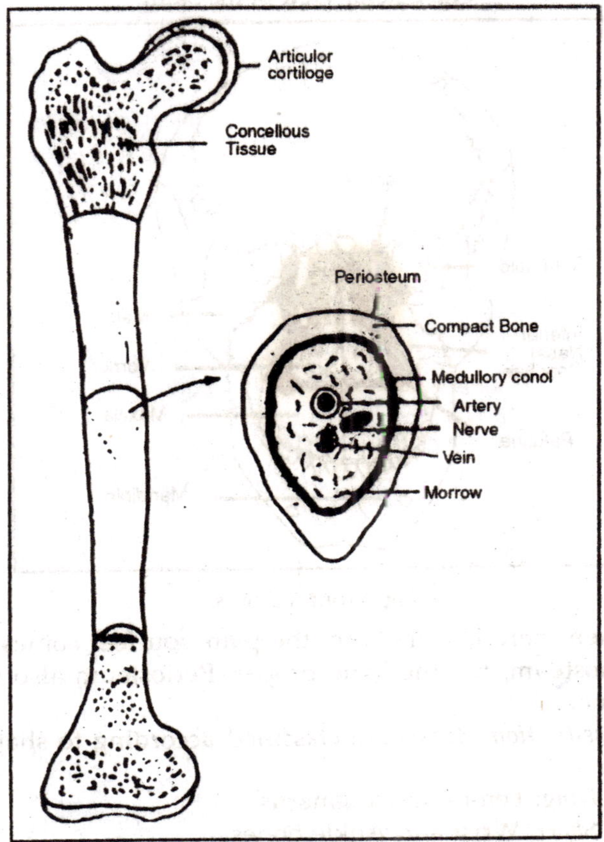

Fig. Structure of a Typical Long Bone.

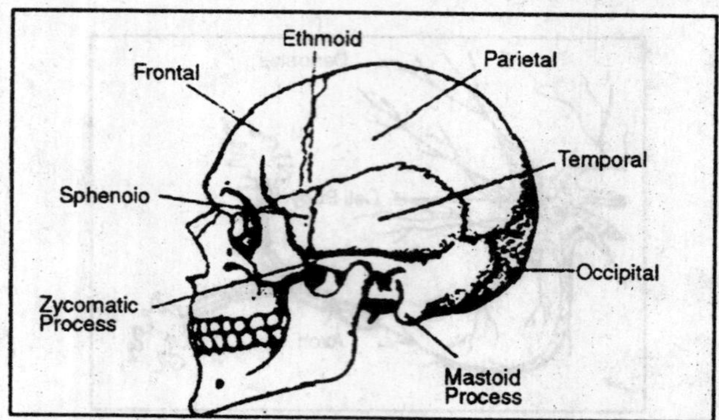

Fig. Lateral View of the Skull

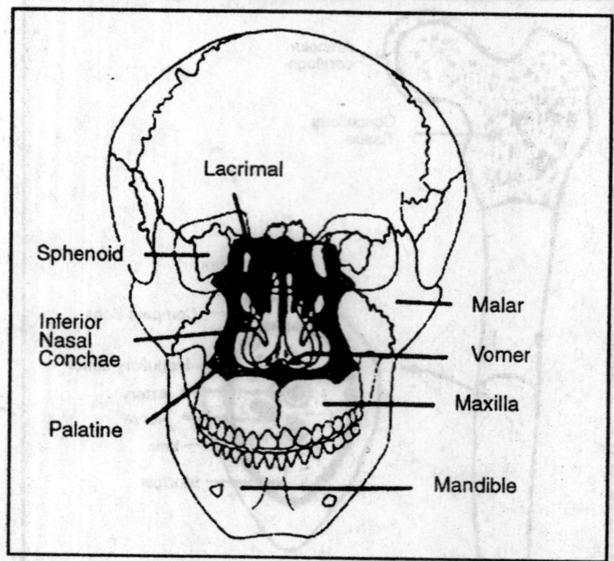

Fig. Frontal Bones.

When there is a fracture, the pain you feel comes from the periosteum, not the bone proper. Periosteum also forms new bone.

Classification: Bones are classified according to shape, as follows:

- *Long*: Femur and Humerus
- *Short*: Wrist and Ankle bones

- *Flat*: Skull, sternum, and scapula
- *Irregular*: Vertebrae, mandible, hyoid, and pelvic bones

DIVISIONS OF SKELETON

The human skeleton is divided into two main divisions, the axial skeleton and the appendicular skeleton. The axial skeleton consists of the skull,. the vertebral column, and the thorax.

The skull bones are further divided into the cranial and facial bones. The appendicular skeleton consists of the bones of the upper and lower extremities.

Axial Skeleton

Skull

Consists of 28 bones, 22 of which form the framework of the head and provide protection for the brain, eyes, and ears; six are ear bones. With the exception of the lower jaw bone (mandible) and the ear bones, all skull bones are joined together and fixed in one position. The seams where they join are known as sutures.

- *Cranial Bones*: The cranium is formed by eight cranial bones, six of which are essential to know. The Frontal Bone, which forms the forehead, contains the frontal sinuses and helps form the eye socket and nasal cavity. The two Parietal Bones form the roof of the skull. The two Temporal Bones, which help form the sides and base of the skull, also house the auditory, or hearing organs. The Occipital Bone forms part of the base and back of the skull and contains a large hole, called the Foramen Magnum. This opening permits passage of the spinal cord from the cranium into the spinal column.
- *Facial Bones:* The two form the upper jaw, nasal walls, and part of the eye socket. These bones contain large cavities called maxillary sinuses. Frequently these sinuses become infected, causing the individual much discomfort. The lower jaw is called the Mandible.

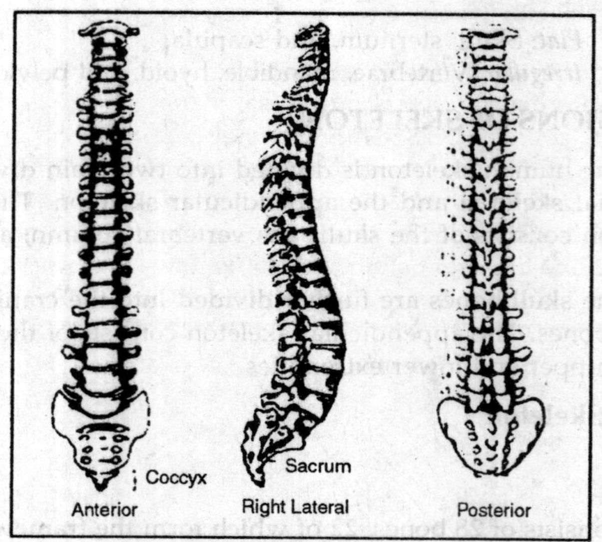

Fig. Vertebral Column.

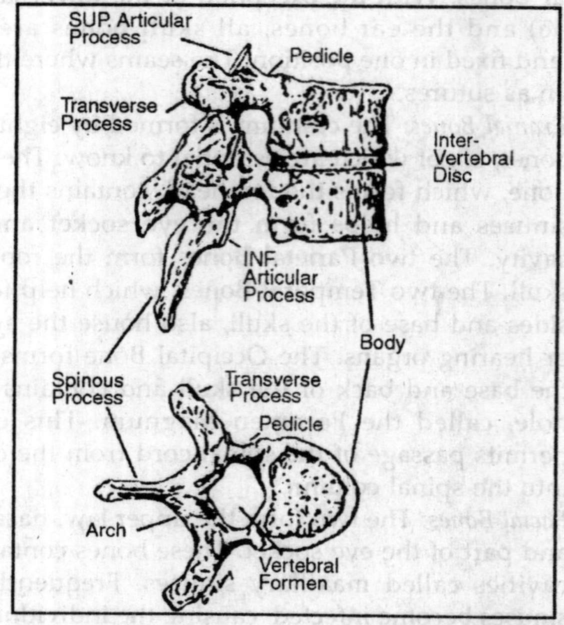

Fig. Vertebra Structure.

Its main function is mastication. Other bones of the face are the Lacrimal and Nasal Bones.

Vertebral (Spinal) Column

It consists of 24 movable or true vertebrae, the sacrum, and the coccyx, or tail bone. The spinal column is divided into five regions in the following order: cervical (neck), thoracic (chest), lumbar (lower back), and sacral and coccygeal (pelvis). The vertebrae protect the spinal cord and the nerves arising from the spinal cord. Each vertebra has an anterior portion, the body, which is the large solid segment of the bone.

This body is for support, not only for the spinal cord, but for other structures of the body as well. Many of the main muscles are attached to the vertebrae. The vertebral foramen is a hole directly behind the body of the vertebrae and forms the passage for the spinal cord. The vertebral projections are for the attachments of muscles and ligaments and to facilitate movement of one vertebra over the fusion of five false vertebrae.

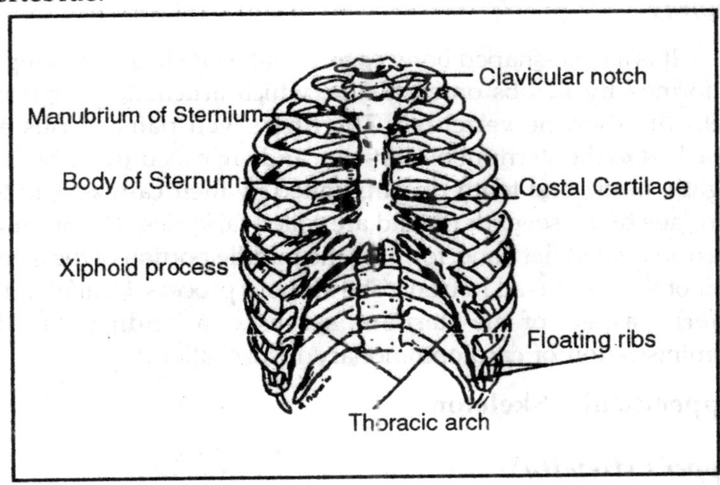

Fig. Thorax, Anterior View

It articulates on another. There are seven cervical vertebrae in the neck. The first is called the Atlas and resembles a bony ring. It supports the head. The second is the highly specialized Axis. It has a bony prominence that fits into the ring of the atlas, thus permitting the head to rotate from side to side. The atlas and the axis are the only named vertebrae, all others are numbered. Each cervical vertebrae has a transverse foramen to allow passage of nerves, the vertebral artery, and a vein.

The seventh cervical vertebra has an especially prominent projection that can easily be felt at the nape of the neck. This makes it possible for physicians to count and identify the vertebrae above and below it. There are 12 vertebrae in the thoracic region.

These articulate with the posterior portion of the 12 ribs to form the posterior wall of the thoracic, or chest, cage. There are five lumbar vertebrae, which are the largest segments of the vertebral column. The Sacrum is the triangular bone immediately below the lumbar vertebrae, formed by each side with the hip bone and with the Coccyx to form the posterior wall of the Pelvis.

Thorax

It is a cone-shaped bony cage, about as wide as it is deep. It is formed by 12 ribs on each side, which articulate posteriorly with the thoracic vertebrae. The first seven pairs of ribs are attached to the sternum by cartilage and are called true ribs. The eighth, ninth, and tenth ribs are united by their cartilages to the cartilage of the seventh rib and are called false ribs. The Sternum is an elongated flat bone, forming the middle portion of the upper half of the chest wall in front. The xiphoid process, located at the inferior aspect of the sternum, serves as a landmark in the administration of cardiopulmonary resuscitation.

Appendicular Skeleton

Upper Extremity

The upper extremity consists of the shoulder, the arm, the forearm, the wrist, and the hand .

The specific bones that form the framework for the upper extremity are:

Clavicle	Collarbone	2
Scapula	Shoulder blade	2
Humerus	Arm bone	2
Radius and ulna	Forearm bones	4
Carpals	Wrist bones	16
Metacarpal	Bones of the palm	10
Phalanges	Finger bones	28

The Clavicle forms the front part of the shoulder girdle. It lies nearly horizontally just above the first rib and is shaped like a flat letter S. The clavicle is a thin brace bone that fractures easily. Its inner end is round and attached to the sternum; its outer end is flattened and fixed to the scapula.

The Scapula is a triangular bone that lies in the upper part of the back on both sides, between the second and seventh ribs, forming the posterior portion of the shoulder girdle. Its lateral corner forms part of the shoulder joint, articulating with the humerus.

The Humerus is the longest bone of the upper extremity and is often called the arm bone. It articulates with the shoulder girdle to for-m the shoulder joint and with the bones of the forearm to form the elbow. Its anatomical portions include a head, a rounded portion that fits into a recess of the scapula called the glenoid fossa; the greater and lesser tuberosities, which are enlargements of the superior end; the surgical neck, a slight narrowing distal to the tuberosities and a frequent site of fractures; the shaft, which is the main part of the humerus; and the distal end, which includes the prominences called epicondyles and the surfaces that articulate with the bones of the forearm.

When the arm is in the anatomical position with the palm turned forward, the Radius is on the lateral, or thumb, side and the Ulna is on the medial, or little finger, side of the forearm. When the hand is pronated (palm turned downward), the bones rotate on each other and cross in the middle. This makes it possible to turn the wrist and hand as in opening doors.

The ulna and the radius articulate at their proximal ends with the humerus, at their distal ends with some of the carpal bones, and with each other at both ends. There are eight Carpal bones, arranged in two rows, forming the wrist. The Metacarpal bones are numbered one to five corresponding with the five fingers, or digits, with which they articulate. The fingers are named as follows: 1st thumb; 2nd index; 3rd middle; 4th ring; and 5th little.

The small bones of the fingers are called Phalanges, and each one of these bones is called a Phalanx. Each finger has three phalanges, except the thumb which has two. The phalanges are named for their anatomical posi'ion proximal phalanx is the bone closest to the hand; the distal phalanx is the bone at the end of the finger; and the middle phalanx, the bone located between the proximal and distal phalanges.

Lower Extremity

The lower extremity includes the bones of the hip, thigh, leg, ankle, and foot.

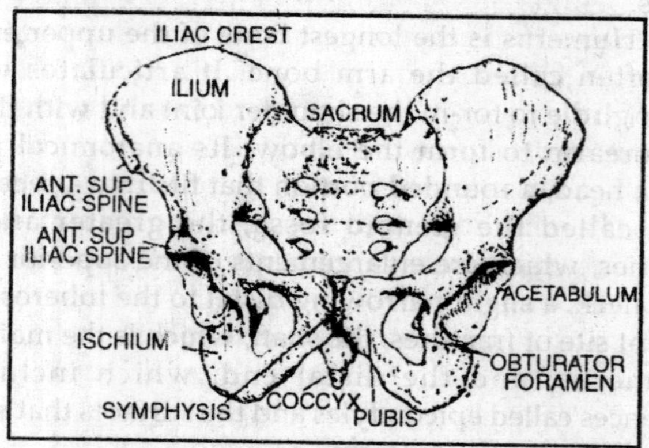

Fig. Pelvic Girdle.

The hip, or Innominate, is a large irregularly shaped bone composed of three parts: the ilium, ischium, and pubis. In children these three parts are separate bones, but in adults they are firmly united to form a cuplike structure, called the Acetabulum, into which the head of the femur fits.

The Ilium forms the outer prominence of the hip bone

(crest of the ilium), the Ischium forms the hard lower part, and the Pubis forms the front part of the pelvis. The area where the two pubic bones meet is called the Symphysis Pubis and is often used in anatomical measurements.

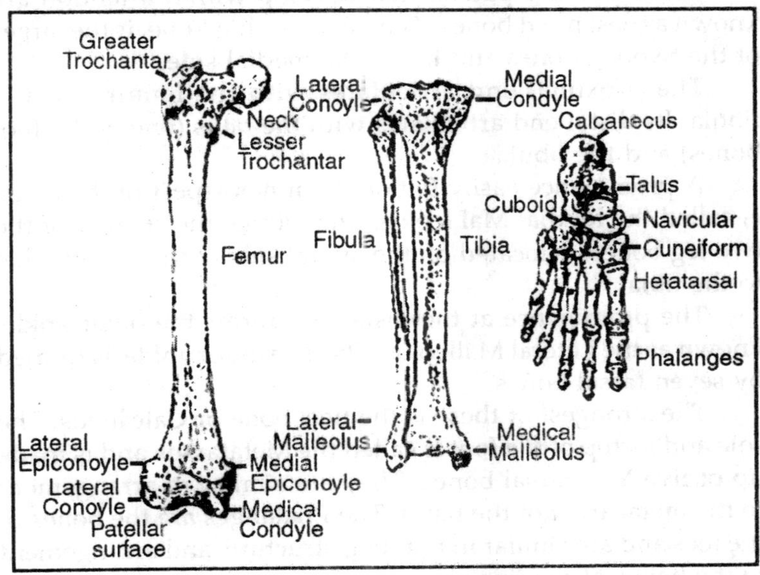

Fig. Bones of the Lower Extremity.

The largest foramen (opening) is located in the hip bone, between the ischium and the pubis, and is called the Obturator Foramen. The crest of the ilium is used in making anatomical and surgical measurements (e.g., location of the appendix, which is approximately halfway between the crest of the ilium and the umbilicus). The Femur, or thigh bone, is the longest bone in the body.

The proximal end is rounded and has a head supported by a constricted neck that fits into the acetabulum. Two processes called the Greater and Lesser Trochanters are at the proximal end for the attachment of muscles. The neck of the femur, located between the head and the trochanters, is the site most frequently fractured. At the distal end are two bony prominences called the Lateral and Medial Condyles, which articulate with the tibia and the patella.

The Patella is a small oval-shaped bone overlying the knee joint. It is enclosed within the tendon of the quadriceps muscle of the thigh.

Bones like the patella that develop within a tendon are known as Sesamoid bones. The Tibia, or shin bone, is the larger of the two leg bones and lies at the medial side.

The proximal end articulates with the femur and the fibula. Its distal end articulates with the talus (one of the foot bones) and the fibula.

A prominence easily felt on the inner aspect of the ankle is called the Medial Mal.leolus. The Fibula, the smaller of the two leg bones, is located on the lateral side of the leg, parallel to the tibia.

The prominence at the distal end forms the outer ankle, known as the Lateral Malleolus. The Tarsus, or ankle, is formed by seven tarsal bones.

The strongest of these is the heel bone or Calcaneus. The sole and instep of the foot is called the Metatarsus and is made up of five Metatarsal bones. They are similar in arrangement to the metacarpal of the hand. The Phalanges are the bones of the toes and are similar in number, structure, and arrangement to the bones of the fingers.

JOINTS

Whenever two bones are attached to each other, a joint is formed. In a freely movable joint, such as the knee or elbow joint, the ends of the bones are covered with a smooth layer of cartilage.

The whole joint is enclosed in a watertight sac or membrane containing a small amount of lubricating fluid. This enables the joint to work with little friction.

The ligaments that reach across the joints from one bone to another keep them from getting out of place. When ligaments are accidentally torn, we call the injury a sprain; when bones are out of place, there is a dislocation; and when bones are chipped or broken, the injury is called a fracture. Joints are classified according to the amount of movement they permit. They may be:

- *Immovable*: Bones of the skull are rigidly interlocked along immovable joint lines known as sutures.

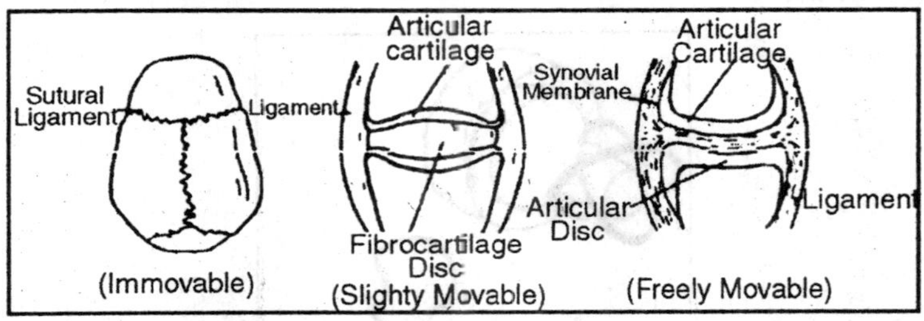

Fig. Typical Joints

- *Slightly Movable*: In these joints the bones are held together by broad flattened disks of cartilage and ligaments (e.g., vertebrae and symphysis pubis).
- *Freely Movable*: Such joints include the knee, hip, and shoulder. These joints are further subdivided into:
- – *Hinge Joints*: Elbow, finger, and knee Ball-and-*Socket*
- – *Joints* : Shoulder and hip

JOINT MOVEMENTS

Joint movements are generally divided into four types:Gliding is the simplest type of motion. It is one surface moving over another without any rotary or angular motion. This motion exists between two contiguous or adjacent surfaces.

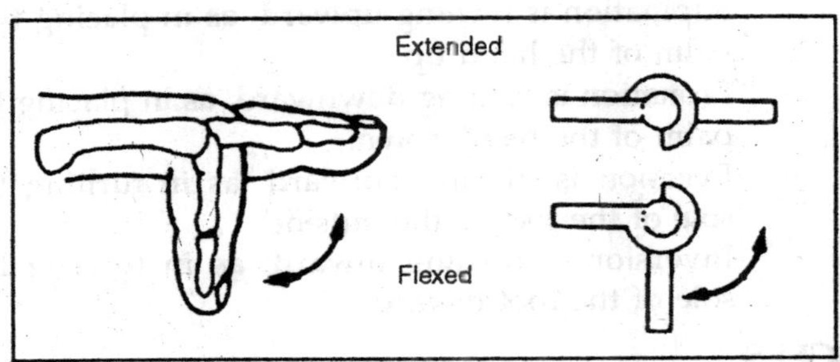

Fig. Inge Joint.

Angular motion decreases or increases the angle between

two adjoining bones. The more common types of angular motion are:

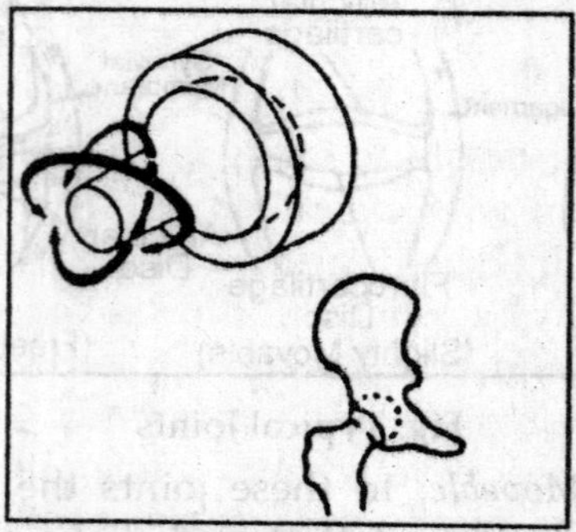

Fig. Ball-and-soCket Joint.

- *Flexion*: Bending the arm or leg.
- *Extension*: Straightening or unbending, as in straightening the forearm, leg, or fingers.
- *Abduction*: Moving an extremity away from the body.
- *Adduction*: Bringing an extremity toward the body.
  - Rotation is a movement in which the bone moves around a central point without being displaced, such as turning the head from side to side.
  - Circumduction is movement of the hips and shoulders. Other types of movement generally used to indicate specific anatomical positions include the following:
  - Supination is turning upward, as in placing the palm of the hand up.
  - Pronation is turning downward, as in placing the palm of the hand down.
  - Eversion is turning outward, as in turning the sole of the foot to the outside.
  - Inversion is turning inward, as in turning the sole of the foot inward.

MUSCLES

Muscles make up about one-half of the total body weight. Their main functions are threefold:

- Providing movement, including internal functions such as peristalsis in the intestines.
- Maintaining body posture through muscle tone, as in the muscles of the head, neck and shoulders, which keep the head up.
- Providing heat through chemical changes that take place during muscle activity, such as mild exercise that warms the body on cold days. addition, muscles are involved in such essential bodily functions as respiration, bloodcirculation, digestion, and even such functions as speaking and seeing.

At one end of some muscles are long white Tendons that attach the muscles to bone. The point of fixed attachment of a muscle to bone is called the Origin. The more flexible attachments, especially to a movable bone, is termed the Insertion. Muscle tissue has a highly developed ability to contraet.

Contractibility enables a muscle to become shorter or thicker, and this ability, along with interaction with other muscles, produces movement in internal and external body parts. Muscle contraction in a tissue or organ produces motion and provides power and speed for body activity. A contracting muscle is referred to as a Prime Mover. A muscle that is relaxing while a prime mover is contracting is called the Antagonist.

Muscular tone, or Tonicity, is a continual state of partial contraction that gives muscles a certain firmness. Isometric muscle contraction occurs when the muscle is stimulated and shortens, but no movement occurs, as when a person tenses his or her muscles against an immovable object. Muscles are also capable of stretching when force is applied (Extensibility) and regaining their original form when that force is removed (Elasticity). All types of muscles respond to stimulus. This property is called Excitability or Irritability.

The mechanical muscular action of shortening or thickening is activated by a stimulus sent through a motor nerve. All muscles are linked to nerve fibers that carry messages from the central nervous system. The chemical action of muscle fibers consists of two stages, Contraction and Recovery. In the contraction stage, two protein substances (actin and myosin) react to provide energy through the breakdown of glycogen into lactic acid. In the recovery stage, oxygen reacts with lactic acid to release carbon dioxide and water.

When a muscle contracts, it produces chemical waste products (carbon dioxide, lactic acid, and acid phosphate), which make the muscle more irritable. If contraction is continued, the muscle will finally cramp up and refuse to move. This condition is known as fatigue. If it is carried too far, the muscle cells will not recover and permanent damage will result.

Muscles, therefore, need rest to allow the blood to carry away the waste materials and bring in fresh glucose, oxygen, and protein to restore the muscle protoplasm and the energy that was used. The importance of exercise for normal muscle activity is clear, but excessive muscle strain is damaging. For example, if a gasoline motor stands idle, it eventually becomes rusty and useless. Similarly, a muscle cell that does not work becomes weak and flabby. On the other hand, a motor that is never allowed to stop and is forced to run too fast or to do too much heavy work soon wears out so that it cannot be repaired.

In the same way, a muscle cell that is forced to work too hard without proper rest will be damaged beyond repair. Violent exercise is never good. Exercise should be adapted to the individual and should never be carried to the point of extreme fatigue.

During exercise, massage, or ordinary activities, the blood supply of muscles is increased. This brings in fresh nutritional material, carries away waste products more rapidly, and enables the muscles to build up and restore their efficiency and tone.

When a muscle dies, it becomes solid and rigid and no longer reacts. This stiffening, which occurs from 10 minutes to several hours after death, is called Rigor Mortis. Muscles seldom act alone; they usually work in muscle groups held together by sheets of a white fibrous tissue call Fascia. There are three types of muscle tissue: skeletal, smooth, and cardiac. Each is designed to perform a specific function. Skeletal Muscles are attached to the bones and give shape to the body.

They are responsible for allowing body movement. This type of muscle is sometimes referred to as Striated because of the striped appearance of the muscle fibers under a microscope. They are also called Voluntary muscles because they are under the control of our conscious will.

These muscles can develop great power. Smooth, or Nonstriated, muscle tissues are found in the walls of the stomach, intestines, urinary bladder, and blood vessels, as well as in the duct glands and in the skin.

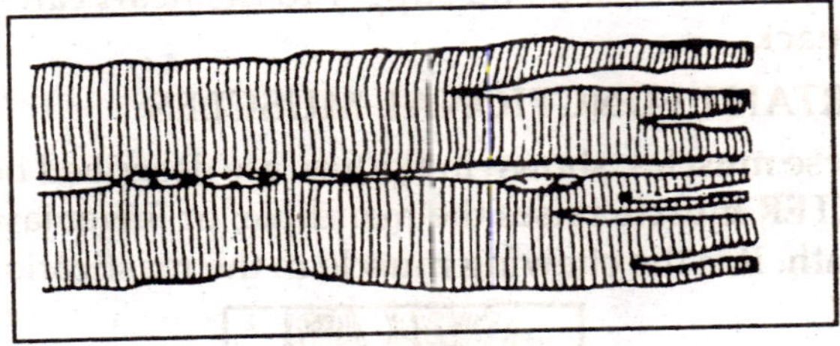

Fig. Striated Muscle Fibers

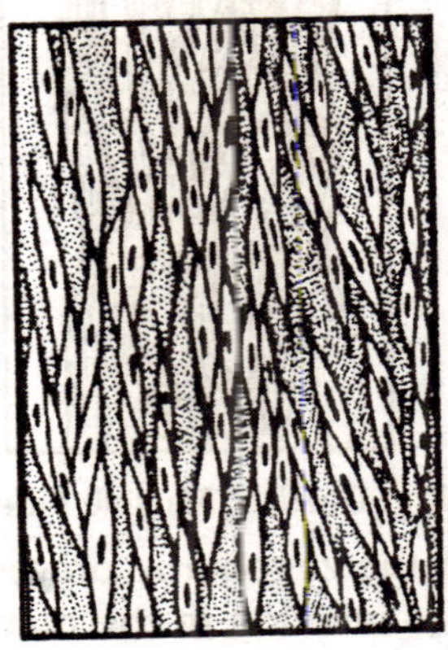

Fig. Smooth Muscle Fibers.

Under a microscope, the smooth muscle fibre lacks the striped appearance of other muscle tissue. This tissue is also called Involuntary muscle because it is not under conscious control. The Cardiac Muscle tissue forms the bulk of the walls and septa (partitions) of the heart, as well as the origins of the great blood vessels.

The fibers of the cardiac muscle differ from those of the skeletal and smooth muscles in that they are shorter and branch into a complicated network.

The cardiac muscle has the most abundant blood supply of any muscle in the body, receiving twice the blood flow of the highly vascular skeletal muscles and far more than the smooth muscles. Cardiac muscles contract to pump blood out of the heart and through the cardiovascular system. Interference with the blood supply to the heart can result in a heart attack.

IMPORTANT FUNCTIONAL MUSCLES

These muscles, shown in figures, are described below. The MASSETER muscle raises the mandible, or lower jaw, to close the mouth. It is the chewing muscle in the mastication of food.

Fig. Cardiac Muscle Fibers.

It originates in the zygomatic process and adjacent parts of the maxilla and is inserted in the mandible. The Temporal muscle assists the masseter and draws the mandible backward. It has its origin in the temporal fossa and is inserted in the coronoid process of the mandible. The Sternoclei-domastoid muscles are located on both sides of the neck. Acting individually, these muscles rotate the head left or right.

Acting together, they bend the head forward toward the chest. The sternocleidomastoid muscle originates in the sternum and clavicle and is inserted in the mastoid process of the temporal bone. This muscle is commonly affected in cases of stiff neck.

The Trapezius muscles are a broad, trapezium-shaped pair of muscles on the upper back, which raise or lower the shoulders. They cover approximately one-third of the back. They originate in a large area, which includes the 12 thoracic vertebrae, the seventh cervical vertebra, and the occipital bone. They have their insertion in the clavicle and scapula.

The Latissimus Dorsi is a broad flat muscle that covers approximately one-third of the back on each side. It rotates the arm inward and draws the arm down and back. It originates from the upper thoracic vertebrae to the sacrum and the posterior portion of the crest of the ilium. Its fibers converge to form a flat tendon that has its insertion in the humerus.

The Pectoralis Major is the large triangular muscle that forms the prominent chest muscle. It rotates the arm inward, pulls a raised arm down toward the chest, and draws the arm across the chest. It originates in the clavicle, sternum, and cartilages of the true ribs, and the external oblique muscle. Its insertion is in the greater tubercle of the humerus.

The Diaphragm is an internal muscle that forms the floor of the thoracic cavity and the ceiling of the abdominal cavity. It is the primary muscle of respiration, modifying the size of the thorax and abdomen vertically. It has three openings for the passage of nerves and blood vessels.

The Deltoid muscle raises the arm and has its origin in the clavicle and the spine of the scapula. Its insertion is on the lateral side of the humerus. It fits like a cap over the shoulder and is a frequent site of intramuscular injections. The Biceps Brachii is the prominent muscle on the anterior surface of the upper arm.

Its origin is in the outer edge of the glenoid cavity and its insertion in the tuberosity of the radius. This muscle rotates the forearm outward (supination) and, with the aid of the brachial muscle, flexes the forearm at the elbow.

The Triceps Brachii is the primary extensor of the forearm

(the antagonist of the biceps brachii). It originates at two points on the humerus and one on the scapula. These three heads join to form the large muscle on the posterior surface of the upper arm. The point of insertion is the olecranon process of the ulna.

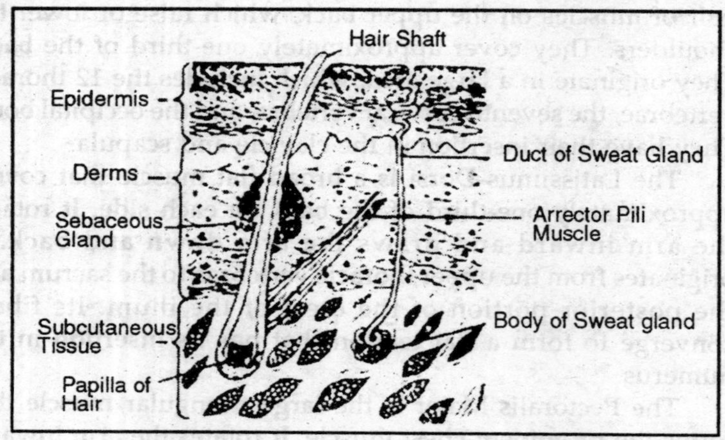

Fig. The Skin.

The Gluteals (Maximus, Minimus, and Medius) are the large muscles of the buttocks, which extend and laterally rotate the thigh, as well as abduct and medially rotate it. They arise from the ilium, the posterior surface of the lower sacrum, and the side of the coccyx. Their points of insertion include the greater trochanter and the gluteal tuberosity of the femur. The gluteus maximus is the site of choice for massive intramuscular injections.

The Quadriceps is a group of four muscles that make up the anterior portion of the thigh. The rectus femoris originates at the ilium; the vastus femoris, v. lateralis, and v. intermedius originate along the femur. All four are inserted into the tuberosity of the tibia through a tendon passing over the knee joint. The quadriceps serves as a strong extensor of the leg at the knee and flexes the thigh.

The Sartorius is the longest muscle in the body. It extends diagonally across the front of the thigh from its origin at the ilium, down to its insertion near the tuberosity of the tibia. Its function is to flex the thigh and rotate it laterally, and to flex the leg and rotate it slightly medially.

The Gracilis is a long slender muscle located on the inner aspect of the thigh. It adducts the thigh and flexes and medially rotates the leg. Its origin is in the symphysis pubis, and its insertion is in the medial surface of the tibia, below the condyle.

The Biceps Femoris (often called the hamstring muscle) originates at the tuberosity of the ischium and the middle third of the femur. It is inserted on the head of the fibula and the lateral condyle of the tibia. It acts, along with other related muscles, to flex the leg at the knee and to extend the thigh at the hip joint.

The Gastrocnemius and Soleus (calf muscles) extend the foot at the ankle. The gastrocnemius originates at two points on the femur; the soleus originates at the head of the fibula and the medial border of the tibia. Both are inserted in a common tendon called the calcaneus, or Achilles tendon.

The Tibialis Anterior originates at the upper half of the tibia and inserts at the first metatarsal and cuneiform bones. It flexes the foot.

The Integumentary System

The skin, or integument, is the outer covering of the body. It consists of two layers, the epidermis and the dermis, and supporting structures and appendages.

Chapter 2

Skin Function

The skin covers almost every visible part of the human body. Even the hair and nails are outgrowths from it. It protects the underlying structures from injury, drying, and invasion by foreign organisms; it contains the peripheral endings of many sensory nerves; and it has limited excretory and absorbing powers. It also plays an important part in regulating body temperature. In addition, the skin is a waterproof covering that prevents excessive water loss, even in very dry climates.

SKIN STRUCTURE

The Epidermis is the outer skin layer. It is made up of tough, flat, scalelike epithelial cells. Four different sublayers of epidermal cells have been identified.

The uppermost is called the horny layer (stratum corneum). It is composed of scaly dead cells that form a protective surface and are gradually sloughed off naturally or by irritation (e.g., sunburn) or abrasion. This scaly layer, if unbroken, can block the passage of almost every known type of germ; however, its protective powers are reduced if the skin is not cleansed regularly.

Two middle layers of cells may be present in a particular area of skin, depending on its thickness (the soles of the feet are the thickest skin, the eyelids the thinnest). In the innermost sublayer, the stratum germinativum, new epidermal cells are constantly being produced to replace the sloughed off cells. These newly formed cells push the older cells outward. As they approach the surface, they become drier or more scalelike.

Because of this constant activity of the deeper cells of the epidermis, any injury of the outer layer of the skin is repaired in a few days without leaving a scar.

Skin pigment, called melanin, which is responsible for skin colour, is found here in this deepest sublayer. The colour and quantity of the melanin are the chief factors in determining one's complexion. The pigment can be darkened by exposure to the ultraviolet rays of the sun (tanning). Freckles are patches of melanin.

The DERMIS, or true skin, lies below the epidermis and gradually blends into the deeper tissues. It is a wide area of connective tissue that contains blood vessels, hair follicles, nerve endings, smooth muscles, and sweat and oil glands. The blood vessels of the dermis can dilate to contain a significant portion of the body's blood supply. This ability, along with the actions of the sweat glands, forms the body's primary temperature regulating mechanism.

The constriction or dilation of these blood vessels also affects blood pressure and the volume of blood available to the internal organs. The skin contains nerve endings that carry impulses to and from the central nervous system. The nerves are distributed to the smooth muscles in the walls of the arteries in the dermis and to the smooth muscles around the sweat glands and hair roots.

Through these nerves, messages about the external environment are carried to the brain. Smooth involuntary muscles are found in the dermis. They are responsible for controlling the skin surface area. When dilated, these muscles allow for maximum skin surface exposure to aid heat loss. When constricted, the skin surface exposure is decreased, thus impeding heat radiation. Repeated muscle contractions (shivering) are also a rapid means of generating body heat.

SKIN APPENDAGES

The appendages of the skin are the nails, hairs, sebaceous glands, sweat glands, and ceruminous glands. The Nails are composed of horny epidermal scales and are found on the dorsal surfaces of the fingers and toes. They protect the many sensitive nerve endings at the ends of these digits. New formation of nail will occur in the epitheliums of the nail bed. As new nail is formed, the whole nail moves forward, becoming longer.

Hair is an epithelial structure found on almost every part of the surface of the body. Its colour depends on the type of melanin present. The hair has two components: the root below the surface and the shaft projecting above the skin.

The root is embedded in a pitlike depression called the hair follicle. Hair grows as a result of the division of the cells of the root. A small muscle, the arrector, fastens to the side of the follicle and is responsible for the gooseflesh appearance of the skin as a reaction to cold or fear. Each hair follicle is associated with two or more sebaceous (oil) glands. Sebaceous Glands are found in most parts of the skin except in the soles of the feet and the palms of the hand.

Their ducts open most frequently into the hair follicles and secrete an oily substance that lubricates the skin and hair, keeping them soft and pliable and preventing bacterial invasion. Sweat Glands are found in almost every part of the skin. They are control mechanisms to reduce the body's heat by evaporation of water from its surface.

The perspiration secreted is a combination of water, salts, fatty acids, and urea. Normally, about one liter of this fluid is excreted daily. However, the amount varies with atmospheric temperature and humidity and the amount of exercise taken.

When the outside temperature is high, or upon exercise, the glands secrete excessive amounts to cool the body through evaporation. When evaporation cannot handle all the sweat that has been excreted, the sweat collects in beads on the surface of the skin. Ceruminous Glands are modified sweat glands found only in the auditory canal. They secrete a yellow, waxy substance called cerumen that protects the eardrum.

CIRCULATORY SYSTEM

The circulatory system, also called the Vascular System, consists of the heart, blood vessels, and lymphatic system. It is the primary fuel supplier of the body. The transportation media is the blood. This system is a closed circuit. At no place does it have access to other tissues of the body except at the capillaries.

Osmosis, the transfer of fluids through the plasma membrane from an area of lower concentration of particles to an area of higher concentration, is the method of feeding body tissues and eliminating waste materials. This occurs in the capillaries, the smallest of the blood vessels.

BLOOD

Blood is fluid tissue composed of formed elements (cells) suspended in plasma. It is pumped by the heart through miles of arteries, capillaries, and veins to all parts of the body. Total blood volume of the average adult is 5 to 6 liters.

Plasma is the liquid part of blood; the whole blood minus cells. Plasma constitutes 50 to 60 per cent of whole blood. It is a clear, slightly alkaline, straw-colored liquid consisting of about 92 per cent water. The remainder is made up mainly of proteins. One of these, fibrinogen, contributes to coagulation. Blood Serum is a clear, pale yellow liquid.

It is the liquid portion of blood after coagulation. Plasma and serum differ in that plasma is whole blood minus the cells, and serum is plasma minus the clotting elements. Red blood cells (RBCs), or Erythrocytes, are small, biconcave, nonnucleated disks, formed in the red bone marrow. Blood of the average man contains 5 million red cells per cubic millimeter.

Women have fewer red cells, 4.5 million per cubic millimeter. Emotional stress, strenuous exercise, high altitudes, and some diseases may cause an increase in the number of RBCs. During the development of the red blood cell, a substance called hemoglobin is combined with it.

Hemoglobin is the key of the red cell's ability to carry oxygen and carbon dioxide. Thus the main function of erythrocytes is the transportation of respiratory gases. The red cells deliver oxygen to the body tissues, holding some oxygen in reserve for an emergency. Carbon dioxide is picked up by the same cells and discharged via the lungs. The colour of the red blood cell is determined by the hemoglobin content. Bright red, or arterial, blood is due to the combination of oxygen and hemoglobin. Dark red, or venous, blood is the result of hemoglobin combining with carbon dioxide. A red blood cell will live only about 100 to 120 days in the body. There are several reasons for its short life span.

This delicate cell has to withstand constant knocking around as it is pumped into the arteries by the heart. It travels through blood vessels at high speed, bumps into other cells, bounces off the walls of arteries and veins, and squeezes through narrow passages. It must adjust to continual pressure changes. Fragments of red blood cells are found in the spleen and other body tissues.

The spleen is the "graveyard" where old, worn out cells are removed from the blood stream. White blood cells (WBCs), or Leukocytes, are almost colorless, nucleated cells originating in the bone marrow and in certain lyrnphoid tissues of the body. There is only one white cell to every 600 red cells. Normal WBC count is 6,000 to 8,000 per cubic millimeter, although the number of white cells maybe 15,000 to 20,000 or higher during infection. Leukocytes are important for the protection of the body against disease.

Their AMEBOID movement permits them to leave the blood stream through the capillary wall and to attack pathogenic bacteria. They can travel anywhere in the body and are often named "the wandering cells." They protect the body tissues by engulfing disease-bearing bacteria and foreign matter, a process called phagocytosis.

When white cells are undermanned, more are produced, causing an increase in their number and a condition known as leukocytosis. Another way they protect the body from disease is by the production of bacteriolysins that dissolve the foreign bacteria. The secondary function of WBCS is to aid in blood clotting.

Blood platelets, or Thrombocytes, are round bodies in the blood that contain no nucleus, only cytoplasm. They are smaller than red blood cells and average about 250,000 per cubic millimeter of blood. They play an important role in the process of blood coagulation, clumping together in the presence of jagged, torn tissue. Blood Coagulation To protect the body from excessive blood loss, blood has its own power to coagulate, or clot. If blood constituents and linings of vessels are normal, circulating blood will not clot. Once blood escapes from its vessels, however, a chemical reaction begins that causes it to become solid.

The clot formed is at first fluid but soon becomes thick and then sets into a soft jelly that quickly becomes firm enough to act as a plug. This plug is the result of a swift, sure mechanism that changes one of the soluble blood proteins, fibrinogen, into an insoluble protein, fibrin, whenever injury occurs.

Other necessary elements for blood clotting are calcium salts, a substance called prothrombin, which is formed in the liver, blood platelets, and various factors necessary for the completion of the successive steps in the coagulation process. Once the fibrin plug is formed, it quickly enmeshes red and white blood cells and draws them tightly together.

Blood serum, a yellowish clear liquid, is squeezed out of the clot as the mass shrinks. Formation of the clot closes the wound, preventing blood loss. A clot also serves as a network for the growth of new tissues in the process of healing. Normal clotting time is 3 to 5 minutes, but if any of the substances necessary for clotting are absent, severe bleeding will occur.

Hemophilia is an inherited disease characterized by delayed clotting of the blood and consequent difficulty in controlling hemorrhage. Hemophiliacs may bleed to death as a result of even a trivial wound.

THE HEART

The heart is a hollow, muscular organ, somewhat larger than the closed fist, located anteriorly in the chest and to the left of the midline. It is shaped like a cone, its base directed upward and to the right, the apex down and to the left. Lying obliquely in the chest, much of the base of the heart is immediately posterior to the sternum.

The heart is enclosed in a membranous sac, the

Pericardium. The smooth surfaces of the heart and pericardium are lubricated by a serous secretion, the pericardial fluid. The inner surface of the heart is lined with a delicate serous membrane, the Endocardium, similar to and continuous with that of the inner lining of blood vessels. The interior of the heart is divided into two parts by a wall called the Interventricular Septum.

In each half is an Upper chamber, the Atrium, which receives blood from the veins, and a lower chamber, the Ventricle, which receives blood from the atrium and pumps it out into the arteries.

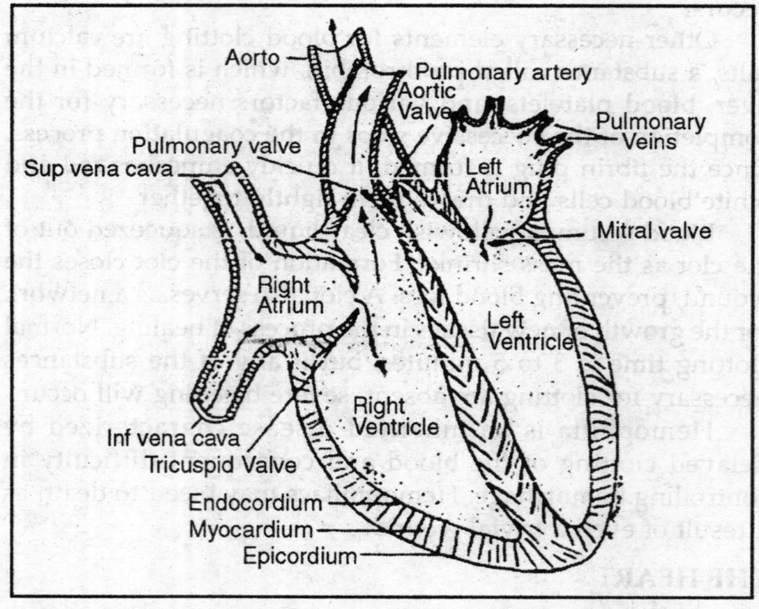

Fig. Diagram of the Heart.

The openings between the chambers on each side of the heart are separated by flaps of tissue that act as valves to prevent backward flow of the continuously forward moving column of blood. The one on the right has three flaps, or cusps, and is called the Tricuspid Valve. The one on the left has two flaps and is called the Mitral, or bicuspid, valve. The outlets of the ventricles are supplied with similar valves. On the right the pulmonary valve is at the origin of the pulmonary artery, and on the left the aortic valve is at the origin of the aorta. Physiologically, the heart acts as four interrelated pumps.

The right atrium receives deoxygenated blood from the body via the superior and inferior vena cavae. It pumps this blood through the tricuspid valve to the right ventricle. The right ventricle pumps the blood past the pulmonary valve through the pulmonary artery to the lungs for oxygenation. The left atrium receives the oxygenated blood from the lungs through four pulmonary veins and pumps it to the left ventricle past the mitral valve.

The left ventricle pumps the blood to all areas of the body via the aortic valve and the aorta. The heart muscle, the Myocardium, is striated like the skeletal muscles of the body, but involuntary in action, like the smooth muscles. The walls of the atria are thin with relatively little muscle fibre because the blood flows from the atria to the ventricles under low pressure.

However, the walls of the ventricles, which comprise the bulk of the heart, are thick and muscular. The wall of the left ventricle is considerably thicker than that of the right, because more force is required to pump the blood into the peripheral systemic circulation than into the lungs located only a short distance from the heart. The heart acts by contraction and relaxation.

It contracts with a wringing motion, forcing blood into the arteries. Each contraction is followed by limited relaxation or dilation. Cardiac muscle never completely relaxes, it always maintains a degree of tone. Contraction of the heart is called Systole and the period of work. Relaxation of the heart with limited dilation is called Diastole and the period of rest.

A complete Cardiac Cycle is the time from onset of one contraction, or heart beat, to the onset of the next. The contractions of the heart are stimulated and maintained by the Sinoatrial Node, commonly called the Pacemaker of the heart, which is a group of hundreds of cells in the upper part of the right atrium that sets off electrical impulses, causing both atria to contract simultaneously. The normal heart rate, or number of contractions, is about 72 beats per minute. The Blood Pressure is the pressure the blood exerts on the walls of the arteries. The highest pressure is called Systolic pressure, because it is caused when the heart is in systole, or contraction. A certain amount of blood pressure is maintained in the arteries even when the heart is relaxed.

This is the Diastolic pressure, because it is present during diastole, or relaxation of the heart.

Normal blood pressure can vary considerably with age, weight, and general condition of the individual. For young adults the systolic pressure is between 120 and 150 mm of mercury, and the diastolic pressure is between 70 and 90 mm of mercury. Women have a lower blood pressure than men. The difference between systolic and diastolic pressure is known as Pulse Pressure.

BLOOD VESSELS

The blood vessels of the body fall into three distinct classifications:

- *Distributors*: Arteries and arterioles
- *Exchangers*: Capillaries
- *Collectors*: Veins and venules

The Arteries are elastic tubes constructed to withstand high pressure. They carry blood away from the heart to all parts of the body. The smallest branches of the arteries are called arterioles.

The Aorta is the large tubelike structure arising from the left ventricle of the heart. It arches upward over the left lung and then down along the spinal column through the thorax and the abdomen, where it divides to send arteries down both legs.

The Coronary Arteries are branches of what is generally called the ascending aorta, and they supply the heart with blood. There are certain branches of the aorta with which you should be familiar, since these often must be compressed to control hemorrhage. You will find a discussion of pressure points in the hemorrhage section of the chapter in this manual entitled "First Aid and Emergency Procedures."

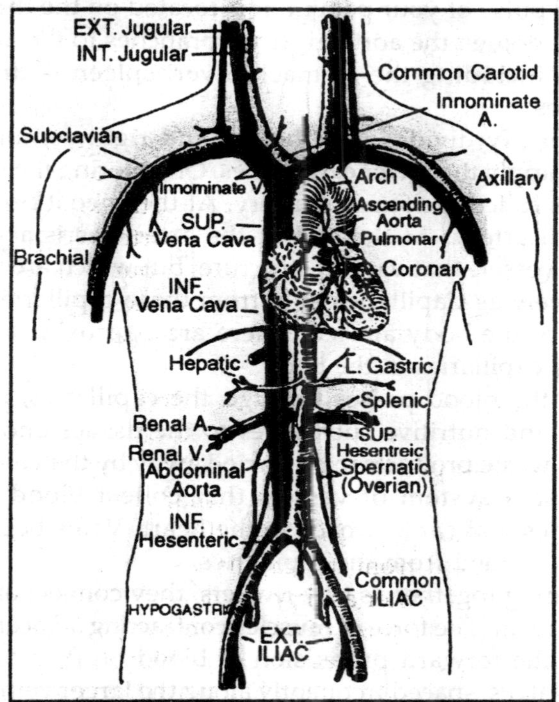

Fig. Arteries and Veins of the Torso.

Three large arteries arise from the aorta as it which supplies the left side of the head. The third arches over the left lung. First is the innominate branch from the arch of the aorta is the left artery, which divides into the right subclavian subclavian, which supplies the left arm. artery to supply the right arm, and the right common carotid to supply the right side of the head. The carotids divide into internal and external The second branch is the left common carotid, branches, the external supplying the muscle and skin of the face and the internal supplying the brain and the eyes.

The subclavian arteries are so named because they run underneath the clavicle. They supply the upper extremity, branching off to the back, chest, neck, and brain through the spinal column. The large artery going to the arm is called the axillary. It divides into the ulnar and radial arteries.

The radial artery is the one at the wrist that you feel to take the pulse of your patient. It is located on the thumb side. In the abdomen the aorta gives off branches to the abdominal viscera, including the stomach, liver, spleen, kidneys, and intestines.

It finally divides into the left and right common iliacs, which supply the lower extremities. On entering the thigh, this artery is called the femoral artery. At the knee it becomes the popliteal artery. At the end of the arterioles is a system of minute vessels that vary in structure, but which are spoken of collectively as Capillaries. It is from these capillaries that the tissues of the body are fed. There are approximately 60,000 miles of capillaries in the body.

As the blood passes through the capillaries, it releases oxygen and nutritive substances to the tissues and takes up various waste products to be carried away by the veins. VEINS comprise a system of vessels that collect blood from the capillaries and carry it back to the heart. Veins begin as tiny venules formed from the capillaries.

Joining together as tiny rivulets, they connect and form a small stream. The force of muscles contracting adjacent to veins aids in the forward propulsion of blood on its return to the heart. Valves, spaced frequently along the larger veins, prevent the backflow of blood.

BLOOD COLLECTION SYSTEM (VENOUS CIRCULATION)

Since arterial blood arises at the heart, we trace arteries from the heart. To return blood to the heart, we trace veins from the small venules back through larger veins. There are three principal venous systems in the body: the pulmonary, portal, and systemic.

The Pulmonary System comprises four vessels, two from each lung, which empty into the left atrium. These are the only veins in the body that carry freshly oxygenated blood.

The Portal System consists of the veins that drain venous blood from the abdominal part of the digestive tract (except the lower rectum), spleen, pancreas, and gallbladder and deliver it to the liver. There it is distributed by a set of venous capillaries.

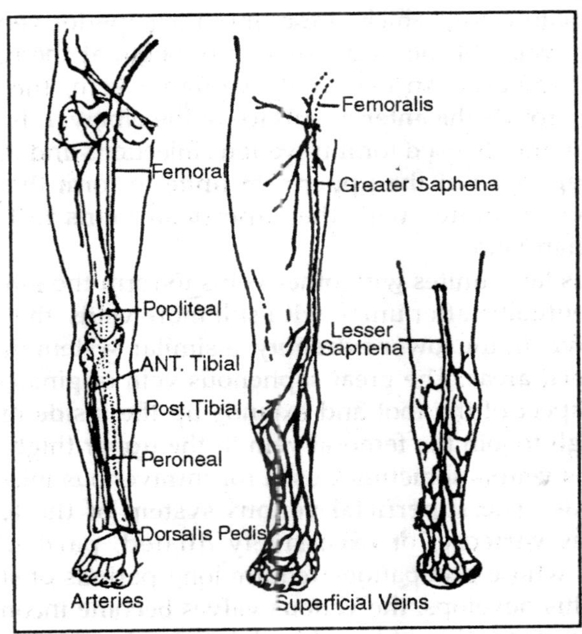

Fig. Arteries and Veins of the Lower Extremity.

The blood in the portal system conveys absorbed substances from the intestinal tract to the liver for storage, alteration, or detoxification. From the liver the blood flows through the hepatic vein to the inferior vena cava.

The Systemic System is divided into the deep and superficial veins. The superficial veins lie immediately under the skin, draining the skin and superficial structures. The deep veins, usually located in the muscle or deeper layers, drain the large muscle masses and various other organs. They usually lie close to the large arteries that supply the various organs of the body and usually have the same name as the artery they accompany.

The superficial veins of the head unite to form the external jugular veins. They drain blood from the scalp, face, and neck, and finally empty into the subclavian veins. The veins draining the brain and internal facial structures are the internal jugular veins. These combine with the subclavian veins to form the innominate veins, which empty into the superior vena cava.

The veins of the upper extremity begin at the hand and extend upward. An extremely valuable vein, the median cubital, crosses the anterior surface of the elbow. It is the vein most commonly used for intravenous injections and infusions. The deep veins of the upper arm unite to form the axillary vein, which unites with the superficial veins to form the subclavian vein.

This later unites with other veins to form the innominate and eventually, after union with still more veins, the superior vena cava. In the lower extremity, a similar system drains the superficial areas. The great saphenous vein originates on the inner aspect of the foot and extends up the inside of the leg and thigh to join the femoral vein in the upper thigh.

This vein is sometimes used for intravenous injections at the ankle. The superficial venous system of the leg often becomes varicose, or excessively dilated, particularly in persons whose occupations require long periods of standing. When this develops, the venous valves become incompetent, allowing stagnation of blood in the dependent extremity.

Under these circumstances varicose ulcers frequently develop. Ligation at several points along the system will force the venous return into the deep venous system and restore normal venous circulation. The veins from the lower extremities unite to form the femoral vein in the thigh, which becomes the external iliac vein in the groin. Higher in this region, it unites with the hypogastric vein from the lower pelvic region to form the common iliac vein.

The two common iliac veins unite to form the inferior vena cava. The veins from the abdominal organs, with the exception of those of the portal system, empty directly or indirectly into the inferior vena cava, while those of the thoracic region eventually empty into the superior vena cava.

LYMPHATIC SYSTEM

All tissue cells of the body are continuously bathed in

interstitial fluid. This fluid is formed by leakage of blood plasma through minute pores of the capillaries. There is a continual interchange of fluids of the blood and tissue spaces with a free interchange of nutrients and other dissolved substances. Most of the tissue fluid returns to the circulation by means of venous capillaries, which feed into larger veins. Large protein molecules that have escaped from the arterial capillaries cannot reenter the circulation through the small pores of the venous capillaries.

However, these large molecules, as well as white blood cells, dead cells, bacterial debris, infected substances, and larger particulate matter, can pass through the larger pores of the lymphatic capillaries and thus enter the lymphatic circulation with the remainder of the tissue fluid.

Lymph

Lymph usually is clear, but following ingestion of a fatty meal the lymph contained in the lymphatic that drain the small intestine appears milky because of the fat globules that have been absorbed. This milky lymph is called Chyle.

Lymph Vessels

Lymph vessels and lymph nodes form a network throughout the body. Capillaries, like veins collect lymph from the tissue spaces and, by means of a system in which small vessels unite to form larger ones, carry it toward the heart, As the lymph vessels increase in size, the walls become stronger until they are composed of three layers, like blood vessels.

Along the path of the larger lymphatic are valves that prevent backflow of lymph. Lymphatic channels from the upper half of the right side of the body converge to form the right lymphatic duct, which empties into the right subclavian vein. Drainage from the remainder of the body is by way of the thoracic duct, which empties into the left subclavian vein.

Lymph Nodes

Lymph nodes, which are frequently called glands but are

not true glands, are small beanshaped bodies of lymphatic tissue found in groups of two to fifteen along the course of the lymph vessels. They usually occur singly just beneath the skin.

Nodes vary in size and act as filters to remove bacteria and particles from the lymph stream. Lymph nodes also participate in the manufacture of white blood cells and thus in the immunity functions of the body.

THE RESPIRATORY SYSTEM

Respiration (breathing) is the exchange of oxygen and carbon dioxide between the atmosphere and the cells of the body. There are two phases of respiration:

- Physical, or mechanical, respiration involves the motion of the diaphragm and rib cage. The musculoskeletal action, which resembles that of a bellows, causes air to be inhaled or exhaled.
- Physiological respiration involves an exchange of gases, oxygen and carbon dioxide, at two points in the body. The first is the transfer that occurs in the lungs between the incoming oxygen and the carbon dioxide present in the capillaries of the lungs (external respiration). The second transfer occurs when the oxygen brought into the body replaces the carbon dioxide build up in the cellular tissue (internal respiration).

Normally, oxygen and carbon dioxide exchange in equal volumes; however, certain physiological conditions may throw this balance off. For example, heavy smokers will find that the ability of their lungs to exchange gases is impaired, leading to shortness of breath and fatigue during even slight physical exertion.

This is the direct result of their inability to draw a sufficient amount of oxygen into the body to replace the carbon dioxide build-up and sustain further muscular exertion. On the other side, hyperventilation brings too much oxygen into the body, overloading the system with oxygen and depleting the carbon dioxide needed for balance.

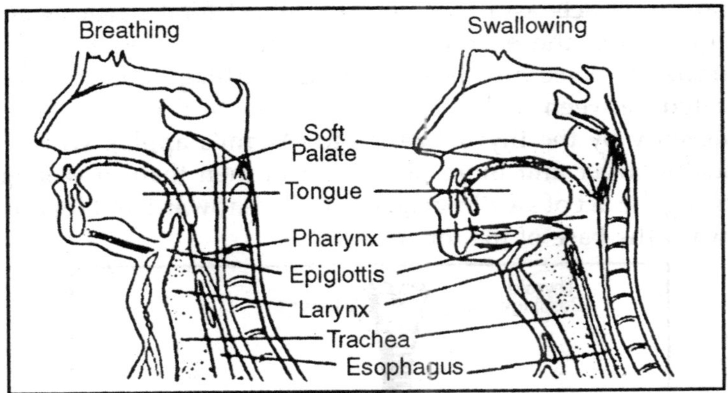

Fig.Commonalities of the upper Respiratory and Digestive Systems.

ANATOMY OF THE RESPIRATORY SYSTEM

Air enters the nasal chambers and the mouth, then passes through the pharynx, larynx, and bronchi into the bronchioles, which form a network around the alveolar air sacs in the lungs. Air enters the Nasal Cavity through the nostrils (Nares). Lining the nasal passages are hairs, which together with the mucous membrane, entrap and filter out dust and other minute particles that could irritate the lungs.

Incoming air is warmed and moistened in the chambers of the nasal cavity to prevent damage to the lungs. The mouth and nose serve as auxiliary respiratory structures. The Pharynx, or throat, serves both the respiratory and digestive systems and aids in speech. It has a mucous membrane lining that traps microscopic particles in the air and aids in adjusting temperature and humidifying inspired air.

The pharynx connects with the mouth and nasal chambers posteriorly. According to its location, it is referred to as:Nasopharynx—posterior to the nasal chambers Oropharynx—posterior to the mouth Laryngopharynx—posterior to the pharynx.

The Epiglottis is a lidlike, cartilaginous structure that covers the entrance to the larynx and separates it from the pharynx. It acts as a trap door to deflect food particles and liquids from the entrance to the larynx and trachea. The Larynx, or voice box, is a triangular cartilaginous structure located between the tongue and the trachea. It is protected anteriorly by the thyroid cartilage (Adam's apple), which is usually larger and more prominent in men than in women. During the act of swallowing, it is pulled upward and forward toward the base of the tongue.

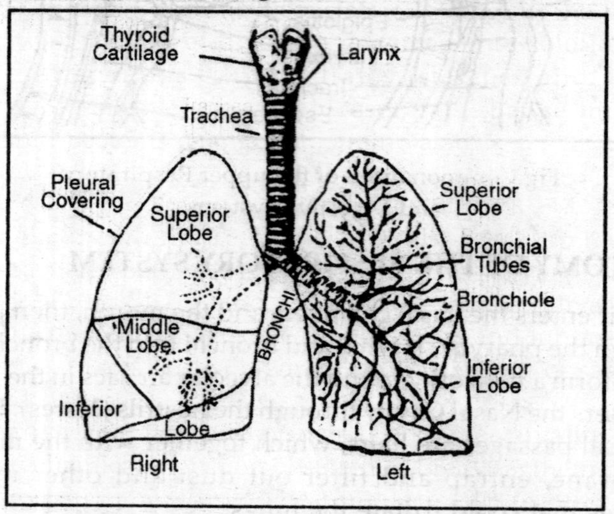

Fig. The Lung and Air Passages

The larynx is responsible for the production of voice. This is accomplished by the passing of air over the vocal cords. The ensuing vibrations can be controlled to produce the sounds of speech or singing. The nose, mouth, throat, bone sinuses, and chest serve as resonating chambers to further refine and individualize the voice.

The Trachea, or windpipe, begins at the lower end of the larynx and terminates by dividing into the right and left bronchi. It is a long tube composed of 16 to 20 C-shaped cartilaginous rings, embedded in a fibrous membrane, that support its walls, preventing their collapse. The trachea has a ciliated mucous membrane lining that entraps dust and foreign material. It also propels secretions and exudates from the lungs to the pharynx, where they can be expectorated. The Bronchi are the terminal branches of the trachea, which carry air to each lung and further divide into the bronchioles. The Bronchioles are much smaller than the bronchi and lack supporting rings of cartilage. They terminate at the alveoli. The Alveoli are thin, microscopic air sacs within the lungs. They are in direct contact with the pulmonary capillaries. It is here that fresh oxygen exchanges with carbon dioxide by means of a diffusion process through the alveolar and capillary cell walls.

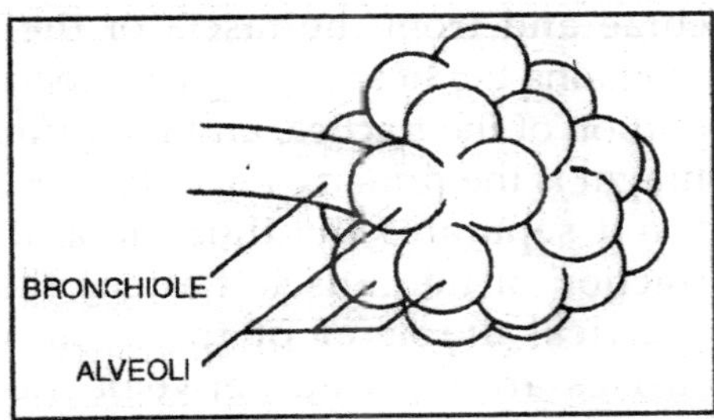

Fig. Bronchiole and aLVeoli.

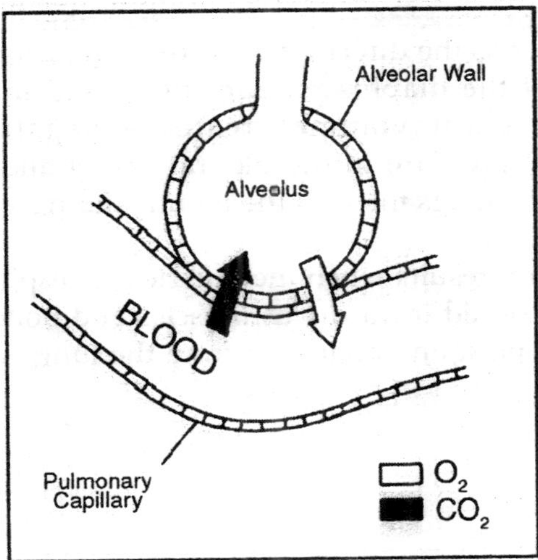

Fig. Pulmonary Exchange at Alveoli.

The Lungs are cone-shaped organs that lie in the thoracic

cavity. Each lung contains thousands of alveoli with their capillaries. The right lung is larger that the left and is divided into superior, middle, and inferior lobes. The left lung has two lobes, the superior and the inferior. The Pleurae are airtight membranes that cover the outer surface of the lungs and line the chest wall.

They secrete a serous fluid that prevents friction during movements of respiration. Pleurisy is a painful inflammation of the pleural lining. The Mediastinum is the interpleural space between the two lungs. It extends from the sternum to the thoracic vertebrae and from the fascia of the neck to the diaphragm. It contains the heart, the great blood vessels, the esophagus, a portion of the trachea, and the primary bronchi.

The Diaphragm is the primary muscle of respiration. It is dome-shaped and separates the thoracic and abdominal cavities. Contraction of the muscle flattens the dome and expands the vertical diameter of the chest cavity. The Intercostal Muscles are situated between the ribs. Their contraction pulls the ribs upward and outward, resulting in an increase in the transverse diameter of the chest (chest expansion).

Inhalation is the direct result of the expansion caused by the action of the diaphragm and intercostal muscles. The increase in chest volume creates a negative (below atmospheric) pressure in the pleural cavity and lungs. Air rushes into the lungs through the mouth and nose to equalize the pressure.

Exhalation results when the muscles of respiration relax. Pressure is exerted inwardly as muscles and bones return to their normal position, forcing air from the lungs.

Chapter 3

The Process of Respiration

The rhythmical movements of breathing are controlled by the respiratory centre in the brain. Nerves from the brain pass down through the neck to the chest wall and diaphragm. The nerve to the diaphragm is called the phrenic nerve; the nerve to the larynx is the vagus nerve; and those to the muscles between the ribs are the intercostal nerves.

The respiratory centre is stimulated by chemical changes in the blood, especially if it becomes acidic. When too much carbon dioxide accumulates in the blood stream, the respiratory centre signals the lungs to breathe faster to get rid of the carbon dioxide. The respiratory centre can also be stimulated or depressed by a signal from the brain. For example, changes in one's emotional state can alter respiration through laughter, crying, emotional shock, or panic. The muscles of respiration normally act automatically, with normal respiration being 14 to 18 cycles per minute.

The lungs, when filled to capacity, hold about 6,500 ml of air, but only 500 ml of air is exchanged with each normal respiration. This exchanged air is called Tidal Air. The amount of air left in the lungs after forceful exhalation is about 1,200 ml and is known as Residual Air. The existence of this reserve is the basis for administering the abdominal thrust maneuver, described in the chapter entitled "First Aid and Emergency Procedures." In this lifesaving procedure, the residual air is used to force a foreign object out of the trachea.

ABNORMALITIES OF BREATHING

The following terms are used to describe breathing and

significant variations in exchanges of respiratory gases: Eupnea is ordinary quiet respiration.

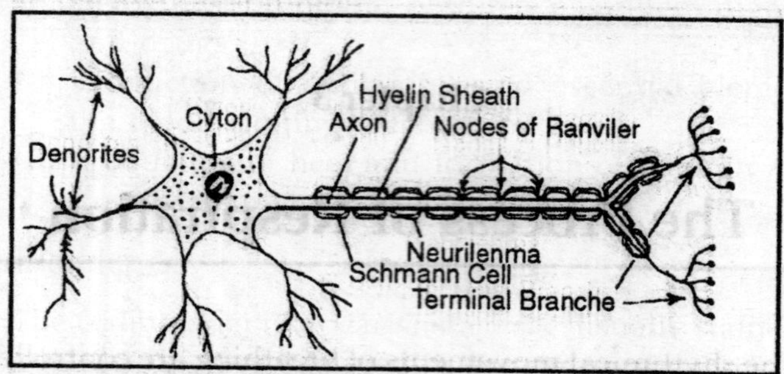

Fig. The Neuron and its Parts.

Bradypnea is abnormal slowness of breathing.

- Tachypnea is excessive rapidity of respiration.
- Hypopnea is abnormal decrease in the depth and rate of the respiratory movements.
- Dyspnea is labored or difficult breathing.
- Hyperpnea is abnormal increase in the depth and rate of the respiratory movements. Apnea is cessation of breathing.
- Cheyne-stokes Respiration are respirations that increase with force and frequency up to acertain point, then decrease until they cease altogether. After a short period of apnea, the respirations begin again, and the cycle is repeated.
- Stertorous Respiration is breathing with abnormal snoring sounds.
- Rales are abnormal respiratory sounds, either moist or dry depending upon the fluid in the air passages, which are classified according to their location as bronchial or laryngeal rales.
- Rhonchus is a rattling sound in the throat due to partial obstruction; it is also a dry, coarse rale in the bronchial tubes.

THE NERVOUS SYSTEM

To effectively support human life, the activities of all the widely diverse cells, tissues, and organs of the body must be monitored, regulated, and coordinated. The interaction of the nervous and endocrine systems provides the needed control. The nervous system is specifically adapted to the rapid transmission of impulses from one area of the body to another.

On the other hand, the endocrine system, working at a far slower pace, maintains body metabolism at a fairly constant level. In this section we will study the structure and functions of the nervous system.

The Neuron

The structure and functional unit of the nervous system is the nerve cell, or neuron, which can be classified into three types. The first is the sensory neuron, which conveys sensory impulses inward from the receptors. The second is the motor neuron, which carries command impulses from a central area to the responding muscles or organs. The third type is the interneuron, which links the sensory neurons to the motor neurons. The neuron is composed of dendrites, a cyton, and an axon.

The Dendrites are thin receptive branches, which vary greatly in size, shape, and number with different types of neurons. They serve as receptors, conveying impulses toward the cyton. The Cyton is the cell body containing the nucleus. The single, thin extension of the cell outward from the cyton is called the Axon. It conducts impulses away from the cyton to its terminal filaments, which transmit the impulses to the dendrites of the next neuron.

Impulse Transmission

When dendrites receive a sufficiently strong stimulus, a short and rapid depolarization of the neuron is triggered. Sodium ions rush through the plasma membrane into the cell, potassium ions leave, and an electrical impulse is formed, which is conducted toward the cyton. The cyton receives the impulse and transmits it to the terminal filaments of the axon. At this point a chemical transmitter such as acetylcholine is released into the Synapse, a space between the axon of the activated nerve and the dendrite receptors of another neuron. This transmitter activates the next nerve. In this manner the impulse is passed from neuron to neuron down the nerve line to a central area at approximately the speed of a bullet. Almost immediately after being activated, the transmitter chemical in the synapse is neutralized by the enzyme acetylcholinesterase, and the first neuron returns to its normal state by pumping out the sodium ions and drawing potassium ions back in through the plasma membrane.

When these actions are completed, the nerve is ready to be triggered again. A particularly strong stimulus will cause the nerve to fire in rapid succession, or will trigger many other neurons, thus giving a feeling of intensity to the perceived sensation.

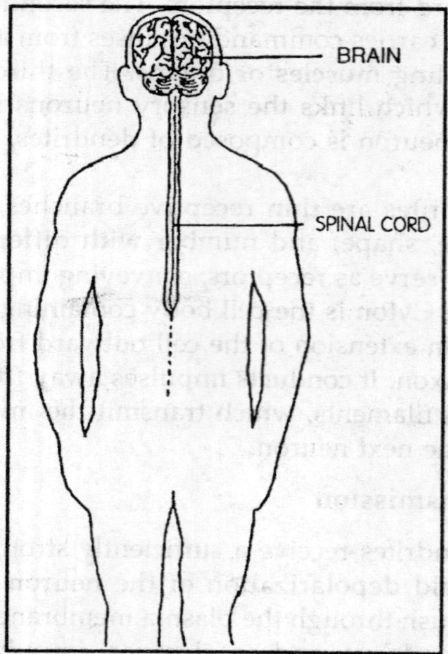

Fig. The Central Nervous System.

CENTRAL NERVOUS SYSTEM

The central nervous system consists of the brain and spinal

cord. The brain is almost entirely enclosed in the skull, but it is connected with the spinal cord, which lies in the canal formed by the vertebral column.

Brain

The brain has two main divisions, the cerebrum and the cerebellum. The cerebrum is the largest and most superiorly situated portion of the brain. It occupies most of the cranial cavity. The outer surface is called the cortex. This portion of the brain is also called gray matter because the nerve fibers are unmyelinated (not covered by a myelin sheath), causing them to appear gray.

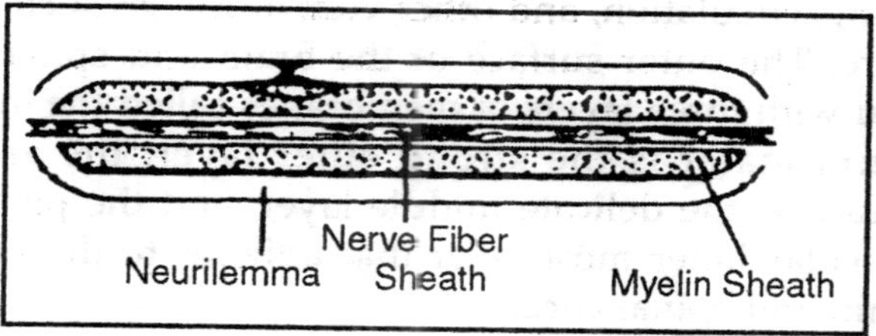

Fig. Sheath of a Neuron.

Beneath this layer is the medulla. This is often called the white matter of the brain, because the nerves are myelinated (covered with a myelin sheath and an outer covering called the neurilemma), which gives them their white appearance. The cortex of the cerebrum is irregular. It bends on itself in folds called convolutions, which are separated from each other by grooves and fissures.

The deep sagittal cleft, a longitudinal fissure, divides the cerebrum into two hemispheres. Other fissures further subdivide the cerebrum into lobes, each of which serves a localized, specific brain function. For example, the frontal lobe is associated with the higher mental processes such as memory, the parietal lobe is concerned primarily with general sensations, the occipital lobe is related to the sense of sight, and the temporal lobe is concerned with hearing.

The cerebellum is situated posteriorly to the brain stem, which is made up of the pons, midbrain, and medulla oblongata, and inferior to the occipital lobe. It is concerned chiefly with bringing balance, harmony, and coordination to the motions initiated by the cerebrum. Two smaller divisions of the brain, vital to life, are the pens and the medulla oblongata.

The pens consists chiefly of a mass of white fibers connecting the other three parts of the brain—the cerebrum, cerebellum, and medulla oblongata. The medulla oblongata is the inferior portion of the brain, the last division before the beginning of the spinal cord. It connects to the spinal cord at the upper level of the first cervical vertebra (C-1).

In it are the centers for the control of heart action, breathing, circulation, and other vital processes such as blood pressure. The outer surface of the brain and spinal cord is covered with three layers of membranes called the meninges. The dura mater is the strong outer layer; the arachnoid membrane is the delicate middle layer; and the pia mater is the vascular inner most layer that adheres to the surface of the brain and spinal cord.

Inflammation of the meninges is called meningitis. The type depends upon whether the brain, spinal cord, or both are affected. Cerebrospinal fluid is formed by a plexus (network) of blood vessels in the central ventricles of the brain. It is a clear, watery solution similar to blood plasma.

The total quantity bathing the spinal cord is about 75 ml. It is constantly being produced and reabsorbed. It circulates over the 3-31 surface of the brain and spinal cord and serves as a protective cushion as well as a means of exchange for nutrients and waste materials.

Spinal Cord

The spinal cord is continuous with the medulla oblongata and extends from the foramen magnum, down inside the atlas, to the lower border of the first lumbar vertebra, where it tapers to a point. The cord is surrounded by the bony walls of the vertebral canal. It is unsheathed in the three protective meninges and surrounded by adipose tissue and blood vessels. The cord does not completely fill the vertebral canal, nor does it extend the full length of it. The nerve roots serving the lumbar and sacral regions must pass some distance down the canal before making their exit.

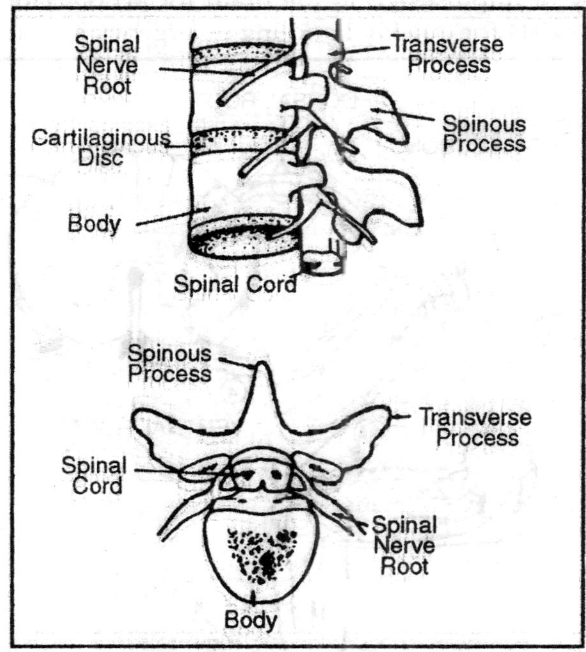

Fig. Spinal Cord.

A cross section of the spinal cord shows white and gray matter. The outer white matter is composed of bundles of myelinated nerve fibers arranged in functionally specialized tracts. It establishes motor communication between the brain and the body parts.

The inner gray unmyelinated matter is shaped roughly like the letter H. It establishes sensory communication between the brain and the spinal nerves, conducting sensory impulses from the body parts. It also plays an integral role in the autonomic nervous system and in the reflex arc, both of which will be discussed later.

The spinal cord may be thought of as an electric cable containing many wires (nerves) that connect parts of the body with each other and with the brain. Sensations received by a sensory nerve are brought to the spinal cord, and the impulse is transferred either to the brain or to a motor nerve. The majority of impulses go to the brain for action. However, a system exists for quickly handling emergency situation.

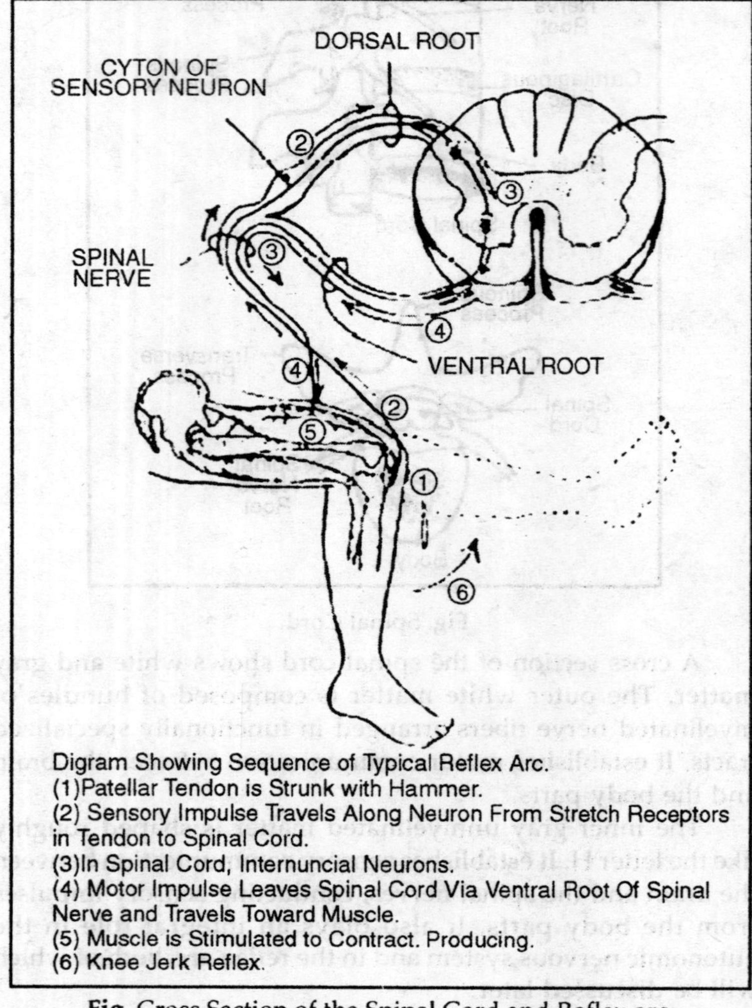

Fig. Cross Section of the Spinal Cord and Reflex arc.

It is called the reflex arc. If you touch a hot stove, you

must remove the hand from the heat source immediately or the skin will burn very quickly. But the passage of a sense impulse to the brain and back again to a motor nerve takes time.

The reflex arc is set up to respond instantaneously to emergency situations like the one just described. The sensation of hot travels to the spinal cord on a sensory nerve, where it is picked up by an interneuron in the gray matter, which triggers the appropriate nerve to stimulate a muscle reflex drawing the hand away.

Another example of the reflex arc is shown in figure. The reflex arc works well in simple situations requiring no action of the brain. Consider, however, what action is involved if the individual touching the stove pulls back and, in so doing, loses his or her balance and has to grab a chair to regain stability. Then the entire spinal cord is involved.

Additional impulses must travel to the brain, then down to the muscles of the legs and arms to enable him or her to maintain balance and to hold on to a steadying object. While all this is going on, the stimulus is relayed through the sympathetic autonomic nerve fibers to the adrenal glands, causing adrenalin to flow, which stimulates heart action, and to the brain, making the individual conscious of pain. In this example the spinal cord has functioned not only as a centre for spinal relaxes, but also as a conduction pathway for other areas of the spinal cord to the autonomic nervous system and to the brain.

PERIPHERAL NERVOUS SYSTEM

The peripheral nervous system is made up of 12 pairs of cranial nerves and 31 pairs of spinal nerves arising from the brain and spinal cord, respectively. These nerves carry both voluntary and involuntary impulses.

Cranial Nerves

The 12 pairs of cranial nerves are sensory, motor, or mixed (sensory and motor).

- The Olfactory nerve (sensory) conveys the sense of

smell from the mucous membrane in the upper nose to the olfactory centre of the brain.

- The Optic nerve (sensory) conveys the sensation of sight from the retinal cells of the eye to the visual area of the brain.
- The Oculomotor nerve (motor) controls most muscles that move the eyeball and some of those in the iris of the eye.
- The Trochlear nerve (motor) controls the muscles that turn the eyeball down and to the side.
- The Trigeminal nerve (sensory and some motor) is divided into three branches: ophthalmic, maxillary, and mandibular. It sometimes is called the great sensory nerve of the head because it supplies the sense of touch, pain, heat, and cold to the skin of the face, eyelids, cornea, conjunctival, tongue, teeth, and mucous membranes of the head. A branch of the mandibular division supplies motor fibers to the muscles of mastication.
- The Abducens nerve (motor) controls the muscles that turn the eye outward.
- The facial nerve (motor and sensory) control the muscles of the face, scalp, and ears. It contains autonomic motor fibers, which cause the salivary glands to secrete, and sensory fibers, which carry taste sensations from the anterior two-thirds of the tongue to the brain.
- The Acoustic (vestibulocochlear) nerve (sensory) is the nerve of hearing and equilibrium.
- The Glossopharyngeal nerve (motor and sensory) carries sensation from the pharynx and posterior one-third of the tongue and transmits motor impulses to the parotid gland and to one of the small muscles of swallowing. The Vagus nerve (motor and some sensory) is composed of motor fibers (some of which are parasympathetic) and sensory fibers. It extends down through the neck to the pharynx, larynx, trachea, esophagus, and thoracic and

abdominal viscera. The Accessory nerve (motor) supplies nerves to muscles of the neck (sternocleidomastoid, trapezius,pharyngeal, and laryngeal).

- The Hypoglossal nerve (motor) controls the musclesof the tongue.

Spinal Nerves

Spinal nerves arise from the spinal cord and leave the vertebral canal in the spaces between the vertebrae. These nerves send fibers to sensory surfaces and all muscles of the trunk and extremities. Also, involuntary fibers go to the smooth muscles and glands of the gastrointestinal tract, urogenital system, and cardiovascular system. There are 31 pairs of spinal nerves: 8 cervical, 12 thoracic, 5 lumbar, 5 sacral, and 1 coccygeal. The lower spinal nerves going to the legs and feet extend below the level of the spinal cord. The nerve roots arising from the lumbar and sacral regions pass some distance down the canal before making their exit.

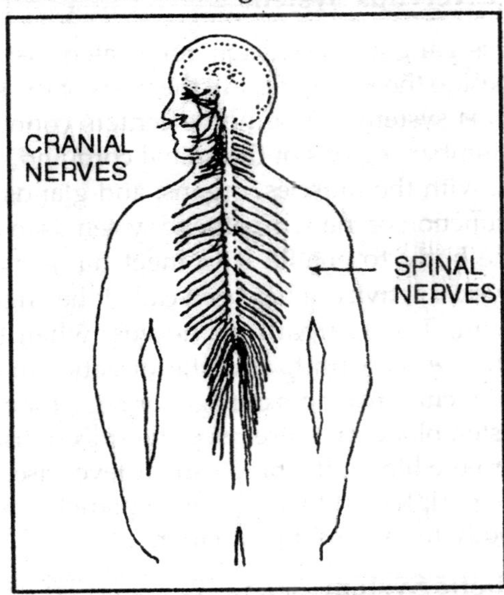

Fig. The peripheral nervous system.

This bundle of nerve roots is called the cauda equina

because it resembles a horse's tail. The various roots emerge through openings in the sacrum and extend to the areas they supply. Spinal nerves contain all types of sensory and motor fibers of both the voluntary and autonomic nervous systems.

In some regions of the body they interlace in a thick network called a plexus. The cervical plexus is located in the neck, and the brachial plexus is in the shoulder. In the pelvic region are the lumbar, sacral, and pudendal plexuses.

AUTONOMIC NERVOUS SYSTEM

The autonomic nervous system, as its name implies, functions automatically. It helps to regulate the smooth muscles, cardiac muscle, digestive tube, blood vessels, sweat and digestive glands, and certain endocrine glands. It is not directly under the control of the brain but usually works in harmony with the nerves that are underthebrain's control. The autonomic nervous system is divided into the sympathetic and parasympathetic systems.

Sympathetic Nervous System

Numerous ganglia (nerve centers) located just outside the spinal cord, beside the vertebrae, are the basis of the sympathetic (thoracolumbar) system. These nerve centers connect with the thoracic and lumbar regions of the spinal cord and, through the spinal nerves, with the muscles, organs, and glands they affect. Because one function of the sympathetic system is to increase the activity of the body to enable it to meet danger or undergo strenuous physical activity, it has been called the "fight or flight" nervous system. The sympathetic nerves, when stimulated, usually discharge as a unit, and the effects can be noticed especially under circumstances of fright or rage; for example, the heart beats faster, blood pressure rises, the spleen discharges red blood cells into the blood, the blood sugar level rises, the pupils dilate, and the peripheral blood vessels constrict. These changes prepare the body for a stressful situation

Parasympathetic System

The ganglia of the parasympathetic system are located in

the midportion of the brain, the medulla oblongata, and the sacral regions. For this reason the parasympathetic system is sometimes called the craniosacral system.

The ganglia in the midbrain and medulla oblongata send impulses out along cranial nerves (oculomotor, facial, glossopharyngeal, and vagus). The sacral ganglia stem from the second, third, and fourth sacral nerves. The parasympathetic nerves do not all discharge at once. They aim more toward conserving and restoring energy.

Their actions slow the heart beat, lower the blood pressure, stimulate gastrointestinal movements and secretion, aid absorption, constrict the pupils, dilate peripheral blood vessels, and empty the bladder and rectum. Overall they promote the autonomic restoration of body systems to normal functioning after sympathetic stimulation. The sympathetic and parasympathetic systems counterbalance each other to preserve a harmonious balance of body functions and activities.

THE SENSORY SYSTEM

The sensory system functions to inform areas of the cerebral cortex of changes that are taking place within the body or in the external environment.

The special sensory receptors are designed to respond only to a special individual stimulus such as sound waves, light, taste, smell, pressure, heat, cold, pain, or touch. Positional changes, balance, hunger, and thirst sensations are also detected and passed on to the brain.

Smell

Odor is perceived upon stimulation of the receptor cells in the olfactory membrane of the nose. The olfactory receptors are very sensitive, but they are also easily fatigued. This explains why odors that are initially very noticeable are not sensed after a short time. Smell is not as well developed in man as in other mammals.

Taste

The taste buds are located in the tongue. The sensation of

taste is limited to sour, sweet, bitter, and salty. Many foods and drinks tasted are actually smelled, and their taste depends upon their odor. This can be demonstrated by pinching the nose shut when eating onions. Sight can also affect taste. Several drops of green food coloring in a glass of milk will make it all but unpalatable, even though the true taste has not been affected.

SIGHT

The eye, the organ of sight, is a specialized structure for the reception of light. It is assisted in its function by accessory structures, such as the ocular muscles, eyelids, conjunctival, and lacrimal apparatus.

Table—Functions of the Autonomic Nervous System.

Sympathetic	Parasympathetic
Dilates pupils.	Constricts pupils.
Lessens tonus of ciliary muscles eyes may accommodate to see distant objects.	Contracts ciliary so the muscles so the eyes may accommodate to see objects near at hand.
Dilates bronchi.	Constricts bronchi.
Quickens and strengthens the action of the heart.	Slows the action of the heart.
Contracts blood vessels of the skin and viscera so that more blood goes to the skeletal and cardiac muscles where it is needed for "fight or flight."	Dilates blood vessels (except cardiac).
Relaxes gastrointestinal tract and bladder.	Increases contraction of gastrointestinal tract and muscle tone of the bladder.
Decreases secretions of the gastrointestinal glands.	Increases secretions of gastrointestinal glands.
Increases secretion of sweat glands.	No action on sweat glands.
Causes contraction of sphincters to prevent emptying of bowels or bladder.	Relaxes sphincters so that waste matter can be excreted.

Structure of The Eye

The eye is a hollow ball, or globe, which consists of various tissues that perform specific functions. The globe, or eyeball, is composed of three layers.

Outer Layer: The outer layer of the eye is called the sclera. It is the tough, fibrous, protective portion of the globe, commonly called the white of the eye. Anteriorly, the outer layer is transparent and is called the cornea, or the window of the eye. It permits light to enter the globe. The exposed sclera is covered with a mucous membrane, the conjunctival, which is a continuation of the inner lining of the eyelids. The lacrimal gland produces tears that constantly wash the front part of the eye and the conjunctival. The tear gland secretions that do not evaporate flow onward the inner angle of the eye where they drain down ducts into the nose.

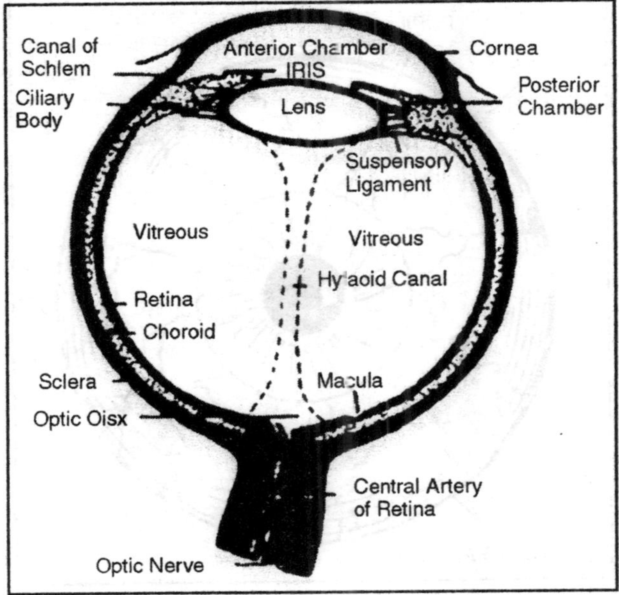

Fig. Cross Section of the Eye

MIDDLE LAYER

The middle layer of the eye is called the choroid. It is a

highly vascular, pigmented tissue that provides nourishment to the inner structures. Continuous with the choroid is the ciliary body, whose muscular structure attaches to the lens by means of suspensory ligaments and produces changes in the thickness of the lens.

This permits the eye to focus to longrange or close-up vision. The iris is continuous with the ciliary body. It is a circular, pigmented muscular structure that gives colour to the eye. The opening in the iris is called the pupil.

The amount of light entering the pupil is regulated through the constriction of radial/circular muscles in the iris. When strong light is flashed into the eye, the circular muscle fibers of the iris contract, reducing the size of the pupil. If the light is dim, the pupil dilates to allow as much of the light in as possible.

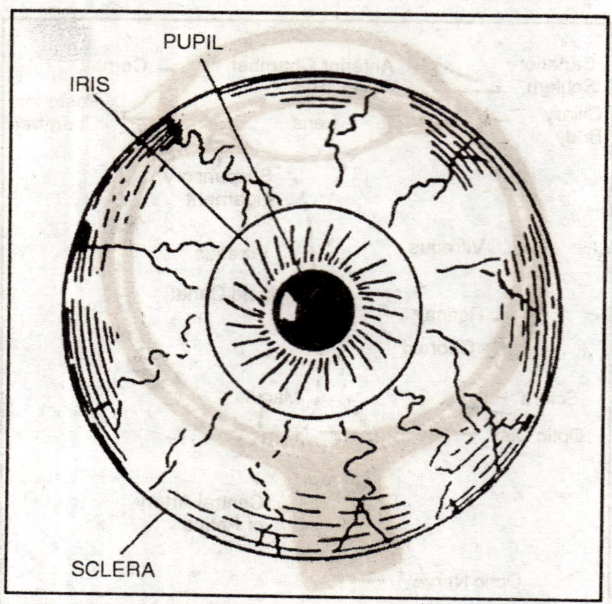

Fig. Eye, Anterior View

The size and reaction of the pupils of the eyes are an important diagnostic tool. The lens is a transparent, biconvex structure suspended directly behind the iris. It separates the interior eye into anterior and posterior cavities. The anterior cavity contains a watery solution called aqueous humour, which helps to give the cornea its curved shape.

The optic globe posterior to the lens is filled with a jellylike substance called vitreous humour, which helps to maintain the shape of the eyeball and prevents misshaping by maintaining intraocular pressure.

INNER LAYER

The inner layer of the eye is called the retina. It contains different layers of nerve cells, rods, and cones that are the receptors of the sense of vision. The retina is continuous with the optic nerve, which enters the back of the globe and carries visual impulses received by the rods and cones to the brain.

The area where the optic nerve enters the eyeball contains no rods and cones and is called the blind spot. The rods respond to low intensities of light and are responsible for night vision. They are located in all areas of the retina, except in the small depression called the fovea centralis, where light entering the eye is focused, and which has the clearest vision.

The cones require higher light intensities for stimulation and are most densely concentrated in the fovea centralis. The cones are responsible for daytime vision.

Vision Process

Deflection or bending of light rays results when light passes through substances of varying densities in the eye (cornea, aqueous humour, crystalline lens, and vitreous humour) The deflection is referred to as refraction. Accommodation is the process performed by the lens that increases or decreases its curvature to refract light rays into focus on the fovea. The constriction of the pupil by the iris regulates the amount of light entering the eye.

This process protects the retina from excessive stimulation and prevents a scattering of light rays that would produce blurred vision. A movement of the globes toward the midline, which causes a viewed object to come into focus on corresponding points of the two retinas, is called convergence.

This gives clear, threedimensional vision. The end receptors or nerve endings in the rods and cones that have been stimulated by light conduct impulses to the occipital lobes of the cerebrum, where they are interpreted into vision.

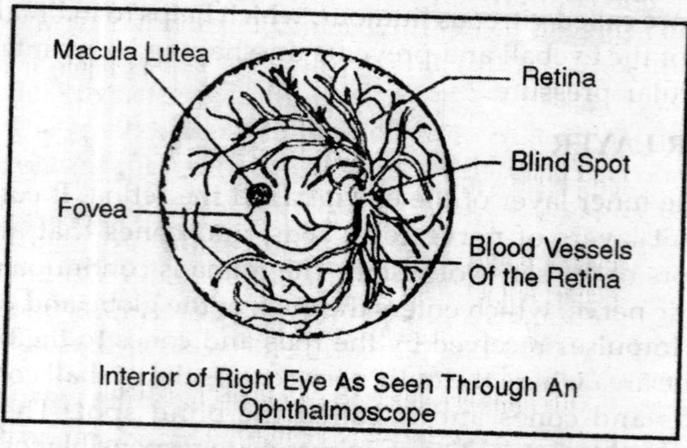

Fig. Eye, Ophthalmoscope View

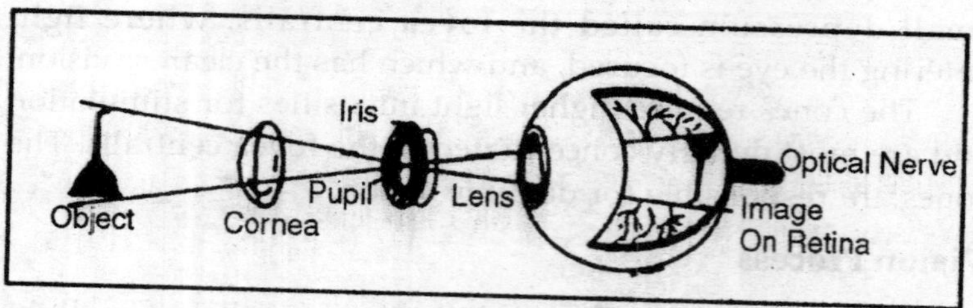

Fig. The Vision Process

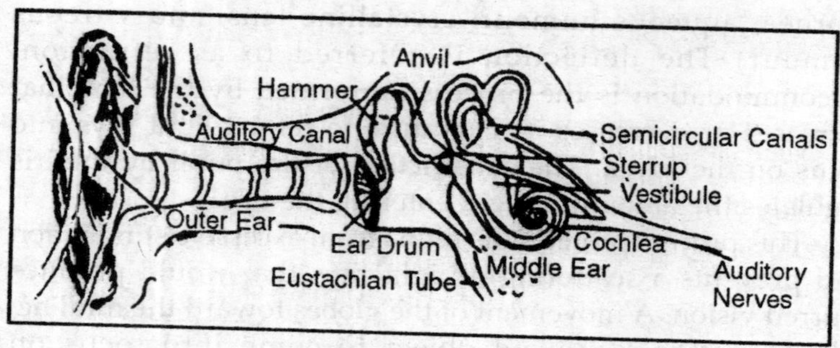

Fig. The Ear

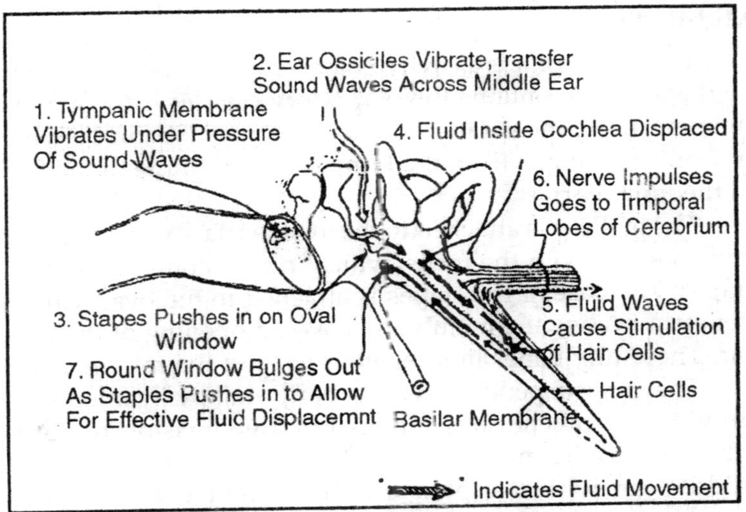

Fig. The Hearing Process

HEARING

The ear is the primary organ of hearing. It is called cerumen.

The cerumen aids in protecting divided into three parts: the external, middle, and the eardrum against foreign bodies and inner ear.

External Ear

The eardrum, or tympanic membrane, is an oval sheet of fibrous epithelial tissue, 10 mm by The external, or outer, ear is composed of two 9 mm in size, which stretches across the inner end parts, the auricle and the external auditory canal. of the external auditory canal and separates the The auricle, or pinna, is a cartilaginous structure outer and middle ear. The sound waves cause the located on each side of the head. The auricle coleardrum to vibrate.

This vibration transfers the lects sound waves from the environment, which sounds from the external environment to the are then conducted by the external auditory canal auditory ossicles.

Middle Ear

The middle ear is a cavity in the temporal bone, lined with epitheliums. It contains three auditory ossicles —the malleus (hammer), the incus (anvil), and the stapes (stirrup)—which transmit vibrations from the tympanic membrane to the fluid in the inner ear.

The malleus is attached to the inner surface of the eardrum and connects with the incus, which in turn connects with the stapes. The base of the stapes is attached to the oval window (fenestra ovalis), the membrane-covered opening of the inner ear. These tiny bones link together to span the middle ear.

They are suspended from its bony wall by ligaments and provide the mechanical means for transmission of sound vibrations to the inner ear. The eustachian tube connects the middle ear with the pharynx. It is lined with a mucous membrane and is about 36 mm long. Its function is to equalize internal and external air pressure.

For example, while riding an elevator in a tall building, you may experience a feeling of pressure in the ear. This is usually relieved by swallowing, which opens the eustachian tube and allows the pressurized air to escape and equalize with the area of lower pressure. Divers who ascend too fast to allow pressure to adjust may experience rupture of their eardrums. The eustachian tube can also be a pathway for infection of the middle ear.

Inner Ear

The inner ear is filled with a fluid called endolymph. Sound vibrations that cause the stapes to move against the oval window create internal ripples that run through the endolymph. These pressurized ripples move to the cochlea, a small snail-shaped structure housing the organ of Corti, the hearing organ.

The cells protruding from the organ of Corti are stimulated by the ripples to convert these mechanical vibrations into nerve impulses, which are relayed through the cochlear (8th cranial) nerve to the auditory area of the cortex in the temporal lobe of the brain. Here they are interpreted as the sounds we hear. Other structures of the inner ear are the three semicircular canals, situated perpendicular to each other. Movement of the endolymph within the canals, caused by general body movements, stimulates nerve endings, which report these changes in body position to the brain, which in turn uses the information to maintain equilibrium.

The round window (fenestra rotunda) is another membranecovered opening of the inner ear. It contracts the middle ear and flexes to accommodate the inner ear ripples caused by the stapes.

TOUCH

Until the beginning of the last century, touch (feeling) was treated as a single sense. Thus warmth or coldness, pressure, and pain, were thought to be part of a single sense of touch or feeling. It was then discovered that different types of nerve ending receptors are widely, but unevenly, distributed in the skin and mucous membranes.

For example, the skin of the back possesses relatively few touch and pressure receptors while the fingertips have a great many. The skin of the face has relatively few cold receptors, and the mucous membranes have few heat receptors. The cornea of the eye is sensitive to pain, and when pain sensation is abolished by a local anesthetic, a sensation of touch can be experienced.

There are five kinds of receptors. The most important, those for the sense of touch, are bare nerve endings next to hairs and specialized encapsulated nerve endings called Meissner's corpuscles. Cold receptors also have encapsulated nerve endings. The receptors for pain are naked nerve filaments and are the most numerous; they are also the only kind present in the deeper tissues, although stimulation of these usually causes the pain to be referred to a skin area. Three kinds of pain may be experienced: superficial or cutaneous pain; deep pain from muscles, tendons, joints, and fascia; and visceral pain.

Other Sense

Certain nerve receptors, located in muscles and tendons,

are stimulated by changes in tension and pressure and continually inform the brain regarding the position of parts of the body (body sense).

Hunger results from rhythmic contractions of the stomach when it has emptied its contents. Blood sugar levels also influence the feeling of hunger. Habit is another factor; for example, persons who habitually snack in midmorning will feel hunger contractions at normal snacktime.

If the snack is not eaten for several days, and adequate food intake continues at mealtime, the hunger contractions at snacktime will diminish. The nervous system also plays a part in controlling hunger, either by depressing the desire for food or by stimulating appetite. The drying of the membranes in the oral cavity influences the sensation of thirst. Although thirst may be due to a lack of water in body tissues, a reduced salivary flow can produce a sensation of thirst.

Special Functions

Speech is controlled by the coordinated action of several nerve functions. The speech centre is located deep in the brain, and from it nerve impulses pass out to the larynx, which contains folds of mucous membranes called vocal cords. When air is forced from the lungs past these folds, certain sounds are produced, and, in conjunction with the movements of the throat, lips, tongue, and teeth, articulate speech results.

Sleep is a period of unconsciousness when the higher physical powers are quiet, although body activities continue. It is usually considered a period of rest in which constructive processes build up and repair the body. Certain changes take place during sleep: respiration is slowed; less blood is sent to the brain and greater amounts to to the extremities; digestion goes on, but at a slower rate; body temperature may drop somewhat; and heart action is slowed.

The Endocrine System

Homeostasis depends on the nervous and endocrine systems, since both are lines of communication for body functions. The endocrine system sends messages by chemical hormones that are carried in the blood stream. These messages aid in the control, development, and integration of body functions. The endocrine system is made up of glands of internal secretion. These are called ductless glands because they have no ducts to carry away their secretions.

The secretion of an endocrine gland is called a hormone. It enters directly into the blood or lymph circulation and eventually reaches the gland, tissue, or organ it controls or influences. Very small quantities of hormones are produced, since only a trace amount is needed to produce the desired effect. Most hormones can be extracted from the glands of animals, and some can be produced synthetically. Medical officers may prescribe these isolated or synthetic hormones for patients who are deficient in them or who might otherwise benefit from their use.

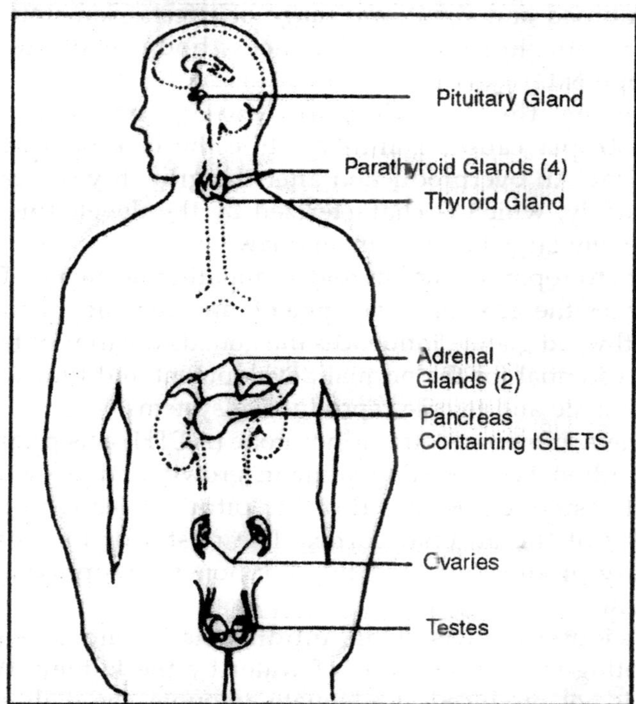

Fig. The Endocrine Glands

The hormone-producing glands include the pituitary, thyroid, parathyroids, adrenals, gonads, and pancreas).

Hypothalamus

The hypothalamus, a structure in the brain, synthesizes chemicals that are secreted to the pituitary gland to stimulate the release of its hormones.

Pituitary Gland

The pituitary is a small, pea-sized gland located at the base of the brain in the sella turcica of the sphenoid bone. It is often called the master gland of the body, because it influences most other endocrine glands. It is divided into two lobes, an anterior and a posterior. The anterior lobe plays the more important role in influencing body functions. The hormones it produces have a broad and significant range of effects. Somatotropin, the growth hormone, influences body growth and development.

During the growth years an overproduction of somatotropin causes giantism while the lack of it causes dwarfism. An overproduction after the growth years causes acromegaly, which is characterized by the development of abnormally large hands, feet, and jaw.

Thyrotropin, or the thyroid-stimulating hormone (TSH), influences the growth, development, and secreting activities of the thyroid gland.. influences the gonads (ovaries or testes) and is essential for the normal development and functioning of both male and female reproductive systems.

The Adrenocorticotropic hormone (ACTH) acts primarily on the adrenal cortex, stimulating its growth and its secretion of corticosteroids. Removal of the pituitary leads to rapid atrophy of the adrenal cortex. The posterior lobe of the pituitary produces at least two hormones, vasopressin and oxytocin.

Vasopressin acts as an antidiuretic hormone (ADH), promoting the conservation of water by the kidney. When ADH is not produced in adequate amounts, the daily urine volume is between 10 and 15 liters instead of the normal 1.5

liters. This condition is known as diabetes insipidus. Oxytocin stimulates contraction of the muscles of the uterus, particularly during pregnancy. It also plays an important role in the production of milk in the mammary glands of nursing mothers.

Thyroid Gland

The thyroid, shaped like a butterfly, lies in the anterior part of the neck, below the larynx. It consists of two lobes, one on each side of the upper trachea, connected by a strip of tissue called the isthmus. The thyroid secretes the iodinecontaining hormone Thyroxin, which controls the rate of cell metabolism.

Excessive secretion of thyroxin raises the metabolic rate and causes hyperthyroidism, a condition characterized by a fast pulse rate, dizziness, increased basal metabolism, profuse sweating, tremors, nervousness, and a tremendous appetite yet a loss of weight.

The thyroid may become enlarged. Iodine is essential for the formation of thyroxin. To prevent simple goiter, iodine-containing foods, such as vegetables, iodized salt, and seafood, are eaten. Hypothyroidism, on the other hand, is caused by an insufficient secretion of thyroxin.

The patient exhibits a decrease in basal metabolism, and sweating is almost absent. There may be a weight gain and constant fatigue. The heart rate may be slow, and there may be an enlargement of the gland, called a simple goiter. There may also be personality changes characterized by slow, lethargic mental functioning. Hypothyroidism in an infant may result in cretinism with impaired mental and physical development.

Parathyroid Glands

Parathyroid glands are four small round bodies located just posterior to the thyroid gland. Their hormone, Parathormone, regulates the calcium and phosphorus content of the blood and bones. The amount of calcium is important in certain tissue activities, such as bone formation, coagulation of blood, maintenance of normal muscular excitability, and milk production in the nursing mother. Diminished function or removal of the parathyroid glands results in a low calcium level in the blood, and in extreme cases death may occur, preceded by strong contraction of the muscles (tetany) and convulsions.

Hyperparathyroidism, an excess of parathyroid hormone in the blood, causes calcium levels in the blood to become elevated by the withdrawal of calcium from the bones, leaving the skeleton demineralized and subject to spontaneous fractures. The excess calcium may be deposited as stones in the kidneys.

Adrenal Glands

The adrenal glands are located on the superior surface of each kidney, fitting like a cap. They consist of an outer portion, the cortex, and an inner portion, the medulla. Adrenal Cortex Specialized cells in the outer layer of the adrenal cortex produce three types of steroid hormones that are of vital importance.

Mineralocorticoids are regulators of fluid and electrolyte balance. They are sometimes called salt and water hormone because they regulate the excretion and absorption of sodium, chlorine, potassium, and water. Glucocorticoids are essential to metabolism.

They increase certain liver functions and have an anti-inflammatory effect. Clinically they are used to suppress inflammatory reactions, to promote healing, and to treat rheumatoid arthritis.

The adrenal cortex also produces sex hormones, some with male characteristics (Androgens), others with female characteristics (Estrogens). These hormones appear in different concentrations in both men and women.

Adrenal Medulla

The adrenal medulla secretes Epinephrine (Adrenalin) in the presence of emotional crises, hypoglycemia (low blood sugar), or low blood pressure. Epinephrine constricts the peripheral vascular system and dilates the blood vessels to the skeletal muscles. Heart rate, respiration rate and depth, blood pressure, blood sugar levels, and metabolism are all increased by epinephrine.

It also stimulates the production of other adrenal cortical hormones. Norepinephrine is also produced in the adrenal medulla. It is a chemical precursor to epinephrine. Its effects are similar to those of epinephrine, but its action differs. Despite these marked influences, the medullary tissue of the adrenal gland is not essential to life, because its various functions can be assumed by other regulatory mechanisms.

GONADS

The male gonads secrete the hormone TESTOSTERONE, which influences the development and maintenance of the accessory organs and the secondary sex characteristics of the male. The female gonads, the Ovaries, produce Estrogen and Progesterone.

Estrogen influences the development and maintenance of the female accessory organs and the secondary sex characteristics and promotes changes in the mucous lining of the uterus (endometrium) during the menstrual cycle. Progesterone prepares the uterus for the reception and development of the fertilized ovum and maintains the lining during pregnancy. It is used in many birth control pills.

PANCREAS

The islands of Langerhans in the pancreas contain two types of endocrine cells, alpha and beta. The alpha cells secrete glucagon, which causes a temporary rise in blood sugar levels. The beta cells secrete insulin, which is essential for carbohydrate metabolism.

Insulin lowers blood sugar levels by increasing tissue utilization of glucose and stimulating the formation and storage of glycogen in the liver.

Together, glucagon and insulin act to regulate sugar metabolism in the body. When the islet cells are destroyed or stop functioning, the sugar absorbed from the intestine remains in the blood and is excreted by the kidneys into the urine.

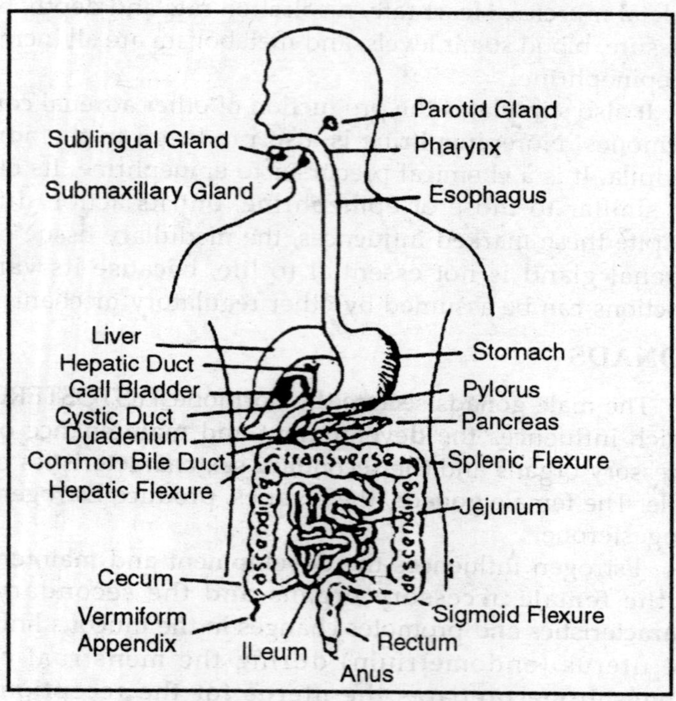

Fig. The Digestive System

It is not used by the body or stored. This condition is called diabetes mellitus, or sugar diabetes. Insulin is given to patients having this disease as part of their ongoing treatment.

Chapter 4

The Digestive System

The digestive system consists of the alimentary tract—mouth, pharynx, esophagus, stomach, intestines, and certain accessory organs of digestion.

Table. Principal digestive juices, source and action

Source	**Digestive Juice**	**Substance acted upon**	**Product**
Salivary Glands	Ptyalin	Starch	Complex Sugar (maltose)
Gastric Glands	Hydrochloric acid (HCL)	Pepsinogen Proteins	Pepsin Spilt Proteins (Proteoses, Peptones)
Liver	Bile	Fats	Emulsified Fats
Pancreas	Amylase	Starch	Complex Sugar (maltose)
	Proteinases (Trypsin chymotrypsin)	Proteins,Split protein	Peptides, Polypeptides
	Lipase	Fats	Fatty acids, glycerol
Intestinal Glands	Carbohydrates (maltase sucare lactase)	Complexsugar (maltose Sucrose lactose)	Simple Sugars (glucose Fructose Galactose)
	Peptidases	Peptides Polypeptides	Amino Acids
	Lipase	Fats	Fatty acids, Glycerol

As food passes through the 9-meterlong alimentary tract, digestion and absorption occur, and eventually waste material is eliminated. Secretions of the accessory organs assist in preparing food for absorption and use by the tissues of the body.

Digestion is both mechanical and chemical. Mechanical digestion occurs when food is chewed, swallowed, and churned by peristalsis. Waste is evacuated when the bowels move. Chemical digestion consists of changing the various foods, with the aid of digestive enzymes, into solutions and simple compounds.Carbohydrates (starches and sugars) change into simple sugars (glucose); fats change into fatty acids; and proteins change into amino acids.

MOUTH

In the mouth the Teeth mechanically break up food into small particles before it is swallowed. The salivary glands—parotid, submaxillary, and sublingual—secrete saliva, which moistens the food, makes it easier to chew, and lubricates the food mass to aid in swallowing. About 1,500 ml of saliva are secreted daily.

Saliva contains one principal enzyme, ptyalin, which initiates chemical digestion of starches, breaking them into the complex sugar maltose. The tongue is a muscular organ attached to the lower jaw at the back of the mouth and is the chief organ of taste. It assists in mastication, swallowing, and speech.

PHARYNX

The pharynx is the passageway between the mouth and the esophagus and is shared with the respiratory tract. The Epiglottis is a cartilaginous flap that closes the opening to the larynx when food is being swallowed down the pharynx. Food is deflected away from the trachea to prevent particle aspiration.

Esophagus

The esophagus is a muscular tube about 25 cm (10 inches)

long. It is the passageway between the pharynx and the stomach. By means of waves of muscular contractions (peristalsis), food is pushed along this tube to the stomach. When peristalsis is reversed, vomiting occurs.

Stomach

The stomach is a saccular enlargement of the gastrointestinal tube, connecting the lower end of the esophagus and the first portion of the small intestine (duodenum). It lies in the left upper quadrant of the abdomen. Muscular rings, or sphincters, at each end of the stomach form valves to close off the stomach and to prevent its contents from escaping in either direction while they are being mixed by peristaltic muscular contractions of the stomach wall.

The sphincter at the esophageal end is the cardiac sphincter; at the duodenal end it is the pyloric sphincter. The stomach acts as an initial storehouse for swallowed material and helps in the chemical breakdown of food substances.

Small glands in the wall of the stomach secrete gastric juice, the principal components of which are hydrochloric acid and pepsinogen. Hydrochloric acid activates pepsin from pepsinogen, kills bacteria that enter the stomach, inhibits the digestive action of ptyalin, and helps regulate the opening and closing of the pyloric sphincter.

The action of pepsin is confined to protein, which it splits. The stomach is half-empty within 1 hour of a normal meal and completely empty in 6 hours. Most food absorption takes place in the small intestine.

There is little food absorption in the stomach. One exception is alcohol, which is absorbed directly through the stomach wall. For this reason intoxication happens quickly when alcohol is taken on an empty stomach.

ABDOMINAL CAVITY

The stomach and intestines are enclosed in the abdominal cavity, the space between the diaphragm and the pelvis. This cavity is lined with serous membrane, the Peritoneum.

The peritoneum covers the intestines and the organs and,

by secreting a serous fluid, prevents friction between adjacent organs. The Mesentery (double folds of peritoneum) extends from the cavity walls to the organs of the abdominal cavity, suspending them in position and carrying blood vessels to the organs.

Small Intestine

The small intestine is a muscular, convoluted (coiled) tube, about 7 meters (23 feet) long and attached to the posterior abdominal wall by its mesentery. The mesentery is gathered together like a folding fan, permitting coiling of the intestine, allowing this long organ to be contained in a relatively small space. The small intestine is divided into three continuous parts: the duodenum, jejunum, and ileum. It receives digestive juices from three accessory organs of digestion: the pancreas, liver, and gallbladder.

The Duodenum is about 25 cm (10 inches) long and forms a C-shaped curve around the head of the pancreas, posterior to the liver. It is lined with a mucous membrane that contains small glands. These glands secrete intestinal juices containing the enzymes carbohydrate, peptidase, and lipase. The Jejunum is the middle part of the small intestine and is about 2.5 meters (7.5 feet) long.

Its enzymes continue the digestive process. The Ileum is the last and longest part of the small intestine. Most of the absorption of food occurs in the ileum where fingerlike projections (villi) provide a large absorption surface. After ingestion it takes 20 minutes to 2 hours for the first portion of the food to pass through the small intestine to the beginning of the large intestine.

Large Intestine

The large intestine is so called because it is larger in diameter than the small intestine. It is considerably shorter, however, being about 1.5 meters (5 feet) long. It is divided into three distinct parts: the cecum, colon, and rectum. The unabsorbed food or waste material passes through the Cecum into the Colon.

The cecum is a pouch at the beginning of the large intestine, located in the lower right portion of the abdominal cavity. Twelve hours after the meal, most of the waste material passes through the colon slowly, building in mass and reaching the rectum 24 hours after the food is ingested.

The Appendix, a long narrow tube with a blind end, is an outpouching of the cecum located near the junction of the ileum and the cecum. It has no known function but frequently becomes infected and an inflammation known as appendicitis develops.

The Rectum is 12.5 cm (5 inches) long and follows the contour of the sacrum and coccyx until t curves back into the short (2.5 to 4 cm) anal canal. The ANUS is the external opening at the lower end of the digestive system. Except during bowel movement (defecation), it is kept closed by a strong muscular ring, the Anal Sphincter.

ACCESSORY ORGANS OF DIGESTION

Pancreas

The Pancreas is a large, elongated gland lying posteriorly to the stomach. Its digestive juices amylase, proteinase, and lipase are secreted through the pancreatic duct into the duodenum and act on all types of food. The pancreas contains a special group of cells called the islands of Langerhans, which secrete the hormone insulin needed for use of sugar by the body.

Liver

The Liver is the largest gland in the body. It is located in the upper abdomen on the right side, just under the diaphragm and superior to the duodenum and pylorus. Of its many functions, the following are important to remember:

- Metabolism of carbohydrates, fats, and proteins preparatory to their use or excretion.
- Formation and excretion of bile salts and pigment from bilirubin, a waste product of red blood cell destruction.

- Storage of blood and water and the products of carbohydrate, protein, and fat metabolism.
- Detoxification of end products of protein digestion and drugs.
- Production of antibodies and essential elements of the blood-clotting mechanism.
- Production of heat and formation of vitamin A from carotin.

Gallbladder

The Gallbladder is a pear-shaped sac, usually stained dark green by the bile it contains. It is located in a hollow on the underside of the liver.

Its duct, the cystic duct, joins the hepatic duct from the liver to form the common bile duct, which enters the duodenum. The gallbladder receives bile from the liver and then concentrates and stores it. It secretes bile when the small intestine is stimulated by the entrance of fats.

Urinary System

The urinary system is the primary filtering system of the body. It consists of two glands, the kidneys, which produce urine; two tubes, the ureters, which drain the urine from the kidneys; a large reservoir, the bladder, where the urine is temporarily stored before it is excreted from the body; and a tube, the urethra, which carries the urine from the bladder to the outside of the body. All these parts, except the length of the urethra, are the same in both sexes.

Kidneys

The importance of the kidney can be realized only when its structure and function are understood. It is the only part of the urinary system in which any changes occur. The bladder, ureters, and urethra store and pass only the products of the kidneys.

The kidneys are two large, bean-shaped organs designed to filter waste materials from the blood. They are located in the upper posterior part of the abdominal cavity, outside the peritoneal sac, one on each side of the spinal column. The upper end of each kidney reaches above the level of the 12th rib. The suprarenal (adrenal) gland sits like a cap on top of each kidney.

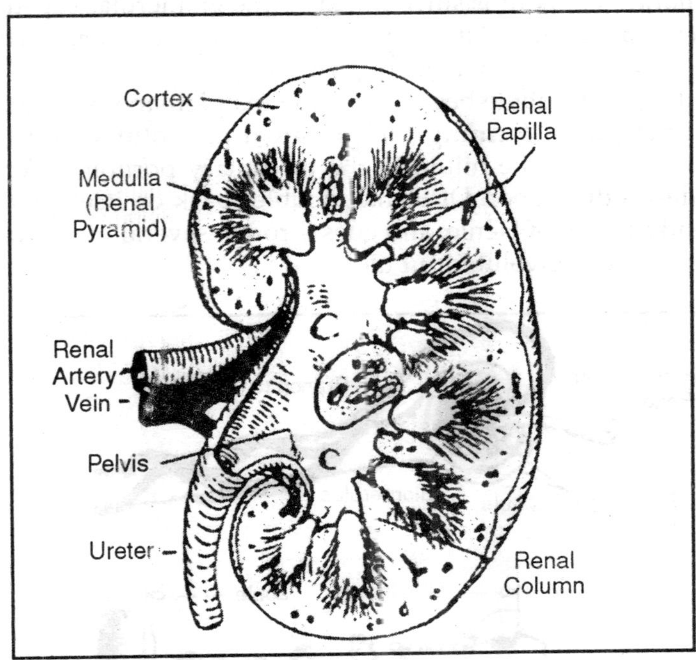

Fig. Cross Section of the Kidney.

Each kidney weighs about 125 to 170 grams. It is protected by a considerable amount of fat and supported by connective tissue and the peritoneum. Attached to the hollow side of each kidney is the dilated upper end of the ureter, forming the renal pelvis.

Structure

The kidney is composed of an external cortical and an internal medullary substance. The cortex or cortical substance is soft and granular and reddish brown. The urine is formed in the cortex.

The medulla or medullary substance is a pyramid-shaped

mass of tubes or tubules that drain the urine to the pelvis of the kidney. Blood enters the kidney through the renal artery and is distributed to the glomerulus.

The Glomerulus, lying in the cortex, consists of a tuft of capillaries. This tuft is surrounded by the glomerular capsule, which is a cuplike dilation of the end of the renal tubule. This combination is called a Malpighian Body.

The renal tubule begins with the malpighian body, takes multiple turns, forming the proximal convoluted tubule, extends toward the hilum in the medullary portion to form the descending Loop Of Henle, doubles back on itself as the ascending loop of Henle, and goes through several more turns as the distal convoluted tubule.

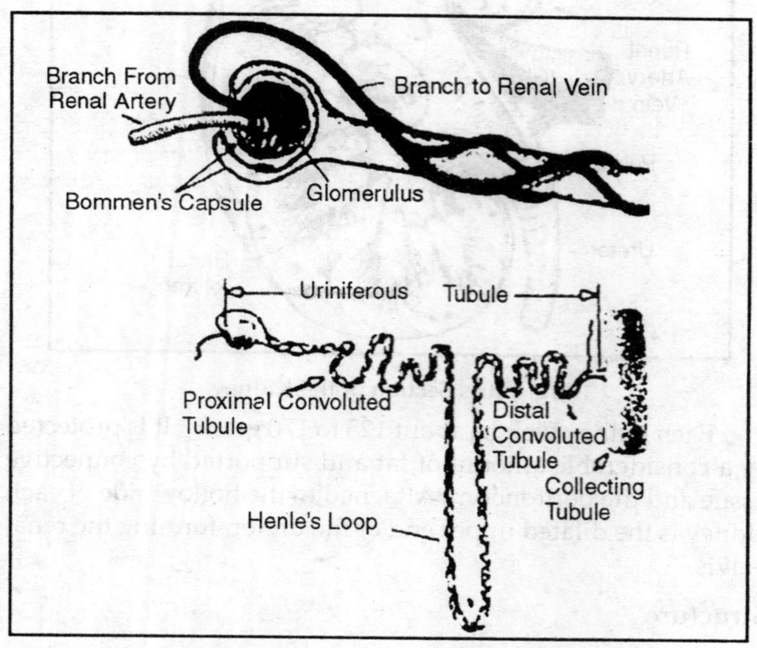

Fig. Functional Unit of the Kidney.

The structural and functional unit of the kidney is called a NEPHRON, of which there are about 1 million in each kidney. For this reason a large portion of the kidney may be destroyed without serious body damage. In addition, the loss or medical donation of one kidney does not seriously affect the body's welfare if the remaining kidney is healthy. Several of the nephrons terminate in one collecting tubule. Several collecting tubules unite to form a renal pyramid, which drains the urine into a branch (calyx) of the renal pelvis.

Function

The kidneys are effective blood purifiers and fluid balance regulators. Besides maintaining a normal pH of the blood (acid-base balance), they keep the blood slightly alkaline by removing excess substances from the blood. For example, if the blood becomes too acid, they will remove acid in the form of salts; if the blood is too alkaline, they will remove alkaline salts.

The main function of the kidneys is to remove the nitrogenous waste products that result when products of proteins are broken up. They also remove excess sugar. The second important function of the kidney is reabsorption of water, salts, sugar, and protein elements of the blood. This selective reabsorption keeps the blood at an acid-base balance and also at a constant concentration of water, salts, and proteins.

This delicate balance is necessary for normal life processes. Controlled reabsorption accounts for the amount of urine that is finally passed from the kidneys. The glomerulus filters gallons of blood each day. It is estimated that 10,000 quarts of blood pass through the kidneys in 24 hours and about 80 gallons of glomerular filtrate are formed. All the water from this filtrate is reabsorbed in the renal tubules except that containing the concentrated waste products.

The amount of urine a normal person excretes varies from 1,000 to 1,500 ml per day, but a person can function normally by excreting only 500 ml per day. The amount of urine excreted varies greatly with temperature, water intake, and state of health. No matter how much water you drink, the blood will always remain at a constant concentration, and the excess water will be excreted by the kidneys.

A large water intake does not put a strain on the kidneys as one might think, instead it eases the load of concentration placed on the kidneys. In blood plasma there is normally 0.03 per cent of urea, while in the urine there is normally 67 times as much, or about 2 per cent. This great increase is caused by the concentration of urea contained in a large kidney area in a relatively small quantity of urine. Beside removing waste products normally found in the body, the kidneys also remove toxic substances, such as certain barbituric acid derivatives, mercury, alcohol, and other drugs. One of the familiar diseases associated with the kidneys is glomerulonephritis, which is caused by protein loss from the body due to damaged glomeruli. Another disease, though not as prevalent, is uremia. This is caused by failure of the kidneys to remove the waste products from the blood, which then accumulate in high concentrations. This condition is serious and sometimes fatal.

Ureters

The ureters are two membranous tubes 1 mm to 1 cm in diameter and about 28 to 34 cm in length. Their only function is to carry urine from each kidney to the urinary bladder.

Bladder

The urinary bladder is a musculomembranous sac located in the pelvic girdle. It functions as a reservoir for urine until it empties through the urethra.

Urethra

The urethra is the tube that carries the urine from the bladder to the exterior. The urinary meatus is the external urethral opening. In the male the urethra is common to the urinary and reproductive systems; in the female it belongs only to the urinary system. The female urethra is about 4 cm long, extending from the bladder to the external orifice in the vestibule. It is embedded in the anterior wall of the vagina and surrounded by the sphincter urethrae. The male urethra is about 20 cm long and is divided into three parts: the prostatic, membranous, and penile portions. The prostatic urethra is surrounded by the prostate gland; it contains the orifices of the prostatic and ejaculatory ducts.

This portion of the male urethra is about 2.5 cm long. The membranous urethra is about 2 cm in length and is surrounded by the external sphincter. The penile urethra, the longest portion, is about 15 cm long. It lies in the ventral portion of the penis, extending to its external opening.

MALE REPRODUCTIVE SYSTEM

The male Reproductive System organs of reproduction are the penis and testes (testicles), and associated ducts and glands.

SCROTUM

The Scrotum is a cutaneous pouch containing the testes and part of the spermatic cord. Immediately beneath the skin is a thin layer of muscular fibers (cremaster), which is controlled by temperature and contracts or relaxes to lower or raise the testes in relation to the body. This muscular activity of the scrotum is necessary to regulate the temperature of the testes, which is important in the maturation of sperm cells.

Testes

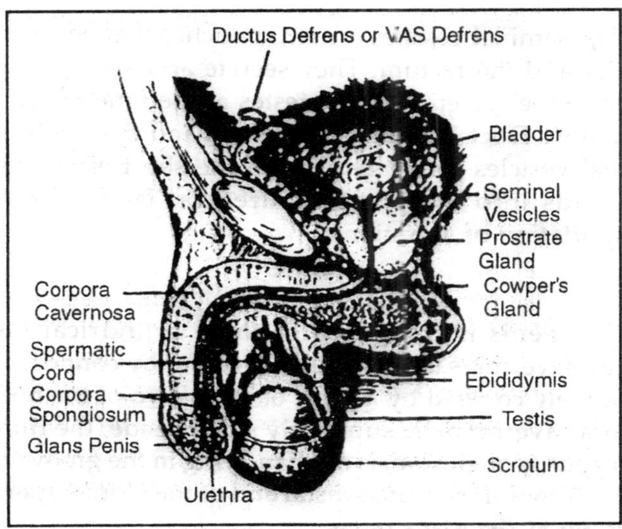

Fig. The Male Reproductive System

The Testes are oval glands suspended by the spermatic cord in a pouch. They perform two functions: production of spermatozoa (sperm) and secretion of the male sex hormone testosterone.

Lying close to the superior pole of each testis is the Epididymis, a ductal system that collects and transmits sperm from the testes.

Spermatic Cords

The two spermatic cords, each of which suspends and supplies a testis, are formed by the ductus deferens, arteries, veins, lymphatics, and nerves, bound together by connective tissue.

Ductus Deferens (Vas Deferens)

The ductus deferens is a small tube that connects the epididymis and ejaculatory duct. It ascends as part of the spermatic cord through the inguinal canal into the pelvic cavity and transmits the sperm to the ejaculatory duct.

Seminal Vesicles

The seminal vesicles are two pouches that lie between the bladder and the rectum. They secrete and store a fluid to be added to the secretion of the testes at the time of ejaculation. Ejaculatory Duct The ductus deferens and the ducts from the seminal vesicles converge to form the short ejaculatory duct that leads into the prostatic urethra. Its function is the transportation of secretions.

Penis

The penis is composed of three cylindrical bodies of spongy cavernous tissue, bound together by connective tissue and loosely covered by a layer of skin. Two of the bodies, the corpora cavernosa, lie superiorly side by side; the third body, the corpus spongiosum, is median, lying in the groove between the other two. The dilated distal end of the corpus spongiosum is known as the glans penis.

The cavernous tissue becomes greatly distended with

blood during sexual excitement, causing erection of the penis. The loose skin of the penis folds back on itself at the distal end, forming the prepuce, or foreskin, and covers the glans. Frequently, the prepuce is surgically removed (circumcision) to prevent irritation and to facilitate cleanliness.

Prostate Gland

The prostate gland is made of smooth muscle and glandular tissue that surrounds the first part of the urethra. It resembles a chestnut in shape and size. It secretes an alkaline fluid to keep the sperm mobile and protect it from the acid secretions of the female vagina. This substance is discharged into the urethra as part of the ejaculate, or semen, during the sexual act.

Bulbourethral Glands (Cowper's Glands)

Cowper's glands are two pea-sized bodies, one on either side of the membranous portion of the urethra, the excretory ducts of which open into the urethra. They secrete a mucouslike alkaline fluid during the sexual act to provide lubrication.

Semen

Semen is composed of sperm and secretions from the seminal vesicles, prostate, and Cowper's glands. It is discharged as the ejaculate during sexual intercourse. There are millions of sperm cells in the semen of each ejaculation, but only one is needed to fertilize the ovum.

It is generally considered that fertilization of the ovum occurs while it is still in the uterine tube. Therefore, it is apparent that sperm cells can move actively in the seminal fluid deposited in the vagina and through the layers of the secretion lining the uterus and the uterine tube. Although the prostate, seminal vesicles, and bulbourethral glands secrete most actively during sexual intercourse, a certain amount is being formed continuously.

During periods of prolonged sexual abstinence, discharge of this accumulation may occur during sleep as a nocturnal emission or "wet dream." This is an entirely normal condition and does not constitute a harmful or disease state; on the other hand, retention of these secretions in no way impairs health or the mental state.

At times, what appears to be semen may drip from the penis on straining to move bowels. This is the secretion of the prostate and seminal vesicles being forced out by the increased pressure within the abdominal cavity and forceful passage of feces through the rectum, which lies close to these structures.

This occurrence does not indicate disease or infection if urethral discharge is present only during such acts of straining. Any continuing discharge should be examined for evidence of infection.

FEMALE REPRODUCTIVE SYSTEM

The female reproductive system includes the ovaries, the fallopian (uterine) tubes, the uterus, the vagina, the external genitalia (vulva), and the breasts (mammary glands), which are not illustrated but will be discussed.

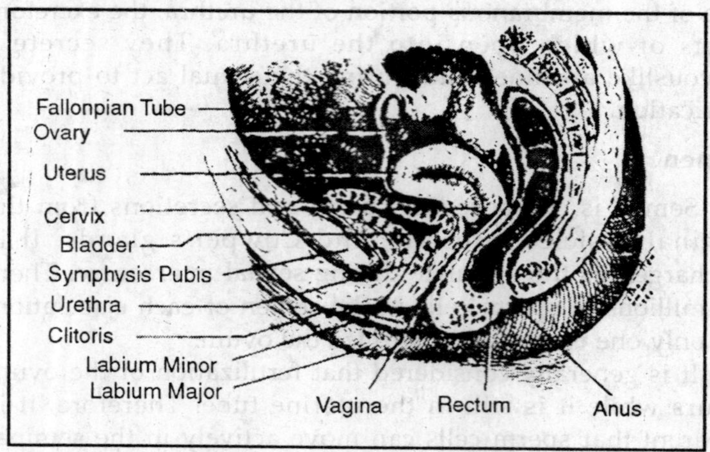

Fig. The Female Reproductive System

External Genitalia

The external genital organs, referred to collectively as the vulva, include the mons pubis, labia majora, labia minors, clitoris, vestibule, Bartholin's glands, and hymen. The mons pubis is the pad of fatty tissue beneath the skin, anterior to the symphysis pubis.

The labia majora are two folds of skin extending from the mons pubis anteriorly to the perineum (the region between the vaginal orifice and the anus). Within these two folds of skin are two smaller folds, called the labia minors, extending from the clitoris to either side of the vaginal orifice. The clitoris is a small body richly endowed with nerves, highly sensitive, and of significance in sexual stimulation.

The clitoris becomes engorged with blood during sexual excitement, but, unlike its male counterpart, the penis, it does not become erect. It is located at the point where the two labia minors meet.

The vestibule is the area between the labia minors into which the urethral and vaginal orifices open. The urinary meatus is the external urethral orifice situated inferior to the clitoris and superior to the reproductive system. vaginal orifice.

The vaginal orifice is situated inferior to the urethra. The Bartholin's glands are the female counterparts of the Cowper's glands in the male. They consist of two small roundish bodies on either side of the vaginal opening.

Each gland is connected with the vagina by means of long ducts and secretes a viscid, alkaline fluid lubricant between the labia minors and the hymen. Finally, the hymen is a fold of mucous membrane that extends across the lower part of the vagina. It is not a very reliable indicator of virginity.

Mammary Glands

The mammary glands, or breasts, are accessory organs of the female reproductive system. They develop during puberty under the influence of the hormones estrogen and progesterone. The breasts are responsible for the secretion of milk (lactation) for the nourishment of newborn infants. Structurally the breasts resemble sweat glands.

At the centre is a nipple containing 15 to 20 depressions, into which ducts from the lobes of the gland empty. During pregnancy hormones secreted by the ovaries cause the glandular tissue to grow in preparation for lactation. After childbirth hormones secreted by the anterior lobe of the pituitary gland stimulate production for 6 to 9 months

Ovaries

The ovaries (female gonads) are two almondshaped glands suspended by ligaments in the upper pelvic cavity, one on either side of the uterus, posterior and inferior to the fallopian tubes. Their prime function is to produce the ova and the female hormone estrogen and progesterone.

Although these hormones are manufactured by the ovaries, their production is controlled by the anterior pituitary gland. These hormones play essential roles in the development of secondary sex characteristics, the reproductive cycle, gestation, and lactation. The graafiau follicles are microscopic pockets in the ovaries. One a month, under hormonal influence, a follicle matures, ruptures, and expels its ovum into the uterus.

Each ovary normally releases an ovum every 56 days, the right and left ovary alternately discharging an ovum every 28 days. The menstrual cycle in most women is therefore 28 days in length.

Fallopian Tubes

The fallopian (uterine) tubes are composed of internal mucous, middle muscular, and outer serous coats that are continuous with the layers of the uterus. They serve as ducts of the ovaries, providing a passageway to the uterus. These tubes are in contact with the ovaries, but are not continuous with them.

Their funnel-shaped openings, called free openings, are fringed with fingerlike processes that pick up an ovum and draw it into the fallopian tubes, where it is transported to the uterus by peristalsis and gravity. Fertilization of an ovum normally takes place in the fallopian tubes.

Uterus

The uterus (womb) is a hollow, pear-shaped organ with

thick, muscular walls. It is lined with a specialized epitheliums, called endometrium, which undergoes partial destruction about every 28 days in the nonpregnant woman. The uterus averages 7 cm in length and 5 cm in width. It has three openings: the openings of the fallopian tubes laterally and the opening into the vagina.

The parts of the uterus are the body, which is the large upper portion, and the cervix, which is the smaller portion that projects into the upper part of the vagina. The cervical opening into the vagina is called the external os. The walls of the uterus arc highly flexible and are composed of three layers that are continuous with the respective layers of the fallopian tubes.

In addition to being the focal point of the endometrial (menstrual) cycle, the uterus is the site of implantation, growth, and development of the fertilized ovum. The muscular walls of the uterus produce powerful rhythmic contractions that are important in the expulsion of the fetus at birth.

Vagina

The vagina is a musculomembranous, collapsible tube capable of great distention. It is lined with mucous membrane that extends from the cervix to the vulva. The canal is about 7.5 cm long, and its lining membrane, which is greatly folded, is continuous with the inner lining of the uterus.

The vagina is the organ that receives the male sperm during intercourse. It also forms the lower portion of the birth canal, stretching widely during delivery. In addition, it serves as an excretory duct for uterine secretions and menstrual flow.

Recurring Cycles

When females reach puberty, they begin to experience the two recurring female cycles, the ovarian and endometrial. As previously mentioned, each ovary produces a mature ovum every 56 days. They expel their ova on an alternating basis, approximately one every 28 days.

The length of this cycle may vary markedly from individual to individual and between cycles of the same individual. On the first days of menstruation, several ova within the graafian follicles begin to mature, and normally one will be expelled 14 days before the next menstrual flow. This is the ovarian cycle.

The endometrial cycle centers around the periodic development and breakdown of the endometrial lining of the uterus. The first phase of the cycle is the menses, or menstruation. It begins when the endometrial lining starts to slough off from the walls of the uterus, and it is characterized by bleeding from the vagina.

This is day 1 of the cycle, and this phase usually lasts through day 5. The time between the last day of the menses and ovulation is known as the postmenstrual phase. It lasts from day 6 through day 13 or 14 and is characterized by proliferation of endometrial cells in the uterus, which develop under the influence of the hormone estrogen. Ovulation is the rupture of a graafian follicle with the release of a mature ovum into the fallopian tubes.

It usually occurs on day 14 or 15 of the cycle. The postovulatory (premenstrual) phase is the time between ovulation and the onset of the menses and normally lasts 14 days.

During this phase the ovum travels through the fallopian tubes to the and Thibodeau: Textbook of uterus. If the ovum becomes fertilized during this it will become implanted in and nurtured by the newly developed endometrial lining. However, if fertilization does not take place, the lining deteriorates and eventually sloughs off, marking day 1 of the next cycle.

Chapter 5

First Aid and Emergency Procedures

GENERAL CONSIDERATIONS

First aid and emergency procedures are the professional care of the sick and injured before definitive medical attention can be obtained. Appropriate care may range from an encouraging word to a dramatic struggle to draw a person back from the brink of death. At all times, however, it must be remembered that first aid measures are temporary expedients whose purpose is to save life, to prevent further injury, and to preserve resistance and vitality.

These measures are not meant to replace proper medical diagnosis and treatment procedures. A corpsman who understands this point, who knows the limits of the professional care a corpsman can offer, and who is motivated to keep abreast of new first aid equipment and procedures will be able to provide the competent care that will make the differences between life or death, temporary or permanent injury, and rapid recovery or long-term disability.

GENERAL FIRST AID RULES

There are a few general first aid rules that you should follow in any emergency:.

- Take a moment to get organized. On your way to an accident scene, use a few seconds to remember the basic rules of first aid. Remain calm as you take charge of the situation, and act quickly but efficiently. Decide as soon as possible what has to be done and which one of the patient's injuries needs attention first.

- Unless contraindicated, make your preliminary examination in the position and place you find the victim.
- Moving the victim before this check could gravely endanger life, especially if the back or ribs are broken. Of course, if the situation is such that you or the victim is in danger, you must weigh this threat against the potential damage caused by premature transportation.
- If you decide to move the victim, do it quickly and gently to a safe location where proper first aid can be administered.
- In a multivictim situation, limit your preliminary survey to observing for airway patency, breathing, and circulation—the immediate life-threatening conditions.
- Remember, irreversible brain damage can occur within 4 to 6 minutes if breathing has stopped. Bleeding from a severed artery can lethally drain the body in even less time. If both are present and you are alone, quickly handle the major hemorrhage first, and then work to get oxygen back into the system.
- Shock may allow the rescuer a few minutes of grace but is no less deadly in the long run.
- Examine the victim for fractures, especially in the skull, neck, spine, and rib areas. If any are present, prematurely moving the patient can easily lead to increased lung damage, permanent injury, or death. Fractures of the innominate bone or extremities, though not as immediately life- threatening, may pierce vital tissue or blood vessels if mishandled.
- Remove enough clothing to get a clear idea of the extent of the injury.
- Rip along the seams, if possible, or cut. Removal of clothing in the normal way may aggravate hidden

injuries. Respect the victim's modesty as you proceed, and do not allow the victim to become chilled.

- Keep the victim reassured and comfortable. If possible, do not allow the victim to see the wounds. The victim can endure pain and discomfort better if confident in your abilities.
- This is important because under normal conditions the corpsman will not have strong pain relief medications right at hand.
- Avoid touching open wounds or burns with your fingers or unsterile objects, unless clean compresses and bandages are not available and it is imperative to stop severe bleeding.
- Unless contraindicated, position the unconscious or semiconscious victim on his or her side or back, with the head turned to the side to minimize choking or the aspirating of vomitus. Never givean unconscious person any substance by mouth.
- Always carry a litter patient feet first so that the rear bearer can constantly observe the victim for respiratory or circulatory distress.

Assessing The Patient's Condition

The following procedures for assessing a patient's condition under various circumstances are based upon Department of Transportation recommendations. These are general guidelines that can be modified to suit the situation.

Determining The Problem

- If the patient can communicate, determine if the problem is medical or trauma related.
  a. If medical, follow the sequence below.
     - Evaluate diagnostic and vital signs.
     - Develop the patient's history.
     - Examine for the medical problems.
     - Examine for a trauma-related problem.
  b. If trauma-related, follow the sequence below.
     - Evaluate diagnostic and vital signs.

  - Examine the injury.
  - Develop the patient's history.
  - Examine for a medical related problem.
- If the patient cannot communicate, follow the sequence below.
  a. Evaluate diagnostic and vital signs.
  b. Develop the patient's history, then determine if the problem is medical or trauma related.
  c. If medical, examine first for the medical problem then for a trauma related problem.
  d. If trauma related, examine first for the trauma related problem then for a medical problem.

Evaluating The Diagnostic And Vital Signs

- Sequence of taking vital signs
  a. If the patient with a traumatic injury is communicative, assess the injury site after taking vital signs.
  b. If the patient with a medical problem is communicative, take vital signs after the preliminary assessment and in conjunction with the medical history, if possible.
  c. If the patient is noncommunicative, take vital signs immediately after the primary assessment.
- Essential diagnostic and vital signs
  a. Mental status
    - Consciousness—avoid descriptive words like "stupor" or "semiconscious"; be specific.
    - Reaction to stimulus—describe
    - Orientation d. Responsiveness
- Respirations
  a. Tracheal deviation
  b. Rate—tachypnea
  c. Depth
    - Hyperpnea
    - Hypopnea
  d. Dyspnea

e. Breathing sounds
f. Flaring of anterior nares on inspiration
g. Retraction of suprasternal notch on inspiration
Retraction of intercostal spaces

- Pulse
  a. Rate
  b. Rhythm
  c. Strength
- Blood pressure

Examining for Trauma-related Problems

Assess each of the following

- Head
  a. Inspect for
    - Obvious hemorrhage
    - Ecchymosis, erythema, or contusions
    - Scalp lesions
  b. Gently palpate for
    - Lumps
    - Depressions
    - Pain on compression of skull (Do not compress if patient is noncommunicative!)
- Eyes
  a. Inspect for
    - Laceration to lid or globe
    - Foreign matter in eye
    - Unequal pupils (anisocoria)
    - Eye movements
    - Pupillary reaction
  b. Palpate for
    - Swelling in orbital or periorbital area
    - Failure to sense touch in supraorbital and infraorbital areas if patient is communicative
- Ear—inspect for
  a. Discharge from external auditory canal
  b. Ecchymosis over mastoid (Battle's sign)

c. Lacerations
d. Bleeding

- Nose—inspect for
  a. Rhinorrhea
  b. Patent nostrils
  c. Bleeding
  d. Flaring of anterior nares on inspiration
- Mouth
  a. Inspect for
     - Potential airway obstruction
     - Edema or hemotoma
     - Bleeding
     - Teeth or dentures lodged in pharynx
     - Misalignment of teeth
     - Pain when biting teeth together
  b. Palpate for fractures:
     - Zygomatic
     - Mandible
     - Maxilla
- Neck
  a. Inspect for
     - Retraction bones at suprasternal notch on inspiration
     - Deviation of trachea from midline
  b. Auscultate for air sounds in trachea
- Skin—inspect for
  a. Jaundice
  b. Cyanosis
  c. Diaphoresis
  d. Temperature
  e. Moistness
  f. Pallor
- Thorax:
  a. Inspect for
     - Respiration
       (a) Rate—tachypnea
       (b) Depth 1 Hyperpnea 2 Hypopnea
       (c) Retraction of intercostal spaces

- Chest elevation symmetry—flail chest
- Lacerations, puncture, or ecchymosis

b. Palpate (unless there is a suspected spinal injury)
   - Vertebrae and ribs for symmetry and tenderness
   - Anterior to posterior compression of thorax
   - Lateral-to-lateral compression of thorax
   - Compression of clavicle
   - Cranial to chordal compression
   - Pressure of costochondral junction
   - Compression on costovertebral angles

c. Auscultate for lung and heart sounds
   - Lung sounds
   a. Absent or unequal breath
   b. Characteristics
      1. Rales
      2. Rhonchi
      3. Wheezes
      4. Strider
   - Heart sounds

d. Percussion
   - Fluid in thorax
   - Pneumothorax or collapsed lung

- Abdomen:

a. Inspect for
   - Lacerations, ecchymosis, burns, etc.
   - Hematoma
   - Flexion of hips to relieve pain

b. Auscultate bowel sounds

c. Palpate firmly for
   1. Distended abdomen
   2. Guarding
   3. Local tenderness
   4. Rebound pain.

- Extremities:

a. Inspect for
   - Abnormal angulation or bone ends protruding

- Presence of extremity pulse
  (a) Dorsalis pedis
  (b) Radial
- Nail bed colour (cyanosis)
- Impaired sensation
- Inability to move joint
- Lacerations or ecchymosis
- Needle marks or bites

b. Palpate for abnormal reaction

- Central nervous system

a. Inspect for
- Mental state
  (a) Consciousness
  (b) Orientation
  (c) Response to verbal stimulus and pain
- Gross deformities
- Lacerations
- Decerebrate posturing
- Decorticate posturing

b. Palpate for
- Tenderness
- Deformities

Examining For Medical Problems

A. Assess each of the following areas

- Neck

a. Inspect for jugular vein distention

b. Auscultate trachea for adequate airflow

- Thorax and lungs

a. Inspect for evidence of pain while breathing or moving

b. Auscultation
- Rales
- Rhonchi
- Wheezes
- Stridor

c. Palpate to determine symmetry of breathing

d. Percuss for

  - Hemothorax
  - Pneumothorax
- Thorax and heart—auscultate for abnormal heart sounds
- Abdomen
  a. Inspect for
    - Flexion of hips to relieve pain
    - Normal contour during breathing
    - Distention
  b. Auscultate for bowel sounds
  c. Palpate for
    - Distention
    - Guarding
    - Local tenderness
    - Rebound pain
- CNS
  a. Inspect for
    - Mental state
    - Pupil reaction
    - Eye movements
    - Muscle tone
    - Paralysis
  b. Palpate for
    - Loss of feeling
    - Absent reflexes
    - Muscle tone
    - Paralysis

Developing The Medical History

The patient's history is an important information source that will directly influence both the treatment offered by the corpsman at the accident scene and the care given in the hospital. The history is acquired at the accident scene and the care given in the hospital. The history is acquired by observing for clues and careful questioning of the patient, family, and bystanders.

A history is divided into three parts: the history of the immediate situation, the patient's medical history, and the family medical history. (The family history is usually not relevant in the field with a trauma patient.) A history of the present illness is a directed history, striking a balance between allowing the patient to ramble and leading the patient. The purpose is to discover why you were called. In general, the following information must be gathered:

- Gross problem identification
  a. Chief complaint
  b. How does the patient feel?
- Location of the problem
  a. Pain
  b. Other symptoms (e.g., dizziness or shortness of breath)
- Quality of symptom(s)
  a. How does it feel?
  b. What does it resemble?
- Quantity of symptom(s)
  a. Pain intensity
  b. Effect on normal functioning
- Chronology of symptom(s)
  a. Time of onset
  b. Duration
  c. Frequency
- Cause of trauma
  a. What happened?
  b. Any contributing physical cause?
  c. How did injury take place (e.g., patient's head hit corner of table during fall)?
- Scenario of first medical symptoms
  a. Where did first symptoms occur?
  b. What was the patient doing?
- Aggravating and alleviating movements
- Associated complaints
  a. Other symptoms
  b. Affected normal body functions

The following are components of a complete history of a patient's medical problems:

- General health before the current problem

- Name of family physician or location of health records
- Current medications and treatments
- Recent injuries
- Allergies
- Family medical history
    a. General health of family members
    b. Recent family illnesses

First Aid Equipment And Supplies

In a first aid situation, the corpsman must always be ready to improvise. In the majority of emergency situations, standard medical supplies and equipment will not be immediately available or they may run out.

Later sections of this chapter will discuss how material can be used as substitutes. When medical supplies and equipment are available, they will probably be found in an ambulance or in the field medical Unit One bag.

Patient transfer litters

- Wheeled litter
- Folding or collapsible litter

Airway, pharyngeal, adult, child, infant Ambu bag with masks, adult, child, infant Suction equipment, portable and installed Oxygen inhalation equipment, installed and portable

- Oxygen masks, adult, child, infant
- Humidifier
- Connecting tubing
- Regulator and flowmeter

Spine boards, long and short Sterile obstetrical delivery pack Splinting material

a. Pneumatic extremity splints
b. Thomas half-ring or Hare traction splint
c. MAST (pneumatic counter-pressure device)

Wound dressing supplies Acute poisoning kit with activated charcoal and syrup of ipecac in premeasured doses Eye irrigation equipment Snakebite kit as determined by local policy General basic supplies to include pillows, pillowcases, sheets, towels, emesis basin, disposable tissues, bedpan, thermometer, drinking cups, sandbags, blankets, stethoscopes, sphygmomanometer

Table. Contents of an Ambulance Emergency Bag.

Regular Drip	Mini Drip
18-gauge Medicut	Ace wrap
16-gauge Medicut	20-gauge needles
Airways (Various sizes)	Syrup of Ipecac
Sodium chloride ampzules	10 cc syringes
19-gauge butterflies	Trach adapter
Y-connector	Straight connector
Tourniquet	Safety pins
Tongue blades	Alcohol swabs
Klings	Tape
Ammonia ampules	Arm slings
Stethoscope	Extension tubing
Examination gloves	Suction tube
Adult mask	Oxygen tubing
Nasal cannula	4 X 4s
Lubricant	Toomey syringe
Ambu bag	Grease pencil

Table —Medical instrument and supply set, individual (Unit One)

- Descriptions
  a. Weight 9 lbs
  b. Four strong compartments
  c. Adjustable carrying strap
  d. Made of nylon
- Contents
  a. One role wire fabric, 5" X 36"
  b. Two bottles of aspirin, 324 mg, 100s
  c. Three packages of morphine inj. 1/4 g, 5s
  d. One bottle tetracaine hydrochloride ophthalmic sol.
  e. Three bottles povidone-iodine sol. 1/2 fl oz.
  f. Two packages atropine inj.,12s
  g. Two muslin triangular bandages
  h. Two medium battle dressings, 7 1/4 X 8

i. Eight small battle dressings 4 X 7
j. One roll adhesive tape, 3" X 5 yds
k. Six packages of Band-Aids, 6s
l. One pair scissors, bandage
m. One tourniquet
n. One airway, plastic adult/child
o. One thermometer, oral
p. One card of safety pins, medium, 12s
q. One surgical instrument set, minor surgery
r. Two books field medical cards
s. One pencil, black lead, mechanical
t. Two packages gauze, roller, 3" X 5 yds

Contents of an emergency bag that a corpsman might find in an ambulance. Table lists the contents of the Unit One bag. Unique operational requirements or command decisions may modify the make-up of any of the lists. It is up to the corpsman to be familiar with the emergency medical equipment at the command, since the call may come at a moment's notice to use any of these items to help save or sustain a life.

Triage

A final general first aid consideration is triage. Triage is a French word meaning "picking, sorting, or choice" and is used to mean the evaluation and classification of casualties for the purpose of establishing priorities for treatment and evacuation. In the military, there are two basic types of triage: combat and noncombat. In each case, sorting decisions may vary, depending upon the situation.

The person in charge is responsible for the balancing of human lives against the realities of the tactical situation, the level of medical stock on hand, and the realistic capabilities of personnel. Triage is an ongoing process and decisions are made at every stage in the movement of the casualty.

Sorting For Treatment— Tactical

The following discussion refers primarily to the battalion aid station (BAS), where helicopter or rapid land evacuation is not readily available, or to the shipboard battle-dressing station. Immediately upon arrival, sort the casualties into groups in the order listed below:

- *Class I*: Those whose injuries require minor professional treatment that can be done on an outpatient or ambulatory basis. These personnel can be returned to duty in a short period of time.
- *Class II*: Those whose injuries require immediate lifesustaining measures or are of a moderate nature. Initially, they require a minimum amount of time, personnel, and supplies.
- *Class III*: Those for whom definitive treatment can be delayed without jeopardy to life or loss of limb.
- *Class IV*: The hopelessly wounded who would require extensive treatment beyond the immediate medical capabilities. Treatment of these casualties would be to the detriment of others.

Sorting For Treatment— Non-tactical

In a civilian or non-tactical situation, sorting of casualties is somewhat, but not significantly, different from a combat situation. There are three basic classes of injuries and the order of treatment is different.

- *Priority I*: These casualties require immediate life sustaining action.
- *Priority II*: These casualties generally have injuries where treatment can be delayed for a short time.
- *Priority III:* These casualties generally have minor injuries or they have obviously mortal wounds where survival is not expected.

As mentioned before, triage is an ongoing process; depending on the treatment rendered, the amount of time elapsed, and the constitution of the casualty, you may have to reassign priorities. What appears to be a minor wound on initial evaluation may develop into a profound shock, or a casualty that requires immediate treatment may be stabilized and down-graded to a delayed status. respiratory system and heart function.

The primary emphasis is placed on maintaining an open

Airway to counter upper airway obstruction; restoring Breathing to counter respiratory arrest; and restoring Circulation to counter cardiac arrest. These are the ABC's of basic life support.

SORTING FOR EVACUATION

During the Vietnam war, the techniques of helicopter medical evacuation (MEDEVAC) were so improved that most casualties could be evacuated to a major medical facility within minutes of their injury.

This considerably lightened the load of the hospital corpsman in the field, since provision for long-term care before the evacuation was not normally required. However, rapid aeromedical response did not relieve the corpsman of the responsibility for giving the best emergency care within the field limitations in order to stabilize the victim before the helicopter arrived.

Trige was seldom a problem since most of the injured could be evacuated quickly. New developments in warfare, along with changes in the probable theaters of deployment, indicate that the helicopter evacuation system may no longer be viable in a front-line environment.

If this becomes the case, longer ground chains of evacuation to the BAS or division clearing station may be required.

This will increase the need for the life stabilizing activities before each step in the chain and in transit. Evacuation triage will normally be for personnel in the Class II and Class III treatment categories, based on the tactical situation and the nature of the injuries.

Class IV casualties may have to receive their treatment at the BAS level and Class I personnel would be treated on the line. Remember, triage is based on the concept of saving the maximum number of personnel possible. In some cases, a casualty has the potential to survive, but the treatment necessary requires a great deal of time and supplies. As difficult as it may be, you may have to forsake this patient in order to save others that have a greater potential for survival.

BASIC LIFE SUPPORT

Basic life support is the emergency techniques for recognizing and treating failures of the respiratory system and heart function. The primary emphasis is placed on maintaining an open Airway to counter upper airway obstruction; restoring Breathing to counter respiratory arrest; and restoring Circulation to counter cardiac arrest. These are the ABC's of basic life support.

Upper Airway Obstruction

The assurance of breathing takes precedence over all other emergency care measures. The reason for this is simple: If a person cannot breathe, he or she cannot survive. Many factors can cause the patient's airway to become fully or partially obstructed. In the adult, a very common cause of obstruction is improperly chewed food that becomes lodged in the airway; the so-called "cafe coronary." Children have a disturbing tendency to swallow foreign objects during play. Another cause occurs during unconsciousness, when the tongue may fall back and block the pharynx. Normally, the heart will continue to beat until oxygen deficiency becomes acute. Periodic checks of the carotid artery must be made to ensure that circulation is being maintained.

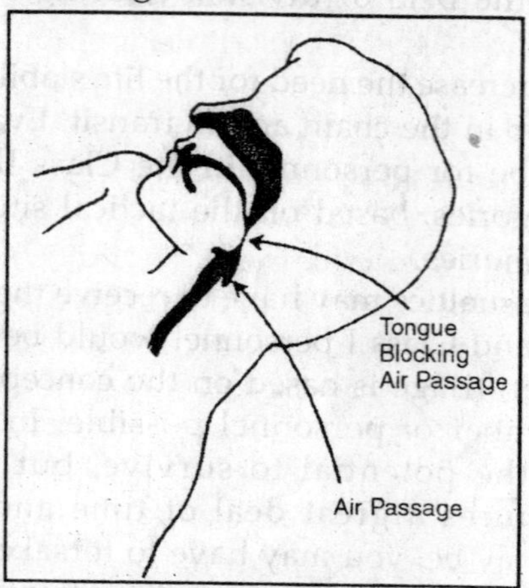

Fig.4-1.—Blocked Airway

Partial Airway Obstruction

The signs of partial airway obstruction include unusual breath sounds, skin discoloration (cyanosis), or changes in breathing pattern. The conscious patient will usually make clutching motions toward the neck, even when the obstruction dews not prevent speech. For the conscious patient with an apparent partial obstruction, encourage him or her to cough.

Note: In cases where the patient has an apparent partial obstruction but cannot cough, begin to treat the patient as if this were a complete obstruction. This also applies to patients who are cyanotic.

Complete Airway Obstruction

The conscious patient will attempt to speak but will be unable to do so, nor will he or she be able to cough. Usually, the patient will display the universal distress signal for choking by clutching at the neck. The unconscious patient with a complete airway obstruction exhibits none of the usual signs of breathing: rise and fall of the chest and air exchange through the nose and/or mouth.

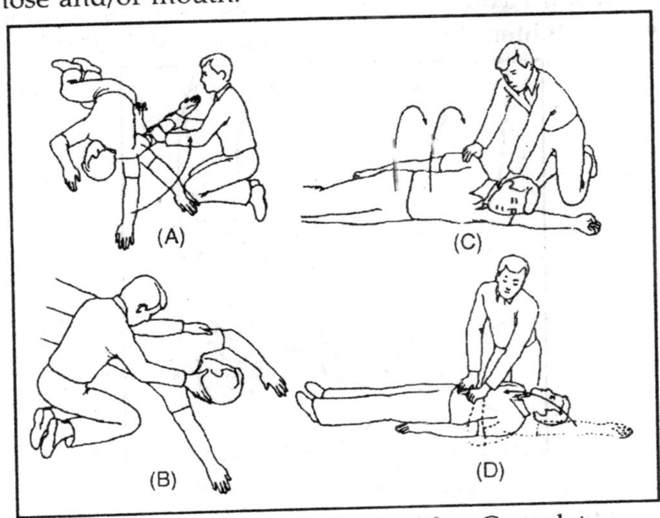

Fig. Unconscious Patient with a Complete Airway obstruction

A complete blockage is also indicated if a perfectly executed attempt to perform artificial ventilation fails to instill air into the lungs.

Opening the Airway

Many problems of airway obstruction, particularly those caused by the tongue, can be corrected simply by repositioning the head and neck. If repositioning does not alleviate the problem, more aggressive measures must be taken.

Note: Before going further, it is imperative that corpsmen remember to check all victims for possible spinal injuries before any repositioning is attempted. If there is no time to immobilize these injuries and the airway cannot be opened with the victim in the present position, then great care must be taken when repositioning.

The head, neck, and back must be moved as a single unit. To do this, adhere to the following steps.

- Kneel to the side of the victim in line with the victim's shoulders but far enough away so that the victim's body will not touch yours when it is rolled toward you.
- Straighten the victim's legs, gently but quickly.

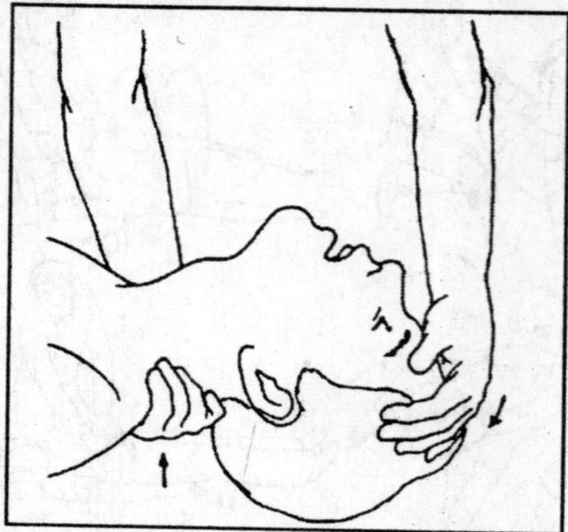

Fig. Opening the Airway

- Move the victim's closest arm along the floor until it reaches straight out past the head.

- Support the back of the victim's head with one hand while you reach over with the other hand to grab the far shoulder.
- Pull the far shoulder toward you while at the same time keeping the head and neck in a natural straight line with the back.

  The head resting on the extended arm will help you in this critical task.

Head Tilt

The head tilt technique of opening the airway is a simple repositioning of the head.

With the patient lying down, place one of your hands on his or her forehead and apply gentle, firm, backward pressure using the palm of your hand.

With your other hand under the victim's neck, lift the neck. This will lift the patient's tongue away from the back of the throat and provide an adequate airway.

Note: This technique is not recommended for patients with suspected neck or spinal injuries.

Jaw Thrust

A second technique for opening the airway is the jaw thrust.

This technique is accomplished by kneeling by the top of the victim's head and placing your fingers behind the angles of the lower jaw, or hooking your fingers under the jaw, then bringing the jaw forward.

Separate the lips with your thumbs to allow breathing through the mouth as well as the nose. This technique is to be used if a neck injury is suspected. Either the head tilt or the jaw thrust will offer some relief for most forms of airway obstruction.

They also prepare the airway for artificial ventilation. If the airway is still seriously obstructed, it may be necessary to try to remove the obstruction by using the abdominal thrust or chest thrust methods indicated for opening a completely blocked airway.

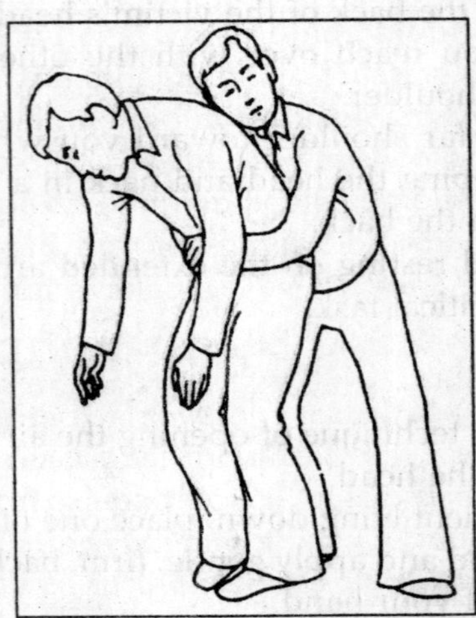

Fig. Position for Standing Abdominal Thrust.

Abdominal Thrusts

The abdominal thrust makes use of the air reserve in the lungs. It is also highly effective in removing water from the lungs of near drowning victims.

ABDOMINAL THRUST STANDING TECHNIQUE

Stand behind the victim and wrap your arms around the victim's waist. Make a fist with one hand and place it thumbside against the abdomen along the midline and slightly above the navel.

Grasp the fist with the other hand. Give four quick upward thrusts to the victim. The obstruction should pop out like a champagne cork.

ABDOMINAL THRUST RECLINING TECHNIQUE

Position yourself for the thrust by straddling the victim at the hips.

Place the heels of your hands one on top of the other, along the midline, slightly above the navel, and give four quick upward thrusts into the abdomen.

Note that the victim must be lying face up. If unsuccessful, repeat the four abdominal thrusts until the obstruction is dislodged.

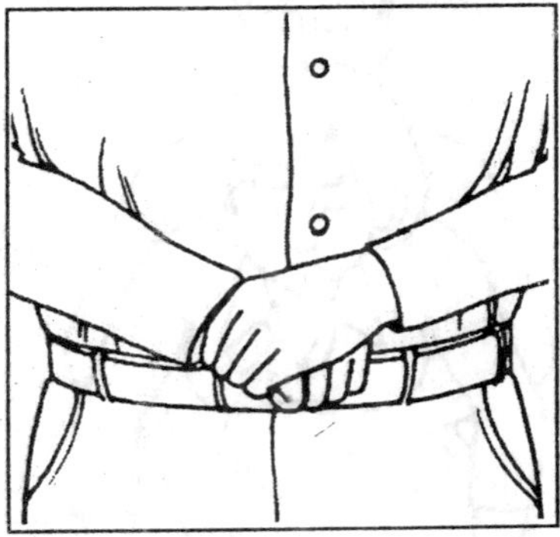

Fig. Correct Hand Position for Abdominal Thrust.

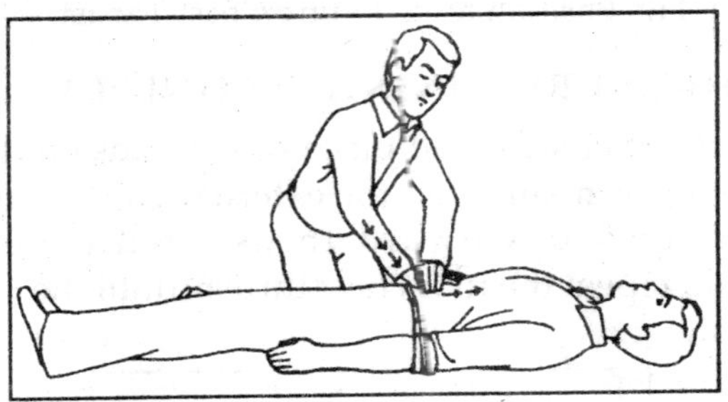

Fig. Position for Reclining Abdominal Thrust.

Chest Thrusts

For obese or pregnant victims, the chest thrust methods are recommended for removing airway obstructions since manual pressure in the abdomen area of these people would either be ineffective or cause internal damage.

Chest Thrust Standing Technique

Bring your arms under the arms of the victim, and encircle the lower chest.

Grasp your wrists, keeping the thumbside close to the victim's chest. Keep your fist on the middle of the sternum, not the lower part. Press the chest with sharp, backward thrusts.

Fig. Position for Standing Chest Thrust.

CHEST THRUST RECLINING TECHNIQUE

Kneel at either side, and place your hands on the chest in exactly the same manner as for external chest compression. Give four quick downward thrusts with the arms. If unsuccessful, repeat the four chest thrusts until the obstruction is dislodged.

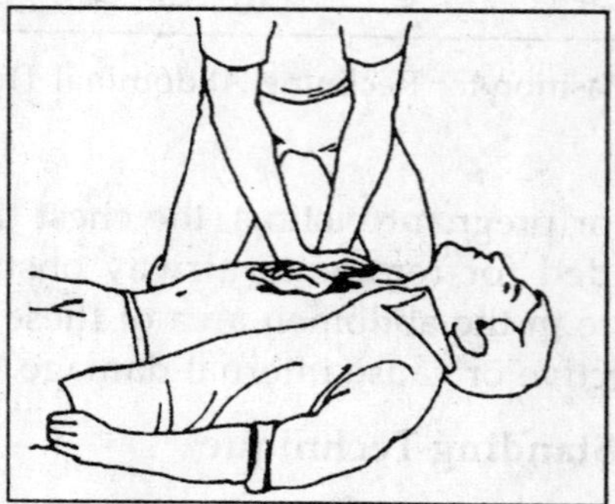

Fig. Position for Reclining Chest Thrust.

BREATHING

The second aspect of basic life support is to restore breathing in cases of respiratory arrest. Failure of the breathing mechanism maybe caused by various factors. They include complete airway obstruction, insufficient oxygen in the air, the inability of the blood to carry oxygen (carbon monoxide poisoning), paralysis of the breathing centre of the brain, and external compression of the body.

Breathing failure is usually, but not always, immediately accompanied by cardiac arrest. Periodic checks of the carotid pulse must be made, and you must be prepared to start cardiopulmonary resuscitation (CPR).

The signs of respiratory arrest are an absence of respiratory effort, a lack of detectable air movement through the nose or mouth, unconsciousness, and a cyanotic discoloration of the lips and nail beds.

Artificial Ventilation

The purpose of artificial ventilation is to provide a method of air exchange until natural breathing is re-established. Artificial ventilation should be given only when natural breathing has been suspended; it must not be given to a person who is breathing naturally.

Do not assume that a person's breathing has stopped merely because the person is unconscious or has been rescued from water, from poisonous gas, or from contact with an electric wire.

Remember: Do Not Give Artificial Ventilation To A Person Who Is Breathing Naturally.

If the victim does not begin spontaneous breathing after using the head tilt or jaw thrust techniques to open the airway, attempt to use artificial ventilation immediately. If ventilation is inadequate, use the thrust techniques to clear the airway, followed by another attempt at artificial ventilation.

Mouth-to-Mouth

To perform mouth-to-mouth ventilation, place one hand under the victim's neck and place. Position for reclining chest thrust. Mouth-to-mouth ventilation. The heel of the other hand on the forehead, using the thumb and index finger to pinch the nostrils shut. Tilt the head back to open the airway.

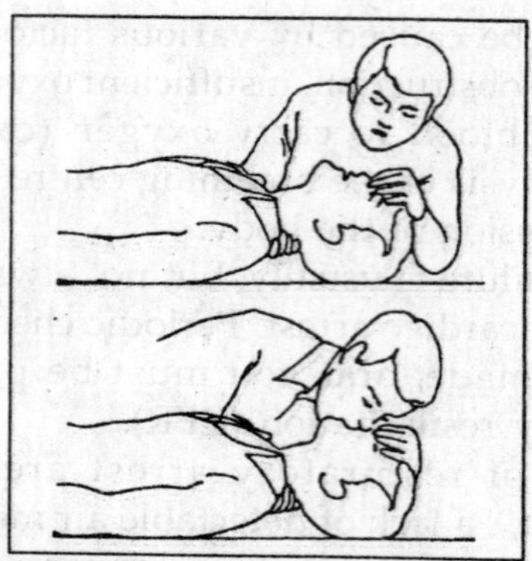

Fig. Mouth-to-mouth Ventilation.

If there is no spontaneous breathing, start artificial ventilation with two ventilations, allowing the lungs to deflate. If the victim still does not respond, then you must fully inflate the lungs at the rate of 12 Ventilations Per Minute Or One Breath Every 5 Seconds. Periodically, check the pupils for reaction to light; constriction is a sign of adequate oxygenation. For infants, seal both the mouth and nose with your mouth. Blow puffs from your cheeks to prevent lung damage. Mouth-to-mouth ventilation can be thrust.

Mouth-to-Nose

Mouth-to-nose administered with the jaw ventilation is effective when the victim has extensive facial or dental injuries; this permits an effective air seal. To administer this method, place the heel of one hand on the victim's forehead and use the other hand to lift the jaw.

After sealing the victim's lips, start artificial ventilation with two breaths, allowing the lungs to deflate. If the victim does not respond, then you must fully inflate the lungs at the rate of 12 ventilations per minute or one breath every 5 seconds until the victim can breathe spontaneously.

Back-Pressure Arm-Lift

The back-pressure arm-lift method is a less effective technique used when other methods are not feasible, such as on a battlefield where gas masks must be worn. Place the victim in the prone position, face to one side, and neck hyperextended with the hands under the head. Quickly clear the mouth of any foreign matter.

Kneel at the victim's head and place your hands on the back so that the heels of your hands lie just below a line between the armpits, with thumbs touching and fingers extending downward and outward.

Rock forward, keeping your arms straight and exert pressure almost directly downward on the victim's back, forcing air out of the lungs. Then rock backward, releasing the pressure and grasping the arm just above the elbows. Continue to rock backward, pulling the arms upward and inward (toward the head) until resistance and tension in the shoulders are noted.

This expands the chest, causing active intake of air (inspiration). Rock forward and release the victim's arms. This causes passive exiting of air (expiration). Repeat the cycle of press, release, lift, and release 12 times a minute until the victim can breathe spontaneously.

Mask-to-Mask

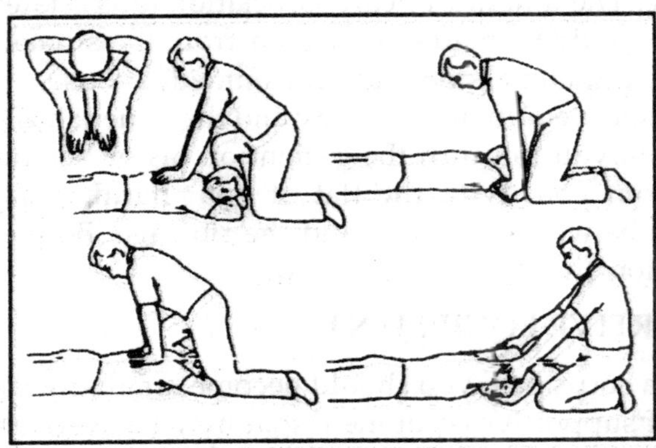

Fig. Back Pressure Arm Lift.

Certain types of gas masks for use in a contaminated environment, such as on a battlefield after a chemical or biological warfare attack, are equipped to allow a corpsman to give a victim artificial ventilation without either the corpsman or the patient being exposed to the unhealthy atmosphere.

This is carried out by a coupling on the face of each mask. When they are joined, an airway is formed, allowing ventilation to proceed.

Gastric Distention

Sometimes during artificial ventilation, air is forced into the stomach instead of into the lungs. The stomach becomes distended (bulges), indicating that the airway is blocked or partially blocked, or that ventilations are too forceful. This problem is more commonly seen in children but can occur with any patient.

A slight bulge is of little worry, but a major distention can cause two serious problems. First is a reduced lung volume; the distended stomach forces the diaphragm up. Second, there is a strong possibility of vomiting.

The best way to avoid gastric distention is to properly position the head and neck and/or limit the volume of ventilations delivered.

Note: The american heart association (aha) states that no attempt should be made to force air from the stomach unless suction equipment is on hand for immedi ate use.

If suction equipment is ready and the patient has a marked distention, you can turn the patient on his or her side facing away from you. With the flat of your hand, apply gentle pressure between the navel and the rib cage. Be prepared to use suction should vomiting occur.

SUPPORTIVE EQUIPMENT

AS a corpsman, you should become familiar with various pieces of supportive equipment that may be available to help you to maintain an open airway and to restore breathing in emergency situation.

They include artificial airways, the bag valve-mask system, the mouth-to-mask system with the oxygen-inlet valve, and suction.

Use of Oxygen (O_2)

In an emergency first aid situation, the corpsman will probably have a size E, 650-liter cylinder available. This is fitted with a yoke-style pressure reducing rcgtilator, with gauges to show tank pressure and flow liters per minute) to the flowmeter rate (adjustable from 0 to 15 A humidifier can be attached nipple to help prevent tissue 4-14 drying caused by the water vapour free oxygen.

An oxygen line can be connected from the flowmeter nipple or humidifier to a number of oxygen delivery devices that will be discussed later.

When available, oxygen should be administered to cardiac arrest patients and to self-ventilating patients who are unable to inhale enough oxygen to prevent hypoxia (oxygen deficiency).

Hypoxia is characterized by tachycardia, nervousness, irritability, and finally cyanosis.

It develops in a wide range of situations from poisoning to shock, crushing chest injuries, cerebrospinal accidents, and heart attack. Oxygen must never by used near open flames since it supports burning. The cylinders must be handled carefully since they are potentially lethal missiles if punctured or broken.

Artificial Airways

The oropharyngeal and nasopharyngeal airways are primarily used to keep the tongue from occluding the airway.

OROPHARYNGEAL AIRWAY

This airway can be used only on unconscious victims because a conscious person will gag on it. They come in various sizes for different age groups (it is important to choose the correct size for the victim), and they are shaped to rest on the contour of the tongue and extend from the lips to the pharynx.

One method of insertion is to depress the tongue with a tongue blade and slide the airway in. Another method is to insert the airway upside down into the victim's mouth; then rotate it 180 degrees as it slides into the pharynx.

NASOPHARYNGEAL AIRWAY

This airway may be used on conscious victims since it is better tolerated because it generally does not stimulate the gag reflex.

Since they are made of flexible material, they are designed to be lubricated and then gently passed up the nostril and down into the pharynx. If the airway meets an obstruction in one nostril, withdraw it and try to pass it up the other nostril.

Bag-Valve-Mask System

The bag-valve-mask system is designed to help ventilate an unconscious victim for long periods, while delivering high concentrations of oxygen. This system can be useful in extended CPR attempts because when using external cardiac compressions, the cardiac output is cut to 25 to 30 per cent of the normal capacity and artificial ventilation does not supply enough oxygen through the circulatory system to maintain life for a long period.

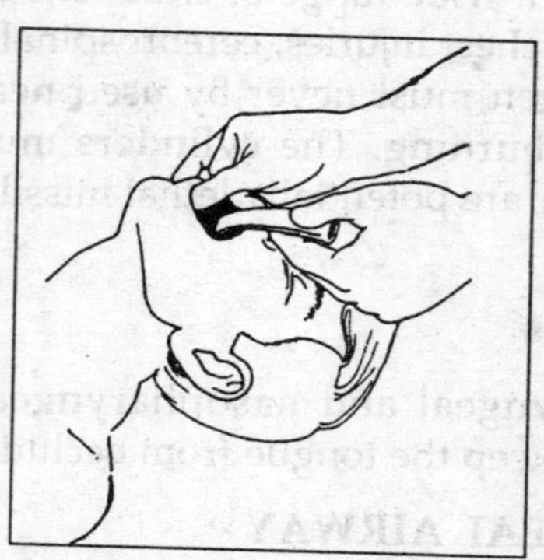

Fig. Placement of an Oropharyngeal Airway.

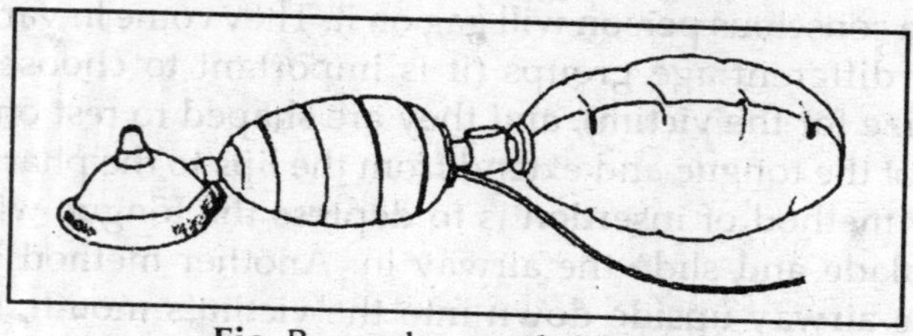

Fig. Bag-valve-mask System.

Various types of bag-valve-mask systems that come in both adult and pediatric sizes are in use in the Navy. Essentially, they consist of a selffilling ventilation bag, an oxygen reservoir, plastic face masks of various sizes, and tubing for connection to an oxygen supply.

The bag-valve-mask system is difficult to use if the corpsman has not had a great deal of practice with it. It must not be used by inexperienced persons.

The system can be hard to clean and reassemble properly, the bagging hand can tire easily, and an airtight seal at the face is hard to maintain, especially if a single rescuer must also keep the airway open.

In addition, the amount of air delivered to the victim is limited to the volume that the hand can displace from the bag (approximately 1 liter per compression).

TECHNIQUE

Hook the bag up to an oxygen supply and adjust the flow from 10 to 15 liters per minute depending on the desired concentration (15 liters per minute will deliver an oxygen concentration of 90 per cent). After hyperextending the neck to open airway or inserting an oropharyngeal airway, place the mask over the face and hold it firmly in position with the index finger and thumb, while the remaining fingers keep the jaw tilted upward.

The other hand is used to compress the bag once every 5 seconds. Observe the chest and abdomen for expansion. If none is observed, the face mask seal may not be airtight, the airway may be blocked, or some component of the bag-valve-mask system may be malfunctioning. Mouth-to-Mask System

A pocket mask designed for mouth-to-mask ventilation, with an oxygen-inlet flow valve, can be used to give oxygen enriched artificial ventilation. Although this system cannot achieve oxygen concentrations as high as the bag-valve-mask system, it has the advantages of providing greater air volume (up to 4 liters per breath), and being far easier to use since both hands can be used to maintain the airway and keep the mask firmly in place.

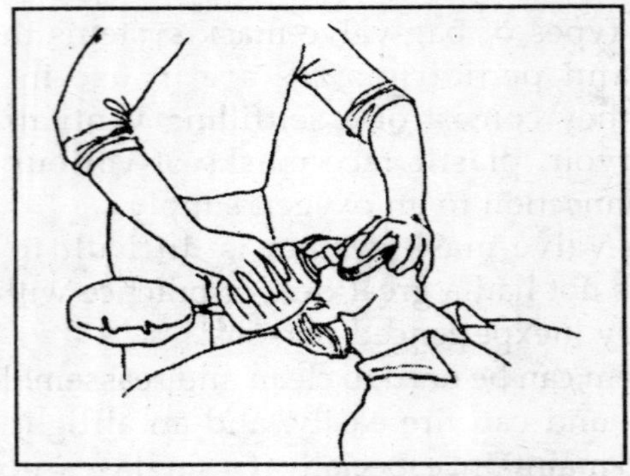

Fig. Bag-Valve-Mask System in Use.

TECHNIQUE

Standing behind the head of the victim, open the airway by tilting the head backward. Place the mask over the victim's face (for adults, the apex goes over the bridge of the nose; for infants, the apex fits over the chin, with the base resting on the bridge of the nose).

Form an airtight seal for the mask and keep the airway open by pressing down on the mask with both thumbs while using the other fingers to lift the jaw up and back. The corpsman then ventilates into the open chimney of the mask. Oxygen can be added by hooking the valve up to an oxygen supply.

Since the oxygen flow will be diluted by the rescuer's breath in artificial ventilation, the flow rate will have to be adjusted to increase oxygen concentration. At 5 liters per minute, the oxygen concentration will be approximately 50 per cent. At 15 liters per minute, this will increase to 55 per cent. The mask has an elastic strap so it can be used on conscious self-ventilating patients to increase oxygen concentration.

ESOPHAGEAL OBTURATOR AIRWAY (EOA)

An EOA is a semi-flexible large-bore tube approximately 30 cm in length, with 19 holes in the shaft and an inflatable cuff. A soft face mask is attached to one end and the other end is closed. The airway was designed for personnel who are not authorized to place endotracheal tubes. One of the distinct advantages is that it can be inserted blindly through the mouth without having to visualize the larynx. It is also helpful in the prevention of gastric regurgitation. The disadvantages are that the tracheo-bronchial tree cannot be adequately suctioned and there is the possibility of esophageal rupture when the cuff is inflated too fully. The following steps are to be followed when inserting the EOA:

- Hyperventilate the patient.
- Position the head in a neutral position or slightly flexed. do not hyperextend the neck.
- Lift the jaw.
- Insert the tube until the mask is flush with the face.

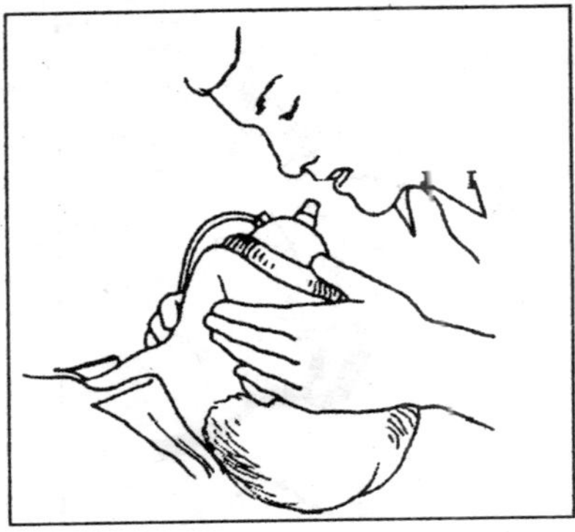

Fig. Mouth-to-mask Breathing.

- Ventilate through the tube and auscultate both lung fields. The EOA is sometimes inserted into the trachea; this is of little worry if recognized and corrected immediately.
- Inflate the cuff (about 35cc of air). Overinflation can possibly rupture the esophagus or may compress the trachea causing an obstruction.
- Ventilate and auscultate again to ensure proper placement.

CRICOTHYROIDOTOMY

A cricothyroidotomy, often known as an emergency

tracheotomy, consists of incising the cricothyroid membrane, which lies just beneath the skin between the thyroid cartilage and the cricoid cartilage.

The cricothyroid membrane can be located easily in most cases. Hyperextend the neck so that the thyroid notch (Adam's apple) becomes prominent anteriorly. Identify the position of the thyroid notch with the index finger. This finger descends in the midline to the prominence of the cricoid cartilage. The depression of the cricothyroid membrane is identified above the superior margin of the cricoid cartilage. A small lateral incision is made at the base of the thyroid cartilage to expose the cricothyroid membrane. This membrane is then excised, taking care not to go too deeply, and a small bore airline is then inserted into the trachea.

Fig. Insertion of Esophageal Obturator Airway.

An alternate method is to use a 12 to 16 gauge intercatheter. Locate the cricothyroid membrane as above and insert the needle into the trachea. Immediately upon penetrating the cricothyroid membrane, thread the plastic catheter into the trachea and remove the needle.

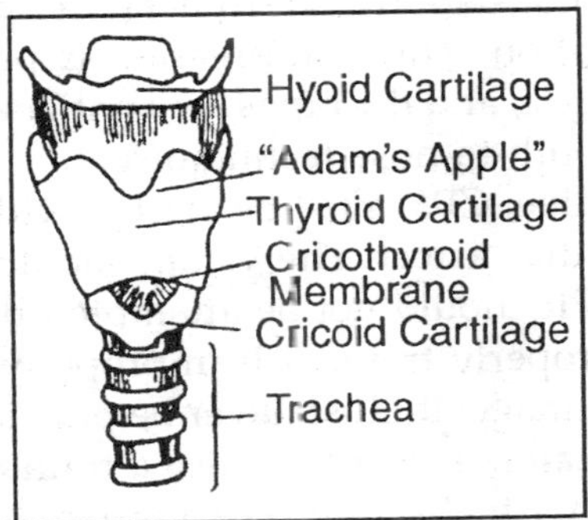

Fig. Structure of the Neck to Identify Cricothyroid Membrane.

The catheter can then be connected to an oxygen line for translaryngeal oxygen jet insufflation. A cricothyroidotomy should not be attempted except as a last resort when other methods of opening the airway are unsuccessful.

Suctioning Devices

In a first aid setting, the hospital corpsman may have access to portable or fixed suctioning devices equipped with flexible tubing, semirigid tips, suction catheters, and nonbreakable collection bottles. The suction pressure should be tested regularly and the equipment kept clean.

TECHNIQUE

After testing the apparatus, attach a catheter or tip, and open the victim's mouth. Carefully insert the end into the pharynx. Apply suction, but for no more than 15 seconds. Suction may be repeated after a few breaths.

CIRCULATION

Cardiac arrest is the complete stoppage of heart function. If the victim is to live, action must be taken immediately to restore heart function. The symptoms include absence of carotid pulse, lack of heartbeat, dilated pupils, and absence of breathing.

A rescuer knowing how to administer cardiopulmonary resuscitation (CPR) greatly increases the chances of a victim's survival. CPR consists of external heart compression and artificial ventilation. This compression is performed on the outside of the chest, and the lungs are ventilated by the mouth-to-mouth or mouth-to-nose techniques.

To be effective, CPR must be started within 4 minutes of the onset of cardiac arrest. The victim should be supine on a firm surface. CPR should not be attempted by a rescuer who has not been properly trained. If improperly done, CPR can cause serious damage. It must never be practiced on a healthy individual for training purposes; use a training aid instead.

To learn this technique, see your medical education department or an American Heart Association or American Red Cross certified corpsman, nurse, or physician

One Rescuer Technique

The rescuer must not assume that an arrest has occurred solely because the victim is lying on the floor and appears to be unconscious. First, try to arouse the victim by gently shaking the shoulders and trying to obtain a response. If there is no response, place the victim supine on a firm surface.

Kneel at a right angle to the victim, and open the airway using the head tilt or jaw thrust methods described previously. Attempt to ventilate. If unsuccessful, reposition the head and again attempt to ventilate. If still unsuccessful, deliver four abdominal or chest thrusts to open the airway. Repeat the thrust sequence until the obstruction is removed. Once the airway has been opened, check for the carotid pulse.

The carotid artery is most easily found by locating the larynx at the front of the neck and then sliding two fingers down the side of the neck toward you. The carotid pulse is felt in the groove between the larynx and the sternocleidomastoid muscle. If the pulse is present, ventilate as necessary. If the pulse is absent, locate the sternum and begin closed cardiac massage.

To locate the sternum, use the middle and index fingers of your lower hand to locate the lower margin of the victim's rib cage on the side closest to you. The fingers are then moved up along the edge of the rib cage to the notch where the ribs meet the sternum in the centre of the lower chest. The middle finger is placed on the notch and the index finger is placed next to it. The heel of the other hand is placed along the midline of the sternum next to the index finger. Remember to keep the heel of your hand off the xiphoid tip of the sternum. A fracture in this area can damage the liver, causing hemorrhage and death. Place the heel of one hand directly on the sternum and the heel of the other on top of the first.

Interlock your fingers or extend them straight out and Keep Them Off The Victim's Chest! Lean or rock forward with the elbows locked and apply vertical pressure to depress the sternum (adult) 1 1/2 to 2 inches.

Then release the pressure, keeping the hands in place on the chest. You will feel less fatigue if you use the proper technique and a more effective compression will result. Ineffective compression occurs when the elbows are not locked, the rescuer is not directly over the sternum, or the hands are improperly placed on the sternum. When one rescuer performs CPR, the ratio of compressions to ventilation is 15 to 2, and it is performed at a rate of 80 compressions per minute to maintain 60 full compression each minute.

Vocalize: "one and, two and, three and,..." until you reach 15. After 15 compressions, you must give the victim 2 ventilation. Continue for four full cycles. Quickly check for the carotid pulse and spontaneous breathing. If there are still no signs of recovery, continue CPR. If a periodic check reveals a return of pulse and respiration, discontinue CPR, but closely monitor the victim and be prepared to start CPR again if required.

Before learning the next technique, review the steps to take for a cardiac arrest involving one rescuer

- Determine whether the victim is conscious.
- Check vital signs.
- Ventilate two times (it may be necessary to remove an airway obstruction at this time).
- Again check vital signs; if there are none, begin the compression-ventilation rate of 15 to 2 for four complete cycles.

- Check pulse, breathing, and pupils; if there is no change, continue the compression-ventilation rate of 15 to 2 until the victim is responsive, you are properly relieved, or you can no longer continue.

Two Rescuer Technique

If there are two people trained in CPR on the scene, one must perform compression while theother performs ventilation.

The ratio for the two person CPR is 5 compressions to 1 ventilation, at a rate of 80 compressions per minute. One rescuer is positioned at the chest area and the other beside the victim's head.

The rescuers should be on opposite sides of the victim to ease position changes when one rescuer gets tired. Changes should be made on cue without interrupting the rhythm. To help avoid confusion, one rescuer must be designated the leader.

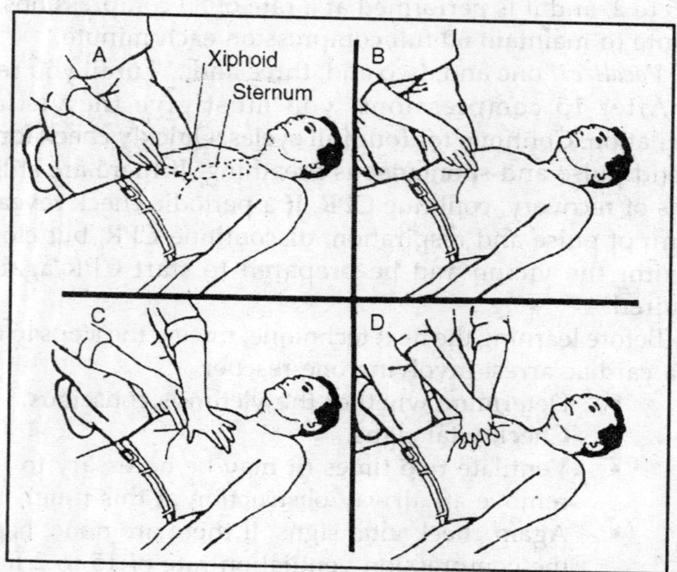

Fig. Locating the Sternum For Closed Cardiac Massage.

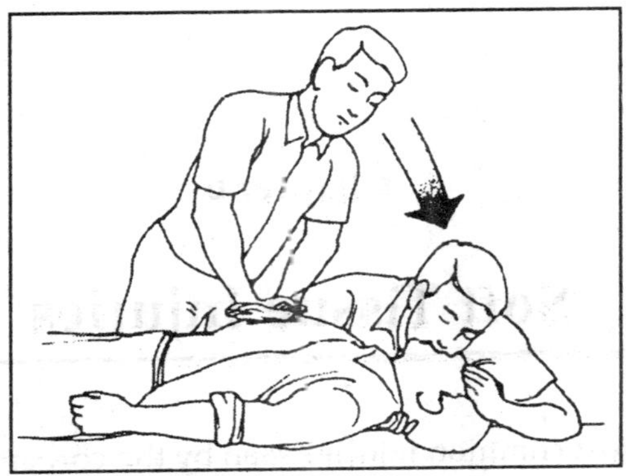

Fig. One-Resuer CPR Technique.

The leader must make the preliminary checks of the victim's vital signs and perform the initial 2 ventilations. The second rescuer will get ready for compression and perform the compressions. When CPR is started, give the compression in a constant, methodical rhythm. The rescuer giving the compressions counts them out loud (one one thousand, two one thousand, three one thousand, four one thousand, five one thousand). As the fifth compression is released, the other rescuer ventilates the victim. Allow a short pause to ventilate the victim.

CPR for Children and Infants

Closed chest cardiac massage for children is similar to that for adults. The primary difference is that the heel of only one hand is used to depress the middle of the sternum from 3/4 to 1 1/2 inches. The other hand can be used to maintain a head tilt that helps ventilation.

For infants, only two fingers are used to depress the middle of the sternum from 1/2 to 3/4 of an inch. For both infants and children, the compression rate increases from 80 to 100 compressions per minute.

The head-tilt or jaw thrust methods of ensuring an open airway will cause the upper back of an infant or small child to arch upward. Additional support for the back is provided by a folded towel, sheet, or blanket.

Chapter 6

Soft Tissue Injuries

The most common injuries seen by the corpsman in a first aid setting are soft tissue injuries with the accompanying hemorrhage, shock, and danger of infection. Any injury that causes a break in the skin, underlying soft tissue structures, or body membranes is known as a Wound.

This section will discuss the classification of wounds, the general and specific treatment of soft tissue injuries, the use of dressings and bandages in treating wounds, and the special problems that arise because of the location of wounds.

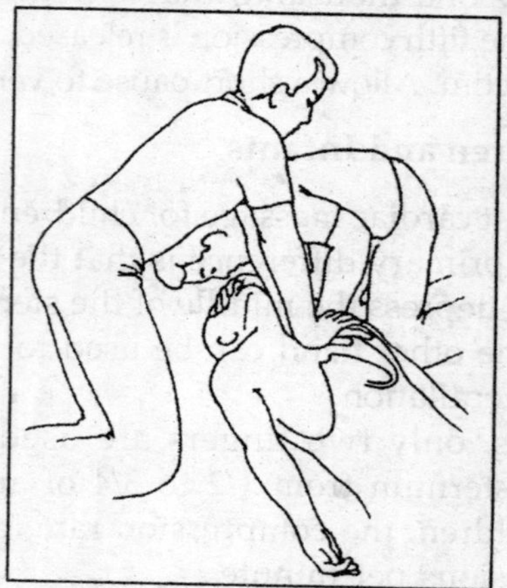

Fig. Two-Rescuer CPR Technique.

CLASSIFICATION OF WOUNDS

Wounds may be classified according to their general condition, size, location, the manner in which the skin or tissue is broken, and the agent that caused the wound. It is usually necessary for you to consider these factors to determine what first aid treatment is appropriate for the wound.

General Condition of. the Wound

If the wound is fresh, first aid treatment consists mainly of stopping the flow of blood, treating for shock, and reducing the risk of infection. If the wound is already infected, first aid consists of keeping the victim quiet, elevating the injured part, and applying a warm wet dressing.

If the wound contains foreign objects, first aid treatment may consist of removing the objects if they are not deeply embedded. DO NOT remove objects embedded in the eyes or the skull, and do not remove impaled objects. Impaled objects must be stabilized with bulky dressing before transport

Size of the Wound

In general, since large wounds are more serious than small ones, they usually involve more severe bleeding, more damage to the underlying organs or tissues, and a greater degree of shock. However, small wounds are sometimes more dangerous than large ones; they may become infected more readily due to neglect. The depth of the wound is also important because it may lead to a complete perforation of an organ or the body, with the additional complication of entrance and exit wounds.

Location of the Wound

Since a wound may involve serious damage to the deeper structures, as well as to the skin and the tissue immediately below it, the location of the wound is important. For example, a knife wound to the chest may puncture a lung and cause interference with breathing.

The same type of wound in the abdomen may result in a dangerous infection in the abdominal cavity, or it might puncture the intestines, liver, kidneys, or other vital organs. A knife wound to the head may cause brain damage, but the same wound in a less vital spot such as an arm or leg might be less important.

Types of Wounds

When you consider the manner in which the skin or tissue is broken, there are six general kinds of wounds: abrasions, incisions, lacerations, punctures, avulsions, and amputations. Many wounds, of course, are combinations of two or more of these basic types.

Abrasions

Abrasions are made when the skin is rubbed or scraped off. Rope burns, floor burns, and skinned knees or elbows are common examples of abrasions. This kind of wound can become infected quite easily because dirt and germs are usually embedded in the tissues

Incisions

Incisions, commonly called Cuts, are wounds made by sharp cutting instruments such as knives, razors, and broken glass. Incisions tend to bleed freely because the blood vessels are cut cleanly and without ragged edges.

There is little damage to the surrounding tissues. Of all classes of wounds, incisions are the least likely to become infected, since the free flow of blood washes out many of the microorganisms (germs) that cause infection.

Lacerations

These wounds are torn, rather than cut. They have ragged, irregular edges and masses of torn tissue underneath. These wounds are usually made by blunt, rather than sharp, objects. A wound made by a dull knife, for instance, is more likely to be a laceration than an incision. Bomb fragments often cause laceration. Many of the wounds caused by accidents with machinery are lacerations; they are often complicated by crushing of the tissues as well. Lacerations are frequently contaminated with dirt, grease, or other material that is ground into the tissue; they are therefore very likely to become infected.

Punctures

Punctures are caused by objects that penetrate into the

tissues while leaving a small surface opening. Wounds made by nails, needles, wire, and bullets are usually punctures. As a rule, small puncture wounds do not bleed freely; however, large puncture wounds may cause severe internal bleeding.

The possibility of infection is great in all puncture wounds, especially if the penetrating object has tetanus bacteria on it. To prevent anaerobic infections, primary closures are not made in the case of puncture wounds.

Avulsions

An avulsion is the tearing away of tissue from a body part. Bleeding is usually heavy. In certain situations, the torn tissue may be surgically reattached.

It can be saved for medical evaluation by wrapping it in a sterile dressing and placing it in a cool container, and rushing it, along with the victim, to a medical facility. Do not allow the avulsed portion to freeze and do not immerse it in water or saline.

Amputations

A traumatic amputation is the nonsurgical removal of the limb from the body. Bleeding is heavy and requires a tourniquet, which will be discussed later, to stop the flow. Shock is certain to develop in these cases.

As with avulsed tissue, wrap the limb in sterile dressings, place it in a cool container, and transport it to the hospital with the victim. Do not allow the limb to be in direct contact with ice, and do not immerse it in water or saline. The limb can often be successfully reattached.

Causes of the Wound

Although it is not always necessary to know what agent or object has caused the wound, it is helpful. Knowing what has caused the wound may give you some idea of the probable size of the wound, its general nature, the extent to which it is likely to become contaminated with foreign matter, and what special dangers must be guarded against.

Of special concern in a wartime setting is the velocity of

wound causing missiles (bullets or shrapnel). A low velocity missile damages only the tissues it comes into contact with. On the other hand, a high velocity missile can do enormous damage by forcing the tissues and body parts away from the track of the missile with a velocity only slightly less than that of the missile itself.

.These tissues, especially bone, may become damagecausing missiles themselves, thus accentuating the destructive effects of the missile. Having classified the wound into one or more of the general categories listed, the corpsman will have a good idea of the nature and extent of the injury, along with any special complications. This information will aid in the treatment of the victim.

MANAGEMENT OF OPEN SOFT TISSUE INJURY

There are three basic rules to be followed in the treatment of practically all open soft tissue injuries: to control hemorrhage, to treat the victim for shock, and to do whatever you can to prevent infection. These will be discussed, along with the proper application of first aid materials and other specific first aid techniques.

Hemorrhage

Hemorrhage is the escape of blood from the vessels of the circulatory system. The average adult body contains about 6 liters of blood. Five hundred milliliters of blood, the amount given by blood donors, can usually be lost without any harmful effect. The loss of 1 liter of blood usually causes shock, but shock may develop if small amounts of blood are lost rapidly, since the circulatory system does not have enough time to compensate adequately. The degree of shock progressively increases as greater amounts of blood escape.

Young children, sick people, or the elderly may be especially susceptible to the loss of even small amounts of blood since their internal systems are in such delicate balance. Capillary blood is usually brick red in colour. If capillaries are cut, the blood oozes out slowly.

Blood from the veins is dark red. Venous bleeding is

characterized by a steady, even flow. If an artery near the surface is cut, the blood, which is bright red in colour, will gush out in spurts that are synchronized with the heartbeats.

If the severed artery is deeply buried, however, the bleeding will appear to be a steady stream. In actual practice, you might find it difficult to decide whether bleeding is venous or arterial, but the distinction is not usually important. The important thing to know is that all bleeding must be controlled as quickly as possible.

External hemorrhage is of greatest importance to the corpsman because it is the most frequently encountered and the easiest to control. It is characterized by a break in the skin and visible bleeding. Internal hemorrhage, which will be discussed later, is far more difficult to recognize and to control.

Control of Hemorrhage

The best way to control external bleeding is by applying a compress to the wound and exerting pressure directly to the wound. If direct pressure does not stop the bleeding, pressure can also be applied at an appropriate pressure point.

At times, elevation of an extremity is also helpful in controlling hemorrhage. The use of splints in conjunction with direct pressure can be beneficial. In those rare cases where bleeding cannot be controlled by any of these methods, you must use a tourniquet.

If bleeding does not stop after a short period, try placing another compress or dressing over the first and securing it firmly in place. If bleeding still will not stop, try applying direct pressure with your hand over the compress or dressing.

Remember that in cases of severe hemorrhage, do not worry too much about finding appropriate materials or about the dangers of infection. The basic problem is to stop rapid exsanguination. If no material is available, simply thrust your hand into the wound. In most situations, direct pressure is the first and best method to use in the control of hemorrhage.

Pressure Points

Bleeding can often be temporarily controlled by applying

hand pressure to the appropriate pressure point. A pressure point is a place where the main artery to the injured part lies near the skin surface and over a bone. Apply pressure at this point with the fingers (digital pressure) or with the heel of the hand; no first aid materials are required.

The object of the pressure is to compress the artery against the bone, thus shutting off the flow of blood from the heart to the wound.

There are 11 principal points on each side of the body where hand or finger pressure can be used to stop hemorrhage. If bleeding occurs on the face below the level of the eyes, apply pressure to the point on the mandible.

To find this pressure point, start at the angle of the jaw and run your finger forward along the lower edge of the mandible until you feel a small notch. The pressure point is in this notch. If bleeding is in the shoulder or in the upper part of the arm, apply pressure with the fingers behind the clavicle.

You can press down against the first rib or forward against the clavicle—either kind of pressure will stop the bleeding. Bleeding between the middle of the upper arm and the elbow should be controlled by applying digital pressure in the inner (body) side of the arm, about halfway between the shoulder and the elbow.

This compresses the artery against the bone of the arm. Bleeding from the hand can be controlled by pressure at the wrist. If it is possible to hold the arm up in the air, the bleeding will be relatively easy to stop.

The artery at this point lies over a bone and quite close to the surface, so pressure with your fingers may be sufficient to stop the bleeding. The proper position for controlling bleeding from the foot. As in the case of bleeding from the hand, elevation is helpful in controlling the bleeding. If bleeding is in the region of the temple or the scalp, use your finger to compress the main artery to the temple against the skull bone at the pressure point just in front of the ear.

The proper position. If the neck is bleeding, apply pressure below the wound, just in front of the prominent neck muscle. Press inward and slightly backward, compressing the main artery of that side of the neck against the bones of the spinal column.

Do not apply pressure at this point unless it is absolutely essential, since there is a great danger of pressing on the windpipe and thus choking the victim. Bleeding from the lower arm can be controlled by applying pressure at the elbow. As mentioned before, bleeding in the upper part of the thigh can sometimes be controlled by applying digital pressure in the middle of the groin. Sometimes, however, it is more effective to use the pressure point of the upper thigh.

If you use this point, apply pressure with the closed fist of one hand and use the other hand to give additional pressure. The artery at this point is deeply buried in some of the heaviest muscle of the body, so a great deal of pressure must be exerted to compress the artery against the bone.

Bleeding between the knee and the foot may be controlled by firm pressure at the knee. If pressure at the side of the knee does not stop the bleeding, hold the front of the knee with one hand and thrust your fist hard against the artery behind the knee.

If necessary, you can place a folded compress or bandage behind the knee, bend the leg back, and hold it in place by a firm bandage. This is a most effective way of controlling bleeding, but it is so uncomfortable for the victim that it should be used only as a last resort.

You should memorize these pressure points so that you will know immediately which point to use for controlling hemorrhage from a particular part of the body. Remember, the correct pressure point is that which is :

- Nearest the Wound,
- Between the Wound and the main part of the Body.

It is very tiring to apply digital pressure, and it can seldom be maintained for more than 15 minutes. Pressure points are recommended for use while direct pressure is being applied to a serious wound by a second rescuer, or after a compress, bandage, or dressing has been applied to the wound, since it will slow the flow of blood to the area, thus giving the direct pressure technique a better chance to stop the hemorrhage. It is also recommended as a stopgap measure until a pressure dressing or a tourniquet can be applied.

Elevation

The elevation of an extremity, where appropriate, can be an effective aid in hemorrhage control when used in conjunction with other methods of control, especially direct pressure. This is because the amount of blood entering the extremity is decreased by the uphill gravitational effect.

Do not elevate an extremity until it is certain that no bones have been broken or until broken bones are properly splinted mmobilization of sharp bone ends reduces further tissue trauma and allows lacerated blood vessels to clot. In addition, the gentle pressure exerted by the splint helps the clotting process by giving additional support to compresses or dressings already in place over open fracture sites. Later in this chapter we will go into the subject of splinting in greater detail.

Tourniquet

A tourniquet is a constricting band that is used to cut off the supply of blood to an injured limb. Use a tourniquet only if the control of hemorrhage by other means proves to be difficult or impossible. A tourniquet must always be applied Above the wound, i.e., towards the trunk, and it must be applied as close to the wound as practical.

Basically, a tourniquet consists of a pad, a band, and a device for tightening the band so that the blood vessels will be compressed. It is best to use a pad, compress, or similar pressure object, if one is available. It goes under the band. It must be placed directly over the artery or it will actually decrease the pressure on the artery and thus allow a greater flow of blood.

If a tourniquet placed over a pressure object does not stop the bleeding, there is a good chance that the pressure object is in the wrong place. If this occurs, shift the object around until the tourniquet, when tightened, will control the bleeding. Any long flat material may be used as the band. It is important that the band be flat: belts, stockings, flat strips of rubber, or neckerchief maybe used; but rope, wire, string, or very narrow pieces of cloth should not be used because they cut into the flesh.

A short stick may be used to twist the band, tightening the tourniquet. To be effective, a tourniquet must be tight enough to stop the arterial blood flow to the limb, so be sure to draw the tourniquet tight enough to stop the bleeding. However, do not make it any tighter than necessary. After you have brought the bleeding under control with the tourniquet, apply a sterile compress or dressing to the wound and fasten it in position with a bandage.

Here are the points to remember about using a tourniquet:

- Don't use a tourniquet unless you can't control the bleeding by any other means.
- Don't use a tourniquet for bleeding from the head, face, neck, or trunk. Use it only on the limbs. tourniquet.

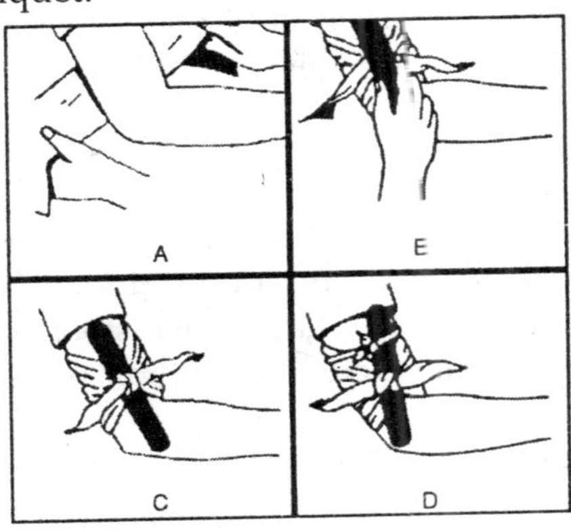

Fig. Applying a Tourniquet.

- Always apply a tourniquet above the woundand as close to the wound as possible. As a general rule, do not place a tourniquet below the knee or elbow except for complete amputations. In certain distal areas of the extremities, nerves lie close to the skin and may be damaged by the compression. Furthermore, rarely does one encounter bleeding distal to the knee or elbow that requires a tourniquet.

- Be sure you draw the tourniquet tight enough to stop the bleeding, but don't make it any tighter than necessary. The pulse beyond the tourniquet should disappear.
- Don't loosen a tourniquet after it has been applied. Transport the victim to a medical facility that can offer proper care.
- Don't cover a tourniquet with a dressing. If it is necessary to cover the injured person in some way, make sure that all the other people concerned with the case know about the tourniquet.Using crayon, skin pencil, or blood, mark a large "T" on the victim's forehead or on a medical tag at- tached to the wrist.

MANAGEMENT OF SOFT TISSUE INJURY

Internal soft tissue injuries may result from deep wounds, blunt trauma, blast exposure, crushing accidents, bone fracture, poison, or sickness. They may range in seriousness from a simple contusion to life-threatening hemorrhage and shock.

Visible indications of internal soft tissue injury include the following:

- Hematemesis vomiting bright red blood.
- Hemoptysis - coughing up bright red blood.
- Melena excretion of tarry black stools.
- Hematochezia - excretion of bright red blood from the rectum.
- Hematuria pass blood in the urine.
- Nonmenstrual vaginal bleeding.
- Epistaxis nosebleed.
- Pooling of the blood near the skin surface.

More often than not, however, there will be no visible signs of injury, and the corpsman will have to infer the probability of internal soft tissue injury from other symptoms that include:

- Pale, moist, clammy skin.
- Subnormal temperature.
- Rapid, feeble pulse.

- Falling blood pressure.
- Dilated, slowly reacting pupils with impaired vision.
- Tinnitus.
- Syncope.
- Dehydration and thirst.
- Yawning and air hunger.
- Anxiety, with a feeling of impending doom.

There is little that a corpsman can do to correct internal soft tissue injuries since they are almost always surgical problems. The hospital corpsman's goal must be to obtain the greatest benefit from the victim's remaining blood supply. The following should be done:

- Treat for shock.
- Keep the victim warm and at rest.
- Replace lost fluids with a suitable blood volume expander (refer to the "Intravenous Therapy" section of the Nursing Procedures Manual); do Not give the victim anything to drink until the extent of the injury is known for certain.
- Give oxygen, if available.
- Splint injured extremities.
- Apply cold compresses to identifiable injured areas.
- Transport the victim to a medical treatment facility as soon as possible.

Dressings and Bandages

A dressing is a pad or bolster of folded linen that is placed in direct contact with the wound.

It should be large enough to cover the entire area of the wound and to extend at least 1 inch in every direction beyond the edges. If the dressing is not large enough, the edges of the wound are almost certain to become contaminated. In most situations, a corpsman will have sterile, prepackaged dressings available.

However, emergencies will sometimes arise when they will be impossible to obtain, or the supplies will run out. In such a situation, use the cleanest cloth available. A freshly laundered handkerchief, towel, or shirt may be used. Unfold these material carefully so that you do not touch the part that goes next to the skin. Always be ready to improvise, but never put materials directly in contact with wounds that are likely to stick to the wound, leave lint, or be difficult to remove.

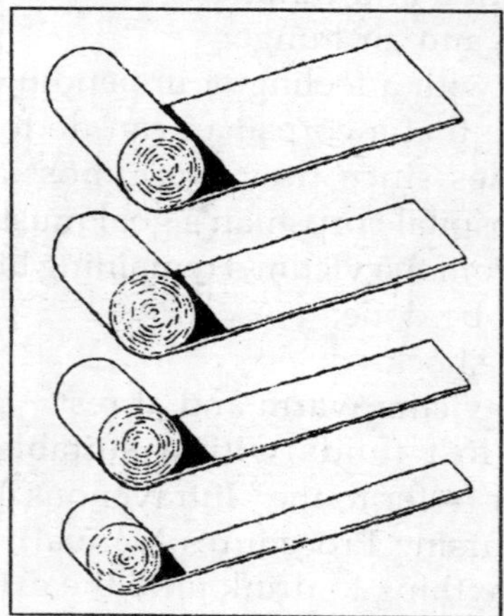

Fig. Roller Bandages.

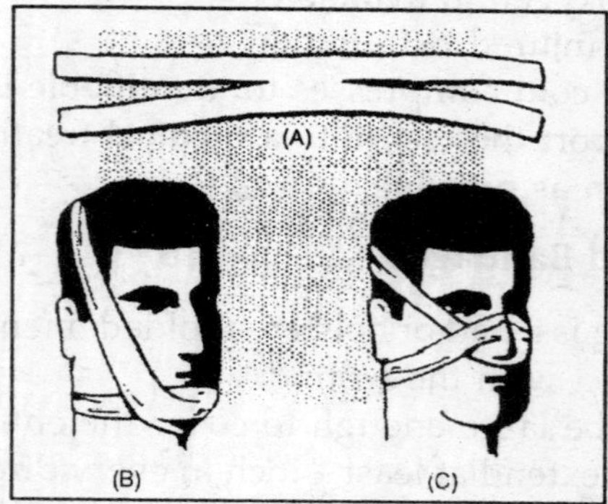

Fig. Four-tailed Bandages.

Bandages are strips or rolls of gauze or other materials that are used for wrapping or binding any part of the body and to hold compresses in place. The types of bandages that are most commonly used are the roller bandage and the triangular bandage that can be used to make the Barton bandage and the cravat bandage.

Roller Bandage

The roller bandage consists of a long strip of material (usually gauze, muslin, or elastic) that is wound into a cylindrical shape. Roller bandages come in various widths and lengths. Most of the roller bandages in the first aid kits have been sterilized, so pieces may be cut off and used as compresses in direct contact with wounds.

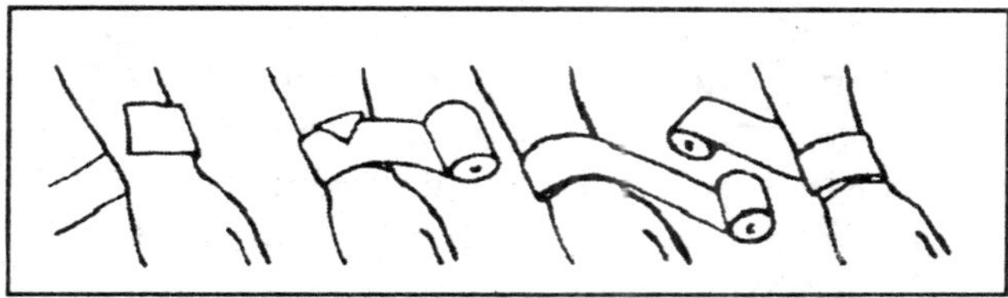

Fig. Applying a Roller Bandage.

If you use a piece of roller bandage in this manner, you must be careful not to touch it with your hands or with any other unsterile object. A piece of roller bandage maybe used to make a four-tailed bandage. This is done by splitting the cloth from each end, leaving as large a centre area as necessary. The four-tailed bandage is often used to hold a compress on the chin. It is good for bandaging any protruding part of the body, because the centre portion of the bandage forms a smoothly fitting pocket when the tails are crossed over. In applying a roller bandage, hold the roll in the right hand so that the loose end is on the bottom; the outside surface of the loose or initial end is next applied to and held on the body part by the left hand.

The roll is then passed around the body part by the right hand, which controls the tension and application of the bandage. Two or three of the initial turns of a roller bandage should overlie each other to secure the bandage and to keep it in place.

In applying the turns of the bandage, it is often necessary to transfer the roll from one hand to the other. Bandages should be applied evenly, firmly, but not too tightly. Excessive pressure may cause interference with the circulation and may lead to disastrous consequences. In bandaging an extremity, it is advisable to leave the fingers or toes exposed so the circulation of these parts may be readily observed.

It is likewise safer to apply a large number of turns of a bandage, rather than to depend upon a few turns applied too firmly t o secure a compress. In applying a wet bandage, or one that may become wet, you must allow for shrinkage. The turns of a bandage should completely cover the skin, as any uncovered areas of skin may become pinched between the turns, with resulting discomfort.

In bandaging any extremity, it is advisable to include the whole member (arm or leg, excepting the fingers or toes) so that uniform pressure may be maintained throughout. It is also desirable in bandaging a limb that the part is placed in the position it will occupy when the dressing is finally completed, as variations in the flexion and extension of the part will cause changes in the pressure of certain parts of the bandage.

The initial turns of a bandage on an extremity (including spica bandages of the hip and shoulder) should be applied securely, and when possible, around the part of the limb that has the smallest circumference. Thus, in bandaging the arm or hand, the initial turns usually are applied around the wrist, and in bandaging the leg or foot, the initial turns are applied immediately above the ankle.

The final turns of a competed bandage usually are secured in the same manner as the initial turns, by employing two or more overlying circular turns. As both edges of the final circular turns are exposed, they should be folded under to present a neat, cufflike appearance.

The terminal end of the completed bandage is turned under and secured to the final turns by either a safety pin or adhesive tape. When these are not available, the end of the bandage may be split lengthwise for several inches, and the two resulting tails may be secured around the part by tying.

Roller Bandage For Elbow

A spica or figure-of-eight type of bandage is used around the elbow joint to retain a compress in the elbow region and to allow a certain amount of movement. Flex the elbow slightly, if you can do so without causing further pain or injury, or anchor a 2or 3-inch bandage above the elbow and encircle the forearm below the elbow with a circular turn.

Continue the bandage upward across the hollow of the elbow to the starting point. Make another circular turn around the upper arm, carry it downward, repeating the figureof-eight procedure, and gradually ascend the arm. Overlap each previous turn about two-thirds of the width of the bandage. Secure the bandage with two circular turns above the elbow and tie. To secure a dressing on the tip of the elbow, reverse the procedure and cross the bandage in the back.

Roller Bandage For Hand And Wrist

For the hand and wrist, a figure-ofeight bandage is ideal. Anchor the dressing,whether it is on the hand or wrist, with several turns of a 2or 3-inch bandage.

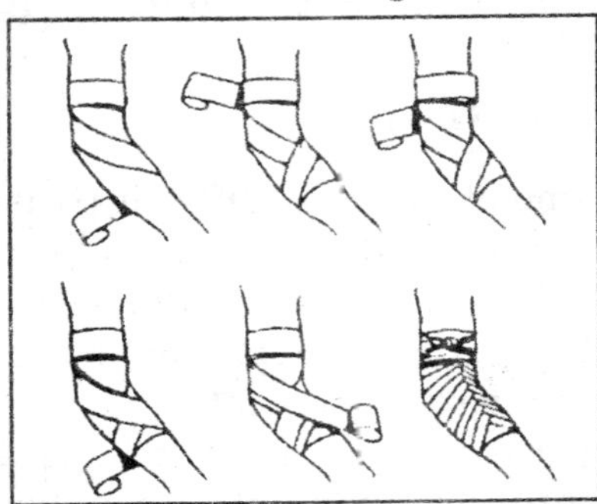

Fig. Roller bandage for the elbow.

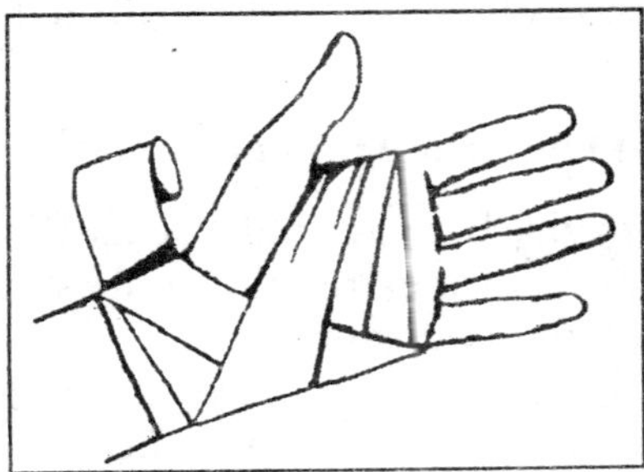

Fig. Roller Bandage for the Hand and Wrist.

If on the hand, anchor the dressing with several turns and continue the bandage diagonally upward and around the wrist and back over the pain. Make as many turns as necessary to secure the compress properly.

Roller Bandage For Ankle And Foot

The figure-of-eight bandage is also used for dressings of the ankle, as well as for supporting a sprain. While keeping the foot at a right angle, start a 3-inch bandage around the instep for several turns to anchor it.

Carry the bandage upward over the instep and around behind the ankle, forward and again across the instep and down under the arch, thus completing one figureof-eight. Continue the figure-of-eight turns, overlapping one-third to one-half its width, with an occasional turn around the ankle, until the compress is secured or until adequate support is obtained.

Roller Bandage For Heel

The heel is one of the most difficult parts of the body to bandage. Place the free end of the bandage on the outer part of the ankle and bring the bandage under the foot and up. Then carry the bandage over the instep, around the heel, and back over the instep to the starting point.

Overlap the lower border of the first loop around the heel and repeat the turn, overlapping the upper border of the loop around the heel. Continue this procedure until the desired number of turns is obtained, and secure with several turns around the lower leg.

Roller Bandage For Arm And Leg

The spiral reverse bandage must be used to cover wounds of the forearms and lower extremities; only such bandages can keep the dressing flat and even.

Make two or three circular turns around the lower and smaller part of the limb to anchor the bandage and start upward, going around making the reverse laps on each turning, overlapping about one-third to one-half the width of the previous turn. Continue as long as each turn lies flat. Continue the spiral and secure the end when completed.

Barton Bandage With the initial end of the roller bandage applied to the head, just behind the right mastoid process, the bandage is carried under the bony prominence at the back of the head, upward and forward back of the left ear, obliquely across the top of the head, and downward in front of the right ear.

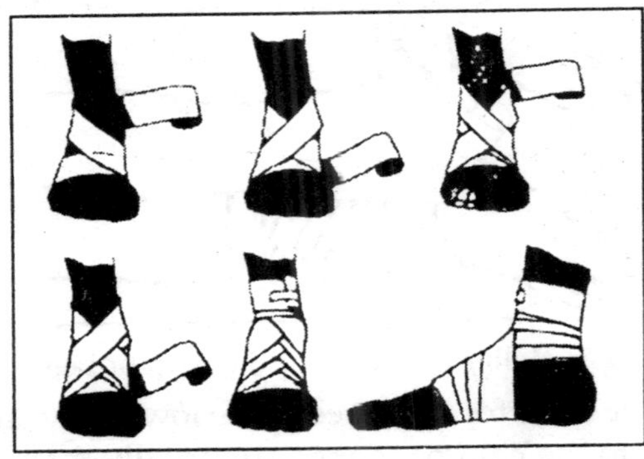

Fig. Roller Bandage for the Ankle and Foot.

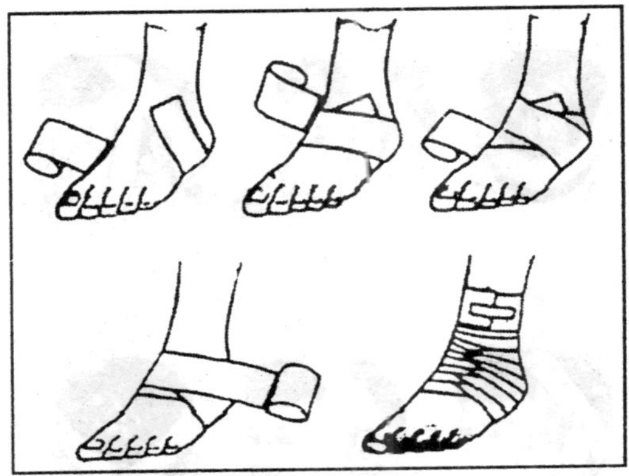

Fig. Roller Bandage for the Heel.

It is then carried under the chin, upward in front of the left ear, obliquely across the top of the head, crossing the first turn in the midline of the head, and then backward and downward to the point of origin behind the right mastoid. Now it is carried around the back of the head under the left ear, around the front of the chin, and under the right ear to the point of origin.

This procedure is repeated several times, each turn exactly overlying the preceding turn. The bandage is secured with a pin or strip of adhesive tape at the crossing on top of the head.

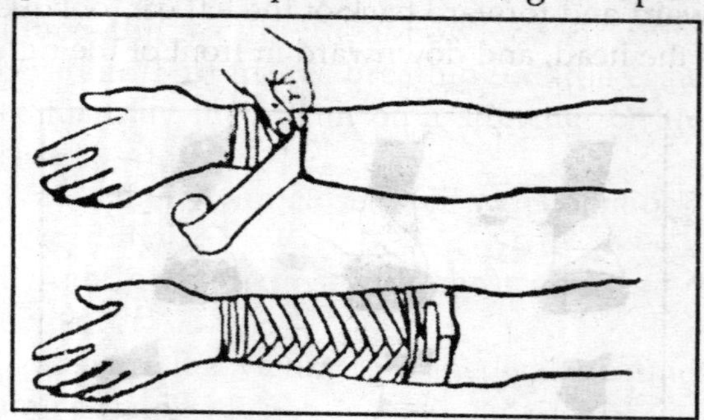

Fig. Roller Bandage for the Arm or Leg.

It may be used for fractures of the lower jaw and to retain compresses to the chin bandages are usually made of muslin.

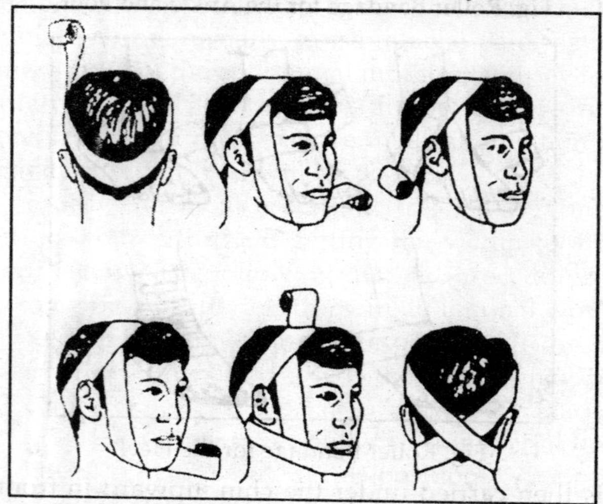

Fig. Triangular Bandage Triangular

They are made by cutting a 36" to 40" square of a piece of cloth and then cutting the square diagonally, thus making two triangular bandages (in sterile packs on the Navy's medical stock list). A smaller bandage may be made by folding a large handkerchief diagonally.

The longest side of the triangular bandage is called the base; the corner directly opposite the middle of the base is called the point; and the other two corners are called ends. The triangular bandage is useful because it can be folded in a variety of ways to fit almost any part of the body. Padding may be added to areas that may become uncomfortable.

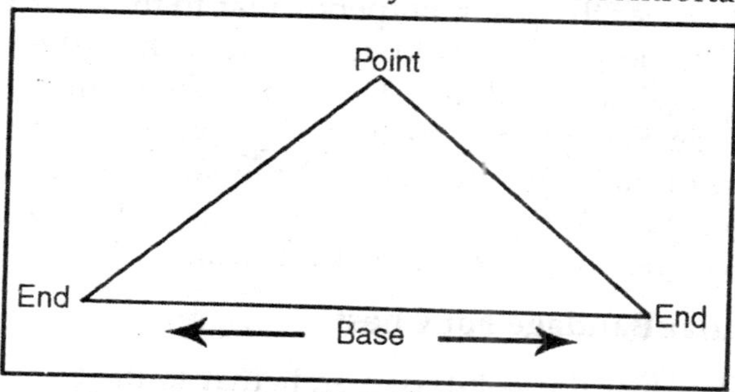

Fig. Triangular Bandage.

Triangular Bandage For Head

This bandage is used to retain compresses on the forehead or scalp. Fold back the base about 2 inches to make a hem. Place the middle of the base on the forehead, just above the eyebrows, with the hem on the outside. Let the point fall over the head and down over the occiput (back of the head).

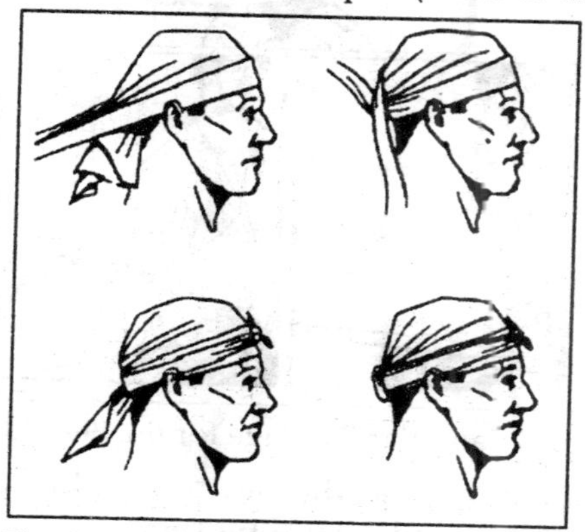

Fig. Triangular Bandage for the Head

Bring the ends of the triangle around the back of the head above the ears, cross them over the point, carry them around the forehead and tie in a Square Knot. Hold the compress firmly with one hand and, with the other, gently pull down the point until the compress is snug; then bring the point up and tuck it over and in the bandage where it crosses the back part of the head.

Triangular Bandage For Shoulder

Cut or tear the point, perpendicular to the base, about 10 inches. Tie the two points loosely around the patient's neck, allowing the base to drape down over the compress on the injured side. Fold the base to the desired width, grasp the ends, and fold or roll the sides toward the shoulder to store the excess bandage. Wrap the ends snugly around the upper arm, and tie on the outside surface of the arm.

Triangular Bandage For Chest

Cut or tear the point, perpendicular to the base about 10 inches. Tie the two points loosely around the patient's neck, allowing the bandage to drape down over the chest.

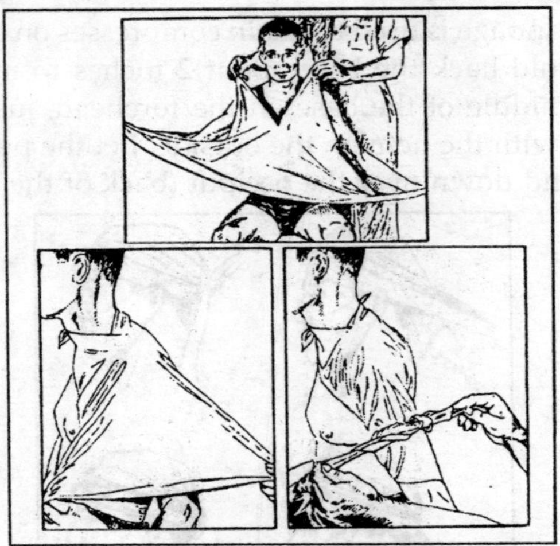

Fig. Triangular Bandage for the Shoulder.

Fold the bandage to the desired width, carry the ends around to the back, and secure by tying.

Triangular Bandage For Hip Or Buttock

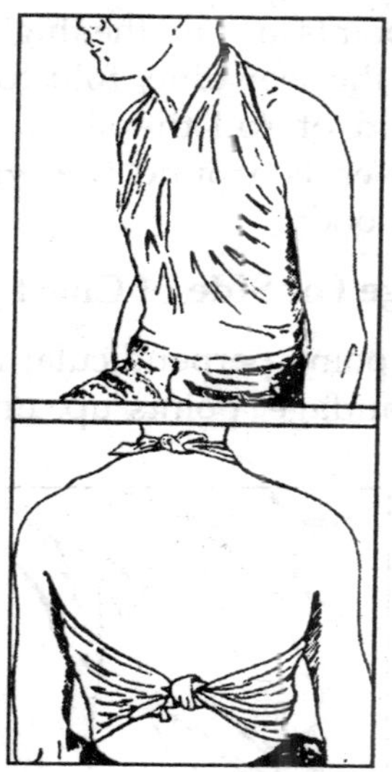

Fig. Triangular Bandage for the Chest

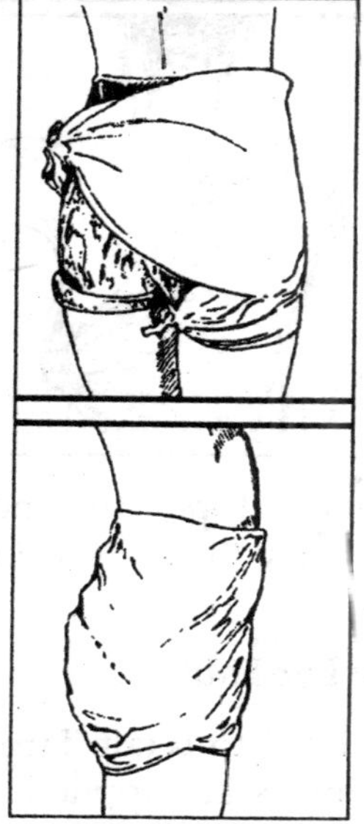

Fig. Triangular Bandage for the Hip or Buttock.

Cut or tear the point, perpendicular to the base, about 10 inches. Tie the two points around the thigh on the injured side. Lift the base up to the waistline, fold to the desired width, grasp the ends, fold or roll the sides to store the excess bandage, carry the ends around the waist, and tie on the opposite side of the body.

Triangular Bandage For Side of Chest

Cut or tear the point, perpendicular to the base, about 10 inches. Place the bandage, points up, under the arm on the injured side.

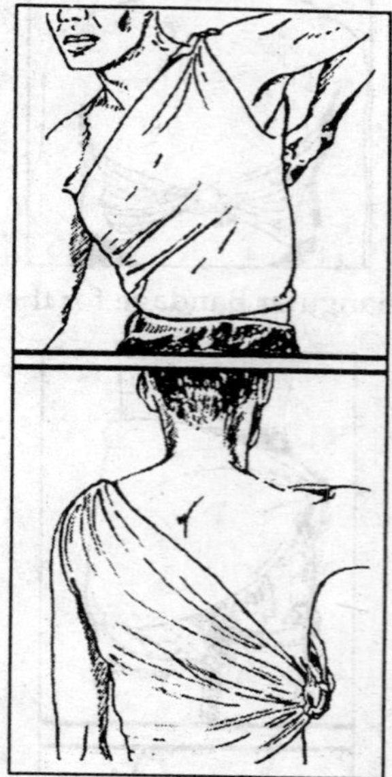

Tie the two points on top of the shoulder. Fold the base to the desired width, carry the ends around the chest, and tie on the opposite side.

Triangular Bandage For Foot

This bandage is used to retain large compresses on the foot. After the compresses are applied, place the foot in the centre of a triangular bandage and carry the point over the ends of the toes and over the upper side of the foot to the ankle.

Fold in excess bandage at the side of the foot, cross the ends, and tie in a square knot in front.

Triangular Bandage For Hand

This bandage is used to retain large dressings on the hand. After the dressings are applied, place the base of the triangle well up in the palmar surface of the wrist.

Carry the point over the ends of the fingers and back of the hand well up on the wrist. Fold the excess bandage at the side of the hand, cross the ends around the wrist, and tie a square knot in front.

Cravat Bandage

To make a cravat bandage, bring the point of the triangular bandage to the middle of the base and continue to fold until a 2 inch width is obtained.

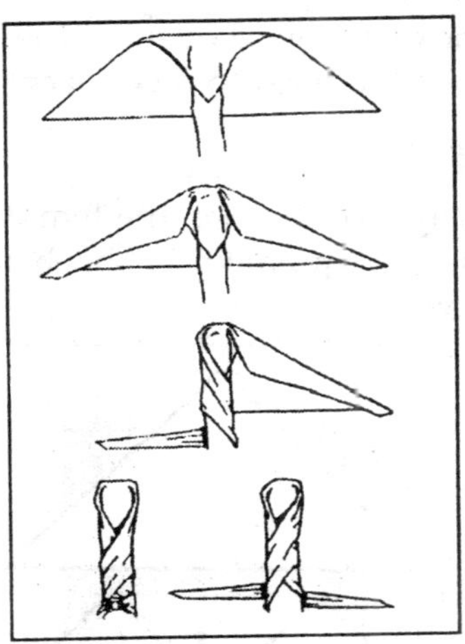

Fig. Triang Ular Bandage for the Foot or Hand.

Cravat Bandage For Head

This bandage is useful to control bleeding from wounds of the scalp or forehead. After placing a compress over the wound, place the centre of the cravat over the compress and carry the ends around to the opposite side; cross them, continue to carry them around to the starting point, and tie in a square knot.

Cravat Bandage for Eye

After applying a compress to the affected eye, place the centre of the cravat over the compress and on a slant so that the lower end is inclined downward. Bring the lower end around under the ear on the opposite side.

Cross the ends in back of the head, bring them forward, and tie them over the compress.

Cravat Bandage for Temple, Cheek and Ear

After a compress is applied to the wound, place the centre of the cravat over it and hold one end over the top of the head, carry the other under the jaw and up the opposite side, over the top of the head, and cross them at right angles over the temple on the injured side.

Continue one end around over the forehead and the other around the back of the head to meet over.

Cravat Bandage

Cravat bandage for the eye. the temple on the uninjured side. Tie the ends in a square knot. This bandage is also called a Modified Barton.

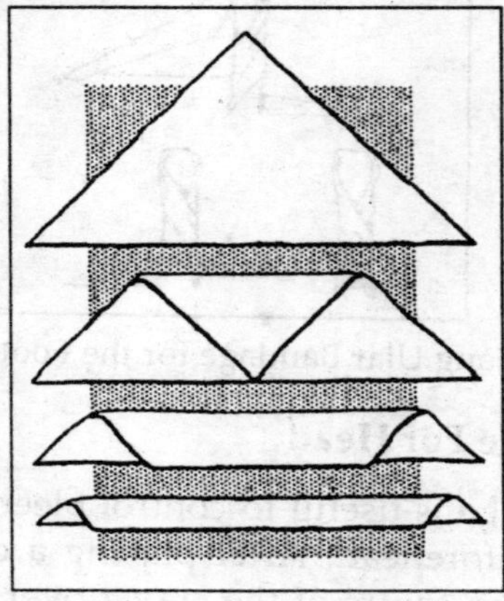

Fig. Cravat bandage

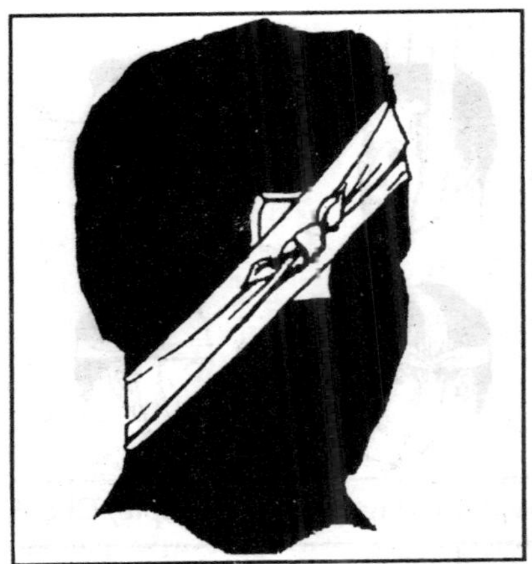

Fig. Cravat Bandage for the Eye.

Cravat Bandage for Elbow or Knee

After applying the compress, and if the injury or pain is not too severe, bend the elbow or knee to a right angle position before applying the bandage.

Place the middle of a rather wide cravat over the point of the elbow or knee, and carry the upper end around the upper part of the elbow or knee, bringing it back to the hollow, and the lower end entirely around the lower part, bringing it back to the hollow. See that the bandage is smooth and fits snug; then tie in a square knot outside of the hollow.

CRAVAT BANDAGE FOR ARM OR LEG.

The width of the cravat you use will depend upon the extent and area of the injury. For a small area, place a compress over the wound and centre the cravat bandage over the compress. Bring the ends around in back, cross them, and tie over the compress.

For a small extremity it may be necessary to make several turns around to use all the bandage for tying. If the wound covers a larger area, hold one end of the bandage above the compress and wind the other end spirally downward across the compress until it is secure, then upward and around again, and tie a knot where both ends meet.

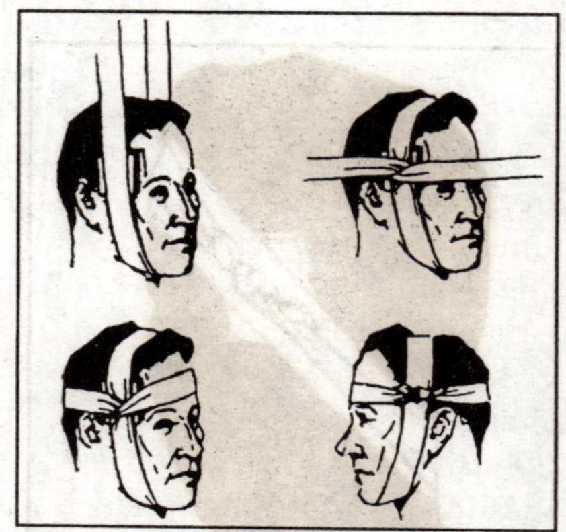

Fig. Cravat Bandage for the Temple, Cheek, or Ear

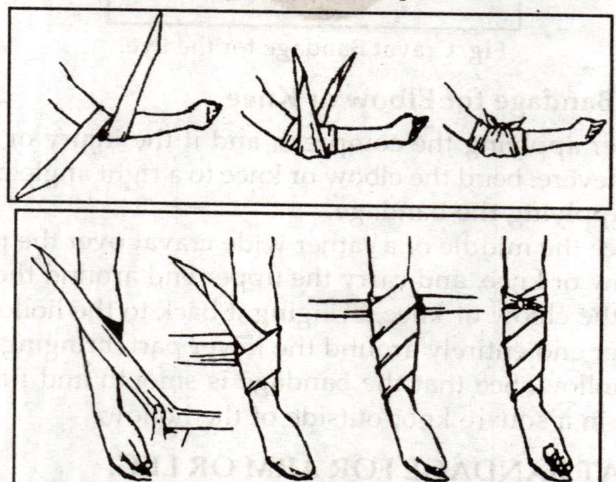

Fig. Cravat Bandage for the Arm, Forearm, Leg or Thigh.

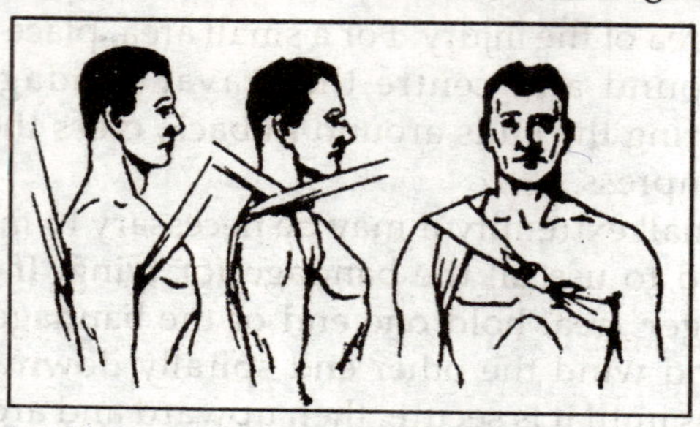

Fig. Cravat Bandage for the Axilla.

CRAVAT BANDAGE FOR AXILLA (ARMPIT)

This cravat is used to hold a compress in the axilla. It is similar to the bandage used to control bleeding from the axilla. Place the centre of the bandage in the axilla over the com-press and carry the ends up over the top of the shoulder and cross them.

Continue across the back and chest, to the opposite axilla and tie them. Do not tie too tightly or the axillary artery will be compressed. adversely affecting the circulation of the arm.

Battle Dressings

A battle dressing is a combination compress and bandage in which a sterile gauze pad is fastened to a gauze, muslin, or adhesive bandage. Most Navy first aid kits contain both large and small battle dressings of this kind.

Any part of a dressing that is to come in direct contact with a wound should be absolutely sterile, i.e., it should be free from microorganisms.

The dressings that you will find in first aid kits have been sterilized, However, if you touch them with your fingers, your clothes, or any other unsterile object, they are no longer sterile. If you drag a dressing across the victim's skin or allow it to slip after it is in place, the dressing is no longer sterile.

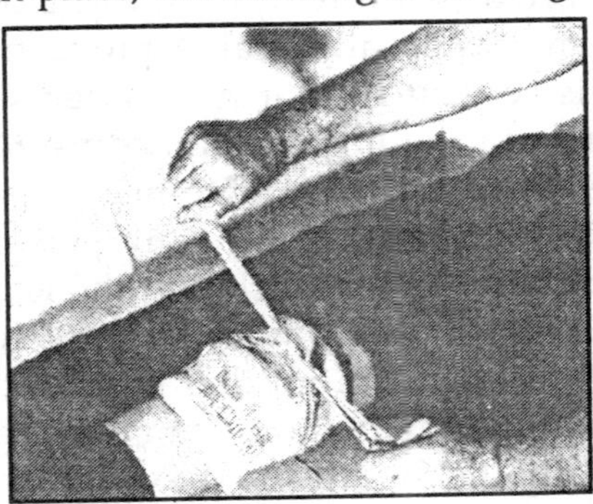

Fig. Battle Dressing

Chapter 7

Special Wounds

Animal Bites A special kind of infection that must be guarded against in case of animal bites is rabies (sometimes called "hydrophobia"). This disease is caused by a virus that is present in the saliva of infected animals. The disease occurs most commonly in wild animals, but it has been found in domestic animals and household pets; in fact, it is probable that all mammals are susceptible to it.

The virus that causes rabies is ordinarily transmitted by a bite, but it can be transmitted by the saliva of an infected animal coming in contact with a fresh wound or with the thin mucous membrane of the lips or nose.

The virus does not penetrate normal unbroken skin. If the skin is broken, Do Not attempt wound closure. If rabies develops in man, it is usually fatal. A preventive treatment is available that is very effective if it is started shortly after the bite; this treatment is outlined in Bumedinst 6220.6 series.

Since the vaccine can be obtained only at a medical treatment facility or a major ship, any person bitten by an animal Must be transferred quickly to the nearest treatment facility for evaluation, along with a complete report of the circumstances surrounding the incident. Remember, prevention is of utmost importance. Immediate local treatment of the wound should be given. Wash the wound and the surrounding area carefully, using sterile gauze, soap, and sterile water.

Use sterile gauze to dry the wound, and then cover the wound with a sterile dressing. Do Not use any chemical disinfectant. Do not attempt to cauterize the wound in any way. All of the animal's saliva must be removed from the victim's skin to prevent further contamination of the wound.

(Caution: Do not allow the animal's saliva to come in contact with open sores or cuts on your hands.) When a person has been bitten by an animal, every effort must be made to catch the animal to keep it confined for a minimum of 8 to 10 days. Do Not kill it if there is any possible chance of catching it alive.

The symptoms of rabies are not always present in the animal at the time the bite occurs, but the saliva may nevertheless contain the rabies virus. It is essential, therefore, that the animal is kept under observation until a diagnosis can be made.

The rabies treatment is given if the animal develops any definite symptoms, if it dies during the observation period, or if for any reason the animal cannot be kept under observation. Remember that any animal bite is dangerous and Must be evaluated at a treatment facility.

SPECIAL CONSIDERATIONS IN WOUND TREATMENT

Shock

Shock is likely to be severe in a person who has lost a large amount of blood or suffered any serious wound. The causes and treatment of shock are explained elsewhere in this chapter.

Infection

Although infection may occur in any wound, it is a particular danger in wounds that do not bleed freely; in wounds in which torn tissue or skin falls back into place and prevents the entrance of air; and in wounds that involve the crushing of tissues. Incisions, in which there is a free flow of blood and relatively little crushing of tissues, are the least likely to become infected.

Battle wounds are especially likely to become infected. They present the problem of devitalized tissue, extravasated blood, foreign bodies such as missile fragments, bits of cloth, dirt, dust, and a variety of bacteria. The devitalized tissue proteins and extravasated blood provide a nutritional medium for the support of bacterial growth and thus are conducive to the development of serious wound infection.

Puncture wounds are also likely to become infected by the germs causing tetanus. There are two types of bacteria commonly causing infection in wounds—aerobic and anaerobic. The former bacterial live and multiply in the presence of air or free oxygen, while the latter are bacterial that live and multiply only in the absence of air.

The principal aerobic bacteria that cause infection, inflammation, and septicemia (blood poisoning) are streptococci and staphylococci, some varieties of which are hemolytic (destroy red blood cells).

The staphylococci and streptococci may be introduced at the time of infliction, or they may be introduced to the wound later, at the time of first aid treatment or in the hospital if nonsterile instruments or dressings are employed. Wash minor wounds immediately with soap and clean water; then dry and paint them with a mild, nonirritating antiseptic. Apply a dressing if necessary.

In the first aid environment, do not attempt to wash or clean a large wound, and do not apply an antiseptic to it since it must be cleaned thoroughly at a medical treatment facility. Simply protect it with a large compress or dressing and transport the victim to a medical treatment facility. After an initial soap and water cleanup, puncture wounds must also be directed to a medical treatment facility for evaluation.

Inflammation

Inflammation is a local reaction to irritation. It occurs in tissues that are injured, but not destroyed. Symptoms include redness, pain, heat, swelling, and sometimes loss of motion. The body's physiologic response to the irritation is to dilate local blood vessels, which increases the blood supply to the area, which in turn causes the skin to appear red and warmer.

As the blood vessels dilate, their injured walls leak blood serum into surrounding tissues, causing edema and pain from increased pressure on nerve endings. In addition, white blood cells increase in the area and act as scavengers (phagocytes) in destroying bacteria and ingesting small particles of dead tissue and foreign matter.

Inflammation may be caused by trauma or mechanical irritation; chemical reaction to venom, poison ivy, acids, or alkalies; heat or cold injuries; microorganism penetration; or other agents such as electricity or solar radiation.

Inflammation should be treated by the following methods:

- Remove the irritating cause.
- Keep the inflamed area at rest and elevated.
- Apply cold for 24 to 48 hours to reduce swelling. Once swelling is reduced, apply heat to soft tissues, which hastens the removal of products of inflammation.
- Apply wet dressings and ointments to soften tissues and to rid the area of the specific causal bacteria.

Abscesses An abscess is a localized collection of pus that forms in cavities created by the disintegration of tissue. Abscesses may follow injury, illness, or irritation. Most are caused by staphylococcal infections and may occur in any area of the body, but are usually on the skin surface.

A Furuncle (boil) is an abscess in the true skin caused by the entry of microorganisms through a hair follicle or sweat gland.

A Carbuncle is a group of furuncular abscesses having multiple sloughs, often interconnected under the true skin. When localized, there are several "heads." Symptoms begin with localized itching and inflammation, followed by swelling, fever, and pain. Redness and swelling localize, and the furuncle or carbuncle becomes hard and painful. Pus forms into a cavity, causing the skin to become taut and discolored.

Treatment for furuncles and carbuncles includes the following:

- Do Not squeeze; this may damage surrounding healthy tissue and spread the infection.
- Use aseptic techniques when handling.
- Relieve pain with aspirin.

- Apply moist hot soaks/dressings (110°F) for 40 minutes, three to four times per day.
- Rest and elevate the infected body part.
- Antibiotic therapy may be ordered by a physician.
- Abscesses should be incised after they have localized (except on the face) to establish drainage. Abscesses in the facial triangle (nose and upper lip) should be seen by a physician.

Eye Wounds

Many eye wounds contain foreign objects. Dirt, coal, cinders, eyelashes, bits of metal, and a variety of other objects may become lodged in the eye. Since even a small piece of dirt is intensely irritating to the eye, the removal of such objects is important. However, the eye is easily damaged. Impairment of vision (or even total loss of vision) can result from fumbling, inexpert attempts to remove foreign objects from the eye. The following precautions Must be observed:

- Do Not allow the victim to rub the eye.
- Do Not press against the eye or manipulate it in any way that might cause the object to become embedded in the tissues of the eye. Be very gentle; roughness is almost sure to cause injury to the eye.
- Do not use such things as knives, toothpicks, matchsticks, or wires to remove the object.
- Do not under any Circum-stances Attempt to Remove an Object that is Embedded in the Eyeball or that has Penetrated The Eye! If you see a splinter or other object sticking out from the eyeball, leave it alone! Only specially trained medical personnel can hope to save the victim's sight if an object has actually penetrated the eyeball.

Small objects that are lodged on the surface of the eye or on the membrane lining the eyelids can usually be removed by the following procedures:

- Try to wash the eye gently with lukewarm, sterile water. A sterile medicine dropper or a sterile syringe can be used for this purpose. Have the victim lie down, with the head turned slightly to one side as shown in figure. Hold the eyelids apart. Direct the flow of water to the INSIDE corner of the eye, and let it run down to the Outside corner. Do not let the water fall directly onto the eyeball.

- Gently pull the lower lid down, and instruct the victim to look up. If you can see the object, try to remove it with the corner of a clean handkerchief or with a small moist cotton swab. You can make the swab by twisting cotton around a wooden applicator, not too tightly, and moistening it with sterile water. Caution: Never use dry cotton anywhere near the eye. It will stick to the eyeball or to the inside of the lids, and you will have the problem of removing it, as well as the original object.
- If you cannot see the object when the lowerlid is pulled down, turn-the upper lid back over a smooth wooden applicator. Tell theVictim to look down. Place the applicator lengthwise across the centre of the upper lid. Grasp the lashes of the upper lid gently but firmly.

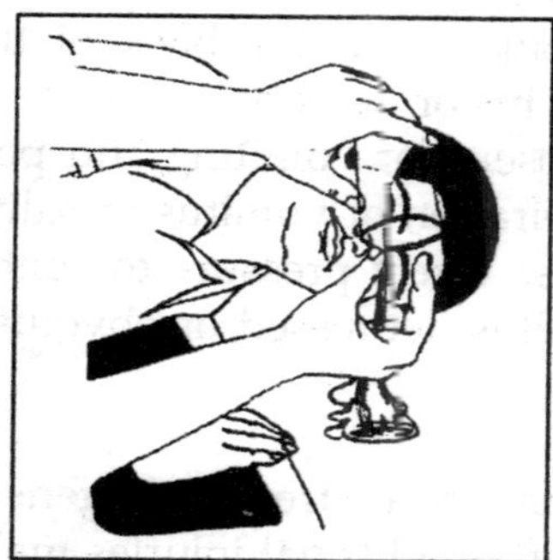

Fig. Patient suffering form Eye Wound

- Press gently with the applicator. Pull up on the eyelashes, turning the lid back over the applicator. If you can see the object, try to remove it with a moist cotton swab or with the corner of a clean handkerchief.

- If the foreign object cannot be removed by any of the above methods, you must Not Make Any Further Attempts to Remov Eit. Instead, place a small, thick gauze dressing over both eyes and hold it in place with a loose ban-dage. This limits movement of the injured eye .
- Get medical help for the victim at the earliest opportunity

Head Wounds

Head wounds must be treated with particular care, since there is always the possibility of brain damage. The general treatment for head wounds is the same as that for other fresh wounds. However, certain special precautions must be observed if you are giving first aid to a person who has suvvered a head wound.

- Never Give Any Medicine.
- Keep the victim lying flat, with the head at the level of the body. Do not raise the feet if the face is flushed. If the victim is having trouble breathing, you may raise the head slightly.
- If the wound is at the back of the head, turn the victim on his or her side.
- Watch closely for vomiting and postiion the head to avoid aspiration of vomitus or saliva into the lungs.
- Do not use direct pressure to control 5. hemorrhage if the skull is depressed or obvoiusly fractured.

Facial Wounds

Wounds of the face are treated, in general, like other fresh wounds. However, in all facial injuries make sure the tongue or injured sodt tissue does not block the airway, causing a breathing obstruction. Keep the nose and throat clear of any obstructing materials and postion the victim so that blood will drain out fo the mouth and nose.

Facial wounds that involve the eyelids or the soft tissue around the eye must be handled carefully to avoid further damage, If the injury does not involve the eyeball, apply a sterile compress and hold it in place with a Firm bandage. If the eyeball appears to be injured, use a Loose bandage. (Remember that you must Never attempt to remove any object that is embedded in the eyeball or that has penetrated it; just apply a dry, sterile compress to cover both eyes and hold it in place with a Loose Bandage). Any person who has suffered a facial wound that involves the eye, the eyelids, or the tissues around the eye must receive medical attention as soon as possible. Be sure to keep the victim lying down; you must use a stretcher for transport.

Chest Wounds

All chest injuries must be considered as serious conditions, for chest injuries may cause severe breathing and bleeding problems. Any victim showing signs of difficulty in breathing without signs of airway obstruction must be inspected for chest injuries.

The most serious chest injury that requires immediate first aid treatment is the Sucking Chest Wound. This is a penetrating injury to the chest that produces a hole in the chest cavity, causing the lung to collapse, which prevents normal breathing functions.

This is an extremely serious condition that will result in death if not treated quickly. Victims with open chest wounds gasp for breath, have difficulty breathing out, and may have a bluish skin colour to their face. A frothy looking blood may bubble from the wound during breathing.

The proper treatment for a sucking chest wound is as follows:

- Immediately seal the wound with a hand or any airtight material available (e.g., ID card). The material must be large enough so that it cannot be sucked into the wound when the victim breaths in.
- Firmly tape the material in place with strips of adhesive tape and secure it with a pressure dressing. It is important that the dressing is airtight, otherwise, it will not relieve the victim's breathing problems. The object of the dressing is to keep air from going

in through the wound. Note: If the victim's condition suddenly deteriorates when you apply the seal, Immediately remove it.

- Give the victim oxygen if it is available and you know how to use it.
- Place the victim in a Fowler's or semiFowler's position. This makes breathing a little easier. During combat lay the victim on a stretcher on the affected side.
- Watch the victim closely for signs of shock and treat accordingly.
- Do not give victims with chest injuries anything to drink.
- Transport the victim to a medical treatment facility immediate}.

Abdominal Wounds

A deep wound in the abdomen is likely to constitute a major emergency since there are many vital organs in this area. Abdomnial wounds usually cause intense pain, nausea and vomiting, spasm of the abdominal muscles, and severe shock. Immediate surgical treatment is almost always required; therefore, the victim must receive medical attention at once, or the chances of survival will be poor.

Give only the most essential first aid treatment and concentrate your efforts on getting the victim to a medical treatment facility. The following first aid procedures may be of help to a person suffering from an abdominal wound:

- Keep the victim in a supine position. [f the intestine is protruding or exposed, the victim may be more comfortable with the knees drawn up. Place a coat, pillow, or some other bulky cloth material under the knees to help maintain this position. Do not Attempt to push the Intestine back in or to Manipulate It In any way!
- If bleeding is severe, try to stop it by applying direct pressure.
- If the intestine is not exposed, cover the wound with

a dry sterile dressing. If the intestine is exposed, apply a sterile compress moistened with sterile water. If no sterile water is available, clean sea water or any water that is fit to drink may be used to moisten the compress. Figure shows an abdominal wound with the intestine protruding.

Figure shows the application of compresses large enough to cover the wound and the surrounding area. The compress should be held in place by a bandage. Fasten the bandage firmly so that the compress will not slip around, but do notapply any more pressure than is necessary severity of shock by making sure that the to hold the compress in position. Large batvictim is comfortably warm and kept in the tle dressings are ideal.

Fig. Applying Compresses to a Protruding Abdominal Wound

- Treat for shock, but do not waste any time doing it. The victim must be transported to a hospital at the earliest possible opor-tunity. However, you can minimize the severity of shock by making sure that the victim is comfortably warm and kept in the supine position. Do not give any-thing to drink. If the victim is thirsty, moisten the mouth with a small amount of water but do not allow any liq-uid to be swallowed.

- Upon the direction of a medical officer, start an intravenous line.

Removing Foreign Objects

Many wounds contain foreign objects. Wood or glass splinters, bullets, metal fragments, bits of wire, fishhooks, nails, tacks, cinders, and small particles from grinding wheels are examples of the variety of objects or materials that are sometimes found in wounds. In some cases, first aid treatment for wounds includes the removal of such objects when they are near the surface and exposed.

However, first aid treatment does not include the removal of deeply embedded objects, powdered glass, or any widely scattered material of this nature. You should never attempt to remove bullets, but you should try to find out whether the bullet remains in the victim; look for both entrance and exit wounds. The general rule to remember is this: Remove foreign objects from a wound when you can do so easily and without causing further damage; but Never Hunt For Or Attempt To Remove Deeply Buried Or Widely Scattered Objects Or Materials except in a definitive care environment.

The following procedure may be used to remove a small object from the skin or tissues if the object is near the surface and clearly visible:

- If Cleanse the skin around the object with soap and water and paint with any available skin antiseptic solution.
- If necessary, pierce the skin with a sharp instrument (a needle, razor, or sharp knife that has been sterilized by passing it through a flame several times).
- Grasping the object at the end, remove it. Tweezers, small pincers, or forceps maybe used for this purpose. (Whatever instrument you use should first be sterilized by boiling if at all possible.)
- If the wound is superficial, apply gentle pressure to encourage bleeding.

- Cover the wound with a dry, sterile dressing.

If the foreign object is under a fingernail or toenail, you may have to cut a V-shaped notch in the nail so that the object can be grasped by the forceps. Do not try to dig the object out from under to nail with a knife or similar instrument. A curved or barbed object such as a fishhook may present special problems. Figure shows one method of removing a fishhook that has become embedded in the flesh.

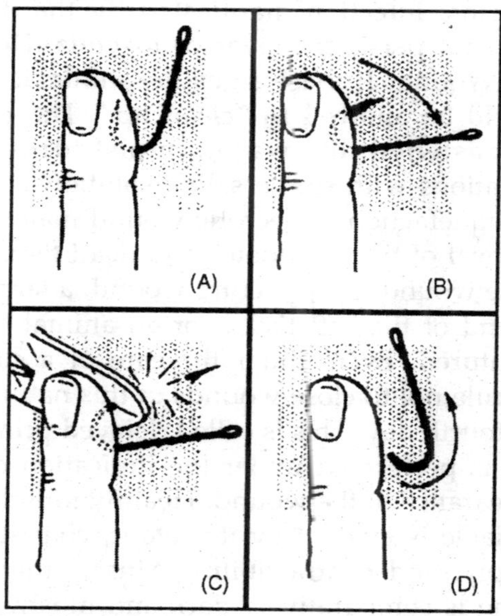

Fig. Removing a Fishhook.

As you can see from figure, the barb on the hook prevents its direct removal. However, if you push the hook forward through the skin, you can clip of the barb with a wire cutter or similar tool. The remainder of the fishhook can then be withdrawn in the manner indicated.

Wound Closing

The care of the wound is largely controlled by the tactical situation, facilities available, and the length of time before proper medical care maybe available. However, if days are to elapse before the patient can be seen by a surgeon, the corpsman should know how to use the various suture procedures and materials and how to select the most appropriate of both.

Before discussing the methods of coaptation (bringing together), some of the contraindications to wound closing should be described:

- If there is reddening and edema of the wound margins, infection manifested by the discharge of pus, and persistent fever or toxemia, Do Not Close The Wound. If these signs are minimal, the wound should be allowed to "clean up." The process may be hastened by warm, moist dressings, and irrigations with sterile saline solutions. These aid in the liquefaction of necrotic wound materials and the removal of thick exudates and dead tissues.
- If the wound is a puncture wound, a large gaping wound of the soft tissue, or an animal bite, leave it unsutured. Even under the care of a surgeon, it is the rule not to close wounds of this nature until after the fourth day. This is called delayed primary closure and is performed under the indication of a healthy appearance of the wound. Healthy muscle tissue that is viable is evident by its colour, consistency, blood supply, and contractibility. Muscle that is dead or dying is comparatively dark and mushy; it does not contract when pinched, nor does it bleed when cut. If this type of tissue is evident, do not close the wound.
- If the wound is deep, consider the support of the surrounding tissue; if there is not enough support to bring the deep fascia together, do not suture because dead (hollow) spaces will be created. In this generally gaping type of wound, muscles, tendons, and nerves are usually involved. Only a surgeon should attempt to close this type of wound.

To a certain extent, firm pressure dressings and immobilization can obliterate hollow spaces. If tendons and nerves do not seem to be involved, absorbable sutures may be placed in the muscle (great care always being exercised to suture muscle fibers end-to-end and to correctly appose them) and the wound is closed in layers. This is extremely delicate surgery and the corpsman should exercise independent judgment on the advisability of attempting it, and then only if he or she has observed and assisted in numerous surgical operations.

If the wound is small, clean, and free from foreign bodies and signs of infection, steps should be taken to close it. All instruments should be checked, cleaned, and thoroughly sterilized. Use a good light and position the patient on the table so that access to the wound will be unhampered. The area around the wound should be cleansed and then prepared with an antiseptic.

The wound area should be draped, whenever possible, to maintain a sterile field in which the corpsman works. The corpsman should wear a cap and mask, scrub his or her hands and forearms, and wear sterile gloves. Suture Materials In modern surgery, many kinds of ligature and suture materials are used.

All can be grouped into two classes:

1. *Nonabsorbable sutures*: Those that cannot be absorbed by the body cells and fluids in which they are embedded during the healing process. When used as buried sutures, they become surrounded or encapsulated in fibrous tissue and remain as innocuous foreign bodies. When used as skin sutures, they are removed after the skin has healed. The most commonly used of this type of sutures and facts associated with them are:
   - *Silk:* Frequent tissue reaction or "spitting" of suture from the wound.
   - *Cotton*: Loses tensile strength with each autoclaving.
   - *Linen*: Better than silk or cotton but more expensive and not as readily available.
   - *Synthetic material*: There are many, such as nylon and dermalon. These are excellent, particularly

for surface use. They cause very little tissue reaction. Their only problem seems to be the tendency for the knots to come untied, so most surgeons tie 3 to 4 square knots in each suture. Nylon is preferred over silk for face and lip areas because silk too often causes tissue reactions.

– *Rust-proof metal*: Usually stainless steel wire or tantalum. This has the least tissue reaction of all suture material and is by far the strongest. The primary problems are the need for wire cutters, and it is more difficult to use because it kinks.

- *Absorbable sutures*: Those that are absorbed or digested by the body cells and tissue fluids in which they are embedded during and after the healing processes. It is this characteristic that enhances their use beneath the skin surfaces and on mucous membranes.Surgical gut fulfills the requirements for the perfect suture more often than any other material.
  – *Manufacture of catgut*: derived from the submucosal connective tissue of the first one-third (about 8 yards) of the small intestine of healthy government inspected sheep. The intestine of the sheep has certain characteristics that make it especially adaptable for surgical use. It is of uniformly fine-grained tissue structure and possesses great tensile strength and elasticity.
  – *Tensile strength of catgut*: this suture material is available in sizes of 6-0 to 0 and 1 to 4, with 6-0 being the smallest diameter and 4 being the largest. The tensile strength increases with the diameter of the suture.
  – *Kinds of surgical gut (catgut)*: this varies from plain catgut, the raw gut that has been gauzed, polished, sterilized, and packaged, to chromic catgut that has undergone various intensities of tanning with one of the salts of chromic acid to delay tissue absorption time. Some examples of

these variations and absorption times are as follows:

a. Type A: Plain, 10 days
b. Type B: Mild chromic, 20 days
c. Type C: Medium chromic, 30 days
d. Type D: Extra chromic, 40 days

Suture Needles

Suture needles may be straight or curved and have either a tapered round point or a cutting edge point. They vary in length, curvature, and diameter for various types of suturing.

- *Sizing*: suture needles are sized by diameter and come in many sizes, depending on use.
- *Taper point*: these cause small amounts of tissue damage and are most often used in deep tissues.
- *Cutting edge point*: this is the preferred needle for suturing the skin because of the toughness of the skin.
- *Atraumatic (atraloc, wedged)*: these needles may either have a cutting edge or taper point and have the suture fixed on the end of the needle by the manufacturer to cause the least tissue trauma.

Preparation of Casualty

- Examine the casualty carefully to determine what materials are needed to properly close the wound.
  a. Select and prepare sterile instruments, needles, and suture materials.
  b. The patient should be securely positioned so that access to the wound and suture tray is optimal. It is usually not necessary to restrain patients for suturing.
  c. Make sure a good light is available.
- Aseptic wound preparation is to be strictly observed. Use mask, cap, and gloves. Thorough cleaning and proper draping is essential.
- Select an anesthetic with care. Consider the patient's tolerance to pain, time of injury, medications the

patient is taking or has been given, and the possible distortion of the tissue when the anesthetic is infiltrated.

The most common local anesthetic used is Xylocaine, which comes in various strengths (0.5%, 1%, 2%) and with or without epinephrine. Injectable containing epinephrine are never to be used on the fingers, toes, ears, or nose because of the vasoconstricting effect of the epinephrine. Epinephrine is also contraindicated in patients with hypertension, diabetes, or heart disease.

The three methods of administration are topical, local infiltration, and nerve block. Topical anesthetics are generally reserved for ophthalmic or plastic surgery and nerve blocks are generally accomplished by an anesthesiologist or anesthetist for the surgical patient. For a corpsman, topical anesthesia is limited to the instillation of eyedrops for mild corneal abrasions after all foreign bodies have been removed.

Do Not attempt to remove embedded foreign bodies. Nerve blocks are limited to digital blocks wherein the nerve trunks that enervate the fingers or toes are anesthetized. The most common method of anesthesia used by a corpsman is the infiltration of the anesthetizing agent around a wound or minor surgical site.

Obtaining a digital block is a fairly simple procedure, but it should not be attempted except under the supervision of a medical officer or after a great deal of practice. The first step is cleansing the injection site with an antiseptic solution. The anesthetizing agent is then infiltrated into the lateral and medial aspects at the base of the digit with a small bore needle (25or 26-gauge), taking care not to inject into the veins or arteries.

Proper placement of the anesthesia should result in a loss of sensitivity in a few minutes. This is tested by asking the patient if he or she can distinguish a sharp sensation or pain when a sharp object is gently applied to the skin. Obtaining local anesthesia is similar except you are anesthetizing nerves immediately adjacent to where you will be working and not nerve trunks.

There are two generally accepted methods of infiltrating the anesthesia. One is through the skin surrounding the margin of the wound and the other is through the wound into the surrounding tissue. In either case, sufficient quantities must be infiltrated to effect anesthesia approximately 1/2 inch around the wound, taking care not to inject into a vein or artery. A note of caution: The maximum recommended amount of Xylocaine to be used is 50 cc for a 1 per cent solution or the equivalent.

General Principles of Wound Suturing

Wounds are closed either primarily or secondarily. A primary closure is within a short time of when the wound occurred; a secondary closure is a delayed closure for up to several days. In general, wounds less than 6 hours old can be closed without the danger of infection. Wounds 6 to 14 hours old may be closed if they are not grossly contaminated and are meticulously cleaned.

Wounds 14 to 24 hours old should not be closed primarily. When reddening and edema of the wound margins, discharge of pus, persistent fever, or toxemia are present, do not close the wound. Do not close primarily a large, gaping, soft tissue wound. This type of wound is certain to contain large quantities of bacteria. These wounds will require warm wet dressings and irrigations, along with aseptic care for 3 to 7 days to clear up the wound. Then a delayed wound closure may be performed.

- Debride the wound area and convert circular wounds to elliptical ones before suturing. Circular wounds cannot be closed with satisfactory cosmetic result.
- Try to convert a jagged laceration to one with smooth edges before suturing it. Make sure that not too much skin is trimmed off that would make the wound difficult to approximate.
- Use the correct technique for placing sutures. The needle holder is applied at approximately one quarter of the distance from the blunt end of the needle. Suturing. with a curved needle is done toward the

person doing the suturing. Insert the needle into the skin at a 90 degree angle and sweep it through an arclike motion, following the general arc of the needle.

- Carefully avoid bruising the skin edges being sutured. Use Adson forceps and very lightly grasp the skin edges. It is improper to use dressingforceps while suturing. Since there are no teeth on the grasping edges of the dressing forceps, the force required to hold the skin firmly may be enough to cause necrosis.
- Do not put sutures in too tightly. Gentle approximation of the skin is all that is necessary. Remember that postoperative edema will occur in and about the wound, making sutures tighter.

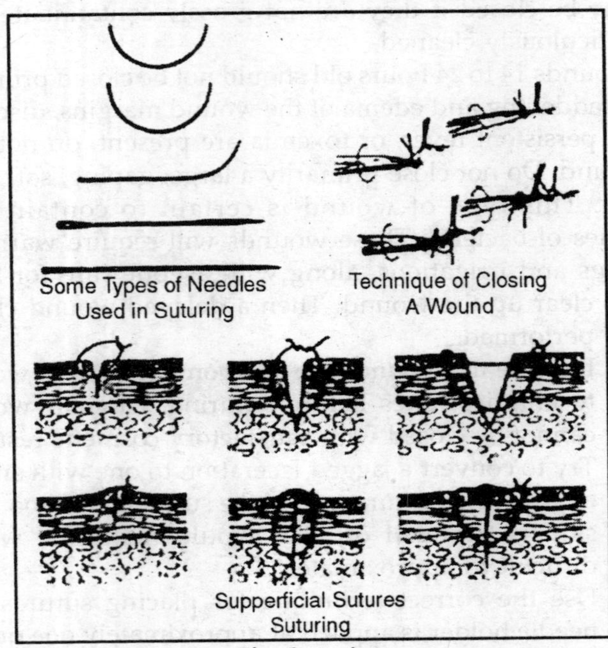

Fig. Suturing.

- If there is a significant chance that the sutured wound may become infected (e.g., bites, delayed closure, grossly contaminated), place a small iodoform or rubber drain in the wound and remove it in 48 hours.

- When suturing, the best cosmetic effect is obtained by using numerous interrupted simple sutures placed 1/8 inch apart. Where cosmetic result is not a consideration, sutures may be slightly further apart. Generally, the distance of the needle bite from the wound edges should be equal to the distance between sutures.
- When subcutaneous sutures are needed, it is proper to use chromic catgut.
- When deciding the type of material to use on skin, use the finest diameter that will satisfactorily hold the tissues.
  - Children under
  - All other faces
  - Body
  - Feet, elbows, knees
  - Child's scalp
  - Adult's scalp
  - Lip
- When cutting sutures, subcutaneous catgut should have a 1/16 inch tail. Silk skin sutures should be cut as short as is practical for removal on the face and lip. Elsewhere, skin sutures may have longer tails for convenience, but a tail over 1/4 inch is unnecessary and tends to collect exudate.
- The following general rules can be used in deciding when to remove sutures: Face: As a general rule, 4 or 5 days. Better cosmetic results are obtained by removing every other suture and any suture with redness around it on the third day and the remainder on the fifth day. Body and scalp: 7 days Soles, palms, back or over joints: 10 days unless excess tissue reaction is apparent around the suture, in which case they should come out sooner. Any suture with pus or infection around it should be removed immediately, since its presence will make the

infection worse. When wire is used, it may be left in safely for 10 to 14 days.

Shock

Shock is the collapse of the cardiovascular system, characterized by circulatory deficiency and depression of vital functions. There are several types of shock.

Hypovolemic shock is due to diminished blood volume; neurogenic shock results from the loss of vascular control by the nervous system; cardiogenic shock is due to inadequate functioning of the heart; septic shock develops in the presence of severe infection; and anaphylactic shock is due to an allergic reaction. Multiple types of shock maybe present in varying degrees in the same patient.

The most frequently encountered and most important type for the corpsman to understand is hemorrhagic shock, a type of hypovolemic shock. In shock, the diminished blood volume causes a markedly lessened cardiac output and reduced peripheral circulation.

This results in a lowered transport of oxygen to the tissues (hypoxia); decreased perfusion, the circulation of blood within an organ; and a lowered transport of waste products away from the tissue cells.

Under these conditions, body cells are able to carry on their normal functions for only a short period of time. Soon they begin to malfunction and then shut down. Certain cells, especially in the heart, brain, liver, and kidneys, are highly susceptible to temporary or permanent damage.

Permanent renal shutdown is an ever present danger in shock. Shock should be expected in all cases of gross hemorrhage, abdominal or chest wounds, crush or blast injuries, extensive large muscle damage, particularly of the extremities, major fractures, traumatic amputations, head injuries, burns involving more than 10 per cent of the body surface area, or any other major injury.

The essence of shock control and prevention is to recognize the onset of the condition and to start treatment before the symptoms fully develop.

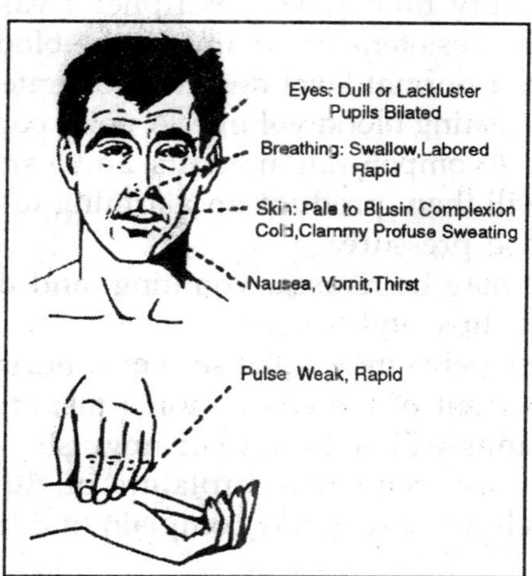

The following are general signs and symptoms of the development of shock:

- *Circulation*: Restlessness and apprehension are early symptoms, often followed by apathy.
- Eyes may be glassy, dull and have dilated pupils (these are also the symptoms of morphine use)
- Breathing may be rapid or labored, often of the gasping "air hunger" type. In the advanced stages of shock, breathing becomes shallow and irregular.
- The face and skin may be very pale or ashen gray; in the dark complexioned, the mucous membranes may be pale. The lips are often cyanotic.
- The skin feels cool and is covered with clammy sweat. The coolness is related to a decrease in the peripheral circulation.
- The pulse tends to become rapid, weak, and thready. If the blood pressure is severely owered, the peripheral pulse may be absent. The pulse rate in hemorrhagic shock may reach 140 or higher. An exception is neurogenic shock, where the pulse rate is slowed, often below 60.
- The blood pressure is usually lowered in moderately severe shock; the systolic pressure drops below 100 while the pulse rises above 100. The body is for

circulatory fluid loss by peripheral vasoconstriction. This process tends to maintain the blood pressure at nearly a normal level despite moderately severe loss of circulating blood volume. A point comes, however, when decompen-sation occurs, and a small additional loss will then produce an alarming and sudden fall in blood pressure.

- There may be nausea, vomiting, and dryness of the mouth, lips, and tongue.
- Surface veins may collapse. Veins normally visible at the front of the elbow, forearms, and the back of the hands will be hard to distinguish.
- There are frequent complaints of thirst. Even the severely wounded may complain of thirst rather than pain.
- The kidneys may shut down. Urine formation either ceases or becomes greatly diminished if the systolic blood pressure falls below 80 for long periods of time.
- The person may faint from inadequate venous blood return to the heart. This may be the result of a temporary gravitational pooling of the blood associated with standing up too quickly.

Hypovolemic Shock

This condition is also known as oligemic or hematogenic shock. The essential feature of all forms of hypovolemic shock is loss of fluid from the circulating blood volume, so that adequate circulation cannot be maintained to all parts of the body.

In cases where there is internal or external hemorrhage due to trauma (hemorrhagic shock) there is a loss of whole blood, including red blood cells. The body tends to restore the circulatory volume by supplying fluid from the body tissues.

There is a resulting progressive fall in the hematocrit (ratio of red blood cells to plasma) and in the red blood cell count due to hemodilution, However, since hemodilution is not an excessively rapid process, the hematocrit is a poor indicator of acute blood loss, i.e., less than 24 hours old, In burn shock, on the other hand, there is a progressively increased hematocrit and red blood cell count due to hemoconcentration from loss of the plasma fraction of the blood into and through the burned area. A third form of hypovolemic shock occurs in cases of severe diarrhea and vomiting, where body fluids and electrolytes (sodium, potassium, and chloride) are lost. This also contributes to a decrease in circulating blood volume.

Neurogenic Shock

Neurogenic shock, sometimes called vasogenic shock, results from the disruption of autonomic nervous system control over vasoconstriction. Under normal conditions the autonomic nervous system keeps the muscles of the veins and arteries partially contracted.

At the onset of most forms of shock, further constriction is signaled. However, the vascular muscles cannot maintain this contraction indefinitely. A number of factors, including increased fluid loss, central nervous system trauma, or emotional shock, can override the autonomic nervous system control.

The veins and arteries immediately dilate, drastically expanding the volume of the circulatory system, with a corresponding reduction of blood pressure. Simple fainting (syncope) is a variation of neurogenic shock.

It often is the result of a temporary gravitational pooling of the blood as a person stands up. As the person falls, blood again rushes to the head, and the problem is solved. It may also be induced by fear or horror, which override the autonomic nervous system control.

Other variations of neurogenic shock that are important to the corpsman are shell shock and bomb shock. These are psychological adjustment reactions to extremely stressful wartime experiences and do not relate to the collapse of the cardiovascular system.

Symptoms range from intense fear to complete dementia and are manifestations of a loss of nervous control. Care is limited to emotional support and evacuation to the care of a psychiatrist or psychologist.

Cardiogenic Shock

Cardiogenic shock is caused by inadequate functioning of the heart, not by loss of circulating blood volume. If the heart muscle is weakened by disease or damaged by trauma or lack of oxygen, as in cases of pulmonary disease, suffocation, or myocardial infarction, the heart will no longer be able to maintain adequate circulatory pressure, even though the volume of fluid is unchanged.

Shock will develop as the pressure falls. Heart attack is an extreme medical emergency all corpsmen must be ready to handle. It will be discussed in greater detail in the "Common Medical Emergencies" section of this chapter.

Septic Shock

Septic shock usually does not develop for 2 to 5 days after an injury and the corpsman will not often see it in a first aid situation. It may appear during the course of peritonitis caused by penetrating abdominal wounds or perforation of the appendix. It may also result from gross wound contamination, rupture of an ulcer, or as a complication of certain types of pneumonia.

Septic shock is the result of vasodilation of small blood vessels in the wound area, or general vasodilation if the infection has entered the bloodstream. In addition to increasing circulatory system volume, the walls of the blood vessels become more permeable, allowing fluids to escape into the tissues. This type of shock carries a poor prognosis and must almost always be treated under the direct supervision of a medical officer.

Anaphylactic Shock

This type of shock occurs when an individual is exposed to a substance to which his or her body is particularly sensitive. In its most severe form, the body goes into an almost instantaneous violent reaction. A burning sensation, itching, and hives spread across the skin.

Severe edema effects body parts and the respiratory system. Blood pressure drops alarmingly, and fainting or coma may develop. The causative agent may be introduced into the body in a number of ways. The injection of medicines, especially penicillin and horseor eggcultured serums, is one route. Another is the injection of venoms by stinging insects and animals. The inhalation of dusts, pollens, or other materials to which a person is sensitive is a third route. Finally, a slightly slower but no less severe reaction may develop from the ingestion of certain foods and medications. Specific treatment of venoms and poisons will be discussed in the "Poisons/Drug Abuse" section of this chapter.

GENERAL TREATMENT PROCEDURES

Intravenous fluid administration is the single most important factor in the treatment of any type of shock except cardiogenic shock. The proper use of intravenous equipment and fluids are discussed in the "Patient Care" chapter of the manual. Ringer's lactate is probably the best solution to use, although normal saline is adequate until properly cross-matched whole blood can be administered.

The electrolyte solutions replace not only the lost blood volume, but also lost extracellular fluid that has been depleted to bolster the shrunken blood volume. If the shock situation is severe enough to warrant immediate administration of intravenous fluids, or transportation to a medical facility will be delayed and a medical officer is not available in the first aid situation to write an administrative order, be conservative. Start the intravenous fluid and let it run at a slow rate of 50 to 60 drops per minute.

If intravenous solutions are unavailable or transportation to a medical treatment facility will be delayed, and there are no contraindications such as gastrointestinal bleeding or unconsciousness, the patient may receive an electrolyte solution by mouth. This may be prepared by adding a teaspoon of salt and half a teaspoon of baking soda to a quart or liter of water. Allow the patient to sip the solution.

Pneumatic Counter-Pressure Devices (MAST)

Commonly known as Medical Anti-Shock Trousers or

Military Anti-Shock Trousers, these devices are designed to correct or counteract certain internal bleeding conditions and hypovolemia.

The garment does this by developing an encircling pressure up to 120 mm Hg around both lower extremities, the pelvis, and the abdomen. The pressure created:

- Slows or stops venous and arterial bleeding in areas of the body enclosed by the pressurized garment.
- Forces available blood from the lower body to the heart, brain, and other vital organs.
- Prevents pooling of blood in the lower extremities.
- Stabilizes fractures of the pelvis and lower extremities.

Some indications for use of the pneumatic counter-pressure devices are as follows:

- Systolic blood pressure less than 80 mm Hg
- Systolic blood pressure less than 100 mm Hg and the patient exhibits the classic signs of shock
- Fracture of the pelvis or lower extremities.

The only absolute contraindication in their use is pulmonary edema, although conditional contraindications include congestive heart failure, heart attack, stroke, pregnancy, abdominal evisceration, massive bleeding into the thoracic cavity, and penetrating wounds where the object is still impaled in the victim.

Application of the anti-shock garment is a relatively simple procedure but requires some important preliminary steps. When the garment is laid out flat, ensure that there are no wrinkles. If clothing is to remain on the patient, remove all sharp and bulky objects from the patient's pockets.

Take vital signs before applying the garment. The garments are inflated only sufficiently to bring the patient's systolic blood pressure to 100 mm Hg and maintain it there. Once the garment is inflated, take vital signs every 5 minutes. The garment is removed only under the direct supervision of a physician, There is no indication for the pre-hospital removal of anti-shock garments.

Other shock treatment procedures to use are as follows:

- Maintain an open airway. Oxygen may also be administered if proper equipment is available.
- Control hemorrhage.
- Check for other injuries that may have been sustained. Remove the victim from the presence of identifiable causative agents.
- Place the victim in a supine position, with the feet slightly higher than the head (shock position). Certain problems, such as breathing difficulties or head injuries, may require other positioning.
- Reduce pain by splinting fractures, providing emotional support, and attending to the victim's comfort. Unless contraindicated, aspirin may be dispensed.
- Conserve body heat.
- Avoid rough handling and transport the victim to a medical treatment facility.
- If transportation to a definitive care facility will be lengthy or delayed, seek the radio or phone advice of a medical officer on whether or not to give fluids by mouth or to start an intravenous line. If this is impossible, use your own judgment. Cardiogenic shock is the only exception to this rule. Do Not start intravenous fluids since volume is sufficient and only function is impaired.
- Constantly monitor and record vital signs every 15 minutes so that you are able to keep track of the victim's progress.

PAIN RELIEF

As a corpsman in the field or on board ship in wartime, you may be issued morphine for the control of shock through relief of severe pain. You will be issued this controlled drug under very strict accountability procedures. Possession of this drug is a medical responsibility that must not be taken lightly.

Morphine Administration

Morphine is the most effective of all painrelieving drugs.

It is most commonly available in syrettes or tubex in premeasured doses. Properly administered in selected patients, it will relieve distressing pain and assist in the prevention of shock.

The adult dose of morphine is 8 to 16 mg repeated, if necessary, in not less than 4 hours. Morphine has several undesirable effects, however, and these must be thoroughly understood by the corpsman.

- Morphine is a severe respiratory depressant and therefore must not be given to patients in moderate or severe shock or to patients in respiratory distress.
- Morphine increases intracranial pressure and may induce vomiting; these effects may be disastrous in head injury cases.
- Morphine causes constriction of the pupils (pinpoint pupils); this effect prevents the use of the pupillary reactions for diagnosis in head injuries.
- Morphine is cardiotoxic and a peripheral vasodilator. It may cause profound hypotension in small doses in the patient in shock.
- Morphine poisoning is an ever-present danger. There is a narrow safety margin between the amounts of morphine that may given therapeutically and the amounts that produce death.
- Morphine causes considerable mental confusion and interferes with the proper exercise of judgment and therefore should not be given to ambulatory patients.
- Morphine is a dangerously habituating drug. It should not be given trivially and must be rigidly accounted for. Under no circumstances should the corpsman administer morphine except in an emergency. Morphine administration to patients in shock or with extensive burns should be rigidly controlled.

Morphine administration by subcutaneous or intramuscular routes may not be absorbed into the bloodstream because of the reduced peripheral circulation, and pain may persist. When this happens, the uninformed often give additional doses, hoping to bring about relief.

Then when resuscitation occurs and the peripheral circulation improves, the stored quantities of morphine are released into the system, and an extremely serious condition (morphine poisoning) ensues.

When other pain-relieving drugs are not available, and the patient in shock or with burns is in severe pain, 16 mg of morphine may be given intramuscularly (followed by massage of the injection site), but the temptation to give more must be resisted.

Doses should not be repeated more than twice and then at least 4 hours apart, unless otherwise ordered by a medical officer.

If the pain from the wound is agonizingly severe, morphine may be given if examination of the patient reveals no:

- Head injury.
- Chest injury, including sucking and nonsucking wounds.
- Wounds of the throat, nasal passages, oral cavity, or jaws wherein blood might obstruct the airway.
- Massive hemorrhage.
- Respiratory impairment, including chemical burns of the respiratory tract. Any casualty having fewer than 16 respirations per minute should not be given morphine.
- Evidence of severe or deepening shock.
- Loss of consciousness.

Overdose is an ever-present danger. For this reason, every casualty who has received morphine should be plainly identified. Write the letter "M" and the hour of injection on the patient's forehead, e.g., M0830. A skin pencil, colored antiseptic, or ink maybe used for this purpose.

The empty morphine syrette or tubex should be attached to the shirt collar or other conspicuous area of the clothing by a safety pin or other means to alert others that the drug has been administered.

Chapter 8

Injuries

INJURIES TO BONES, JOINTS, AND MUSCLES

Many kinds of accidents cause injuries to bones, joints, or muscles. In giving first aid to an injured person, you must always look for signs of fractures (broken bones), dislocations, sprains, strains, and contusions. An essential part of the first aid treatment for fractures consists of immobilizing the injured part with splints so that the sharp ends of broken bones will not move around and cause further damage to nerves, blood vessels, or vital organs.

Splints are also used to immobilize severely injured joints or muscles and to prevent the enlargement of extensive wounds. You must have a general understanding of the use of splints before going on to learn the detailed first aid treatment for injuries to bones, joints, and muscles.

Use of Splints

In an emergency, almost any firm object or material will serve as a splint. Thus, umbrellas, canes, rifles, tent pegs, sticks, oars, wire mesh, boards, corrugated cardboard, and folded newspapers can be used as splints. A fractured leg may sometimes be splinted by fastening it securely to the uninjured leg.

Whenever available, use manufactured spirits such as the pneumatic splints or the traction splints. Splints, whether manufactured or improvised, must fulfill certain requirements. They should be lightweight, strong, fairly rigid, and long enough to reach past the joints above and below the fracture.

They should be wide enough so that the bandages used to hold them in place will not pinch the injured part. Splints must be well padded on the sides touching the body; if they are not properly padded, they will not fit well and will not adequately immobilize the injured part.

If you have to improvise the padding for a splint, you may use clothing, bandages, cotton, blankets, or any other soft material.

If the victim is wearing heavy clothes, you may be able to apply the splint on the outside, allowing the clothing to serve as at least part of the required padding.

Fasten splints in place with bandages, strips of adhesive, tape clothing, or other suitable materials.

If possible, one person should hold the splints in position while another person fastens them. Although splints should be applied snugly, they should NEVER be tight enough to interfere with the circulation of the blood. When you are applying splints to an arm or a leg, try to leave the fingers or toes exposed.

If the tips of the fingers or toes become blue or cold, you will know that the splints or bandages are too tight. You should examine a splinted part approximately every half hour and loosen the fastenings if the circulation appears to be impaired.

Remember that any injured part is likely to swell, and splints or bandages that are applied correctly may later become too tight.

Injuries To Bones

A break in a bone is called a Fracture. There are two main kinds of fractures. A Closed Fracture is one in which the injury is entirely internal; the bone is broken but there is no break in the skin.

An Open Fracture is one in which there is an open wound in the tissues and the skin. Sometimes the open wound is made when a sharp end of the broken bone pushes out through the flesh; sometimes it is made by an object such as a bullet that penetrates from the outside.

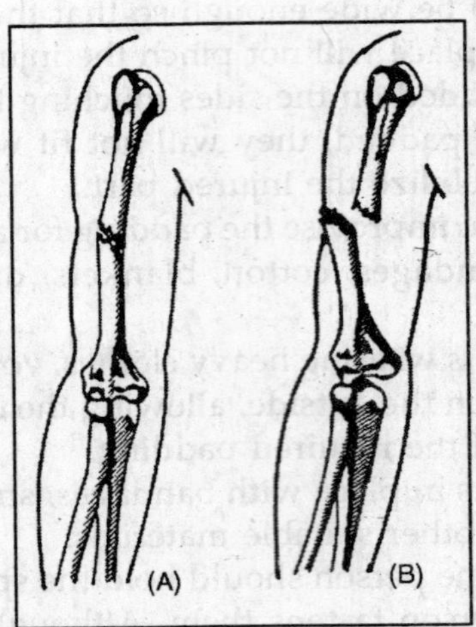

Fig. Closed and Open Fractures

Figure shows closed:

- And open.
- Fractures.

Open fractures are more serious than closed fractures. They usually involve extensive damage to the tissues and are quite likely to become infected. Closed fractures are sometimes turned into open fractures by rough or careless handling of the victim. It is not always easy to recognize a fracture.

All fractures, whether closed or open, are likely to cause severe pain and shock; but the other symptoms may vary considerably. A broken bone sometimes causes the injured part to be deformed or to assume an unnatural position. Pain, discoloration, and swelling may be localized at the fracture site, and there may be a wobbly movement if the bone is broken clear through.

It may be difficult or impossible for the victim to move the injured part; if able to move it, there may be a grating sensation (crepitus) as the ends of the broken bone rub against each other. However, if a bone is cracked rather than broken through, the victim may be able to move the injured part without much difficulty.

An open fracture is easy to recognize if an end of the

broken bone protrudes through the flesh. If the bone does not protrude, however, you might see the external wound but fail to recognize the broken bone.

If you are required to give first aid to a person who has suffered a fracture, you should follow these general rules:

- If there is any possibility that a fracture has been sustained, treat the injury as a fracture until an x-ray can be made.
- Get the victim to a definitive care facility at the first possible opportunity. All fractures require medical treatment.
- Do not move the victim until the injured part has been immobilized by splinting unless the move is necessary to save life or to prevent further injury.
- Treat for shock.
- Do not attempt to locate a fracture by grating the ends of the bone together.
- Do not attempt to set a broken bone, unless a medical officer will not be available for many days.
- When a long bone in the arm or leg is fractured, the limb should be carefully straightened so that splints can be applied unless it appears that further damage will be caused by such a maneuver. Never attempt to straighten the limb by applying force or traction with an improvised windlass or any other device. Pulling gently with your hands along the long axis of the limb is permissible and may be all that is necessary to get the limb back into position.
- Apply splints. If the victim is to be transported only a short distance, or if treatment by a medical officer will not be delayed, it is probably best to leave the clothing on and place emergency splinting over it. However, if the victim must be transported for some distance, or if a considerable period of time will elapse before treatment by a medical officer, it may be better to remove enough clothing so that you can apply well padded splints directly to the injured part. If you decide to remove clothing over the injured

part, cut the clothing or rip it along the seams. In any case, BE CAREFUL! Rough handling of the victim may convert a closed fracture into an open fracture, increase the severity of shock, or cause extensive damage to the blood vessels, nerves, muscles, and other tissues around the broken bone.

- If the fracture is open, you must take care of the wound before you can deal with the fracture. Bleeding from the wound may be profuse, but most bleeding can be stopped by direct pressure on the wound. Other supplemental methods of hemorrhage control are discussed in the section on wounds of this chapter. Use a tourniquet as a last resort. After you have stopped the bleeding, treat the fracture.

Now that we have seen the general rules for treating fractures, we turn to the symptoms and emergency treatment of specific fracture sites.

Fracture of the Forearm

There are two long bones in the forearm, the radius and the ulna. When both are broken, the arm usually appears to be deformed. When only one is broken, the other acts as a splint and the arm retains a more or less natural appearance.

Any fracture of the forearm is likely to result in pain, tenderness, inability to use the forearm, and a kind of wobbly motion at the point of injury. If the fracture is open, a bone may show through. If the fracture is open, stop the bleeding and treat the wound. Apply a sterile dressing over the wound. Carefully straighten the forearm.

(Remember that rough handling of a closed fracture may turn it into an open fracture.) Apply a pneumatic splint if available; if not, apply two well-padded splints to the forearm, one on the top and one on the bottom. Be sure that the splints are long enough to extend from the elbow to the wrist. Use bandages to hold the splints in place. Put the forearm across the chest.

The palm of the hand should be turned in, with the thumb pointing upward. Support the forearm in this position by means of a wide sling and a cravat bandage. The hand should be raised about 4 inches above the level of the elbow. Treat the victim for shock and evacuate as soon as possible.

Fracture of the Upper Arm

The signs of fracture of the upper arm include pain, tenderness, swelling, and a wobbly motion at the point of fracture. If the fracture is near the elbow, the arm is likely to be straight with no bend at the elbow.

Fig. First Aid for a Fractured Forearm.

If the fracture is open, stop the bleeding and treat the wound before attempting to treat the fracture.

Note that treatment of the fracture depends partly upon the location of the Break.

If the fracture is in the upper part of the arm near the shoulder, place a pad or folded towel in the armpit, bandage the arm securely to the body, and support the forearm in a narrow sling. If the fracture is in the middle of the upper arm, you can use one well padded splint on the outside of the arm.

The splint should extend from the shoulder to the elbow. Fasten the splinted arm firmly to the body and support the forearm in a narrow sling. Another way of treating a fracture in the middle of the upper arm is to fasten two wide splints or four narrow one about the arm and support the forearm in a narrow sling. If you use a splint between the arm and the body, be very careful that it does not extend too far up into the armpit; a splint in this position can cause a dangerous compression of the blood vessels and nerves and may be extremely painful to the victim.

If the fracture is at or near the elbow, the arm may be either bent or straight. No matter in what position you find the arm, do not attempt to Straighten it or move it in any way. Splint the arm as carefully as possible in the position in which you find it. This will prevent further nerve and blood vessel damage.

Fig. Splint and Sling for a Fractured Upper Arm.

The only exception to this is if there is no pulse distal to the fracture, in which case gentle traction is applied and then the arm is splinted. Treat the victim for shock and get him or her under the care of a medical officer as soon as possible.

Fracture of the Thigh

The femur is the long bone of the upper part of the leg between the kneecap and the pelvis. When the femur is fractured through, any attempt to move the limb results in a spasm of the muscles and causes excruciating pain. The leg has a wobbly motion, and there is complete loss of control below the fracture.

The limb usually assumes an unnatural position, with the toes pointing outward. By actual measurement, the fractured leg is shorter than the uninjured one because of contraction of the powerful thigh muscles. Serious damage to blood vessels and nerves often results from a fracture of the femur and shock is likely to be severe.

If the fracture is open, stop the bleeding and treat the wound before attempting to treat the fracture itself. Serious bleeding is a special danger in this type of injury, since the broken bone may tear or cut the large artery in the thigh. Carefully straighten the leg.

Apply two splints, one on the outside of the injured leg and one on the inside. The outside splint should reach from the armpit to the foot. The inside splint should reach from the crotch to the foot. The splints should be fastened in five places:

1. Around the ankle;
2. Over the knee;
3. Just below the hip;
4. Around the pelvis; and
5. Just below the armpit.

The legs can then be tied together to support the injured leg as firmly as possible. It is essential that a fractured thigh be splinted before the victim is moved. Manufactured splints, such as the Hare or the Thomas half-ring traction splints are best, but improvised splints may be used. Figure shows how boards may be used as an emergency splint for a fractured thigh.

Remember, do not move the victim until the injured leg has been immobilized. Treat the victim for shock, and evacuate at the earliest possible opportunity.

Fracture of the Lower Leg

When both bones of the lower leg are broken, the usual signs of fracture are likely to be present. When only one bone is broken, the other one acts as a splint and, to some extent, prevents deformity of the leg. However, tenderness, swelling, and pain at the point of fracture are almost always present.

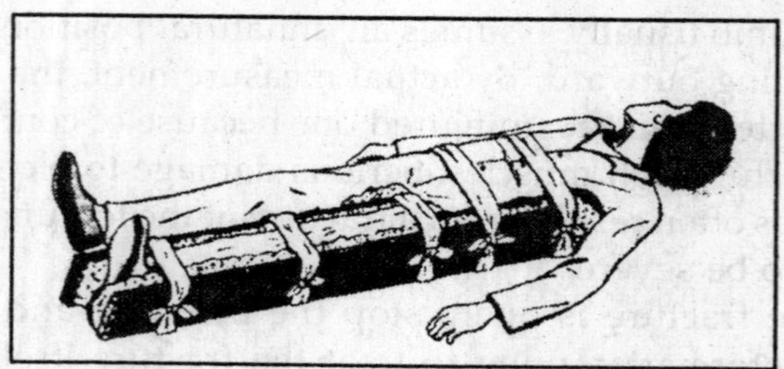

Fig. Splint for a Fractured Femur

A fracture just above the ankle is often mistaken for a sprain. If both bones of the lower leg are broken, an open fracture is very likely to result.

If the fracture is open, stop the bleeding and treat the wound.

Carefully straighten the injured leg. Apply a pneumatic splint if available; if not, apply Three splints—one on each side of the leg and one underneath. Be sure that the splints are well padded, particularly under the knee and at the bones on each side of the ankle.

A pillow and two side splints work very well for treatment of a fractured lower leg. Place the pillow beside the injured leg, then carefully lift the leg and place it in the middle of the pillow. Bring the edges of the pillow around to the front of the leg and pin them together.

Then place one splint on each side of the leg, over the pillow, and fasten them in place with strips of bandage or adhesive tape. Treat the victim for shock and evacuate as soon as possible. When available, you may use the Hare or Thomas half-ring traction splints.

Fracture of the Kneecap

The following first aid treatment should be given for a fractured kneecap (patella): Carefully straighten the injured limb. Immobilize the fracture by placing a padded board under the injured limb. The board should be at least 4 inches wide and should reach from the buttock to the heel. Place extra padding under the knee and just above the heel, as shown in figure.

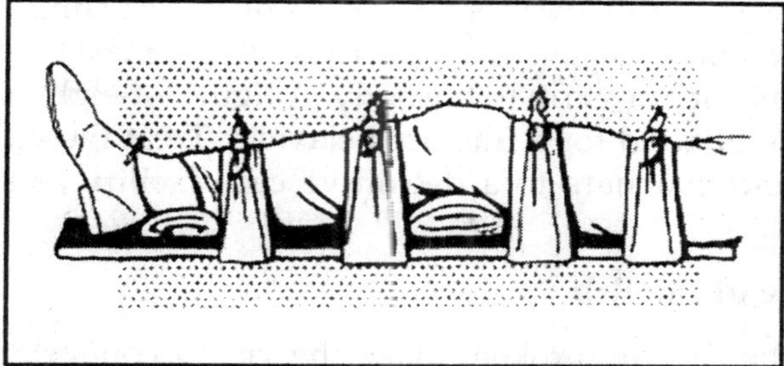

Fig. Immobilization of a Fractured Patella.

Use strips of bandage to fasten the leg to the board in four places:

- Just below the knee.
- Just above the knee.
- At the ankle.
- At the thigh.

Do Not Cover The Knee Itself. Swelling is likely to occur very rapidly,and any bandage or tie fastened over the knee would quickly become too tight. Treat the victim for shock and evacuate as soon as possible.

Fracture of the Clavicle

A person with a fractured clavicle usually shows definite symptoms. When the victim stands, the injured shoulder is lower than the uninjured one. The victim is usually unable to raise the arm above the level of the shoulder and may attempt to support the injured shoulder by holding the elbow of that side in the other hand; this is the characteristic position of a person with a broken clavicle.

Since the clavicle lies immediately under the skin, you may be able to detect the point of fracture by the deformity and localized pain and tenderness. If the fracture is open, stop the flow of blood and treat the wound before attempting to treat the fracture.

Then apply a sling and swathe splint as described below: Bend the victim's arm on the injured side, and place the forearm across the chest. The palm of the hand should be turned in, with the thumb pointed up. The hand should be raised about 4 inches above the level of the elbow. Support the forearm in this position by means of a wide sling. A wide roller bandage (or any wide strip of cloth) may be used to secure the victim's arm to the body. A figure-of-eight bandage may also be used for a fractured clavicle. Treat the victim for shock and evacuate to a definitive care facility as soon as possible.

Fracture of the Rib

If the ribs are broken, make the victim comfortable and quiet so that the greatest danger— the possibility of further damage to the lungs, heart, or chest wall by the broken ends– is minimized.

The common finding in all victims with fractured ribs is pain localized at the site of the fracture. By asking the patient to point out the exact area of the pain, you can often determine the location of the injury.

There may or may not be a rib deformity, chest wall contusion, or laceration of the area. Deep breathing, coughing, or movement is usually painful. The patient generally wishes to remain still and may often lean toward the injured side, with a hand over the fractured area to immobilize the chest and to ease the pain.

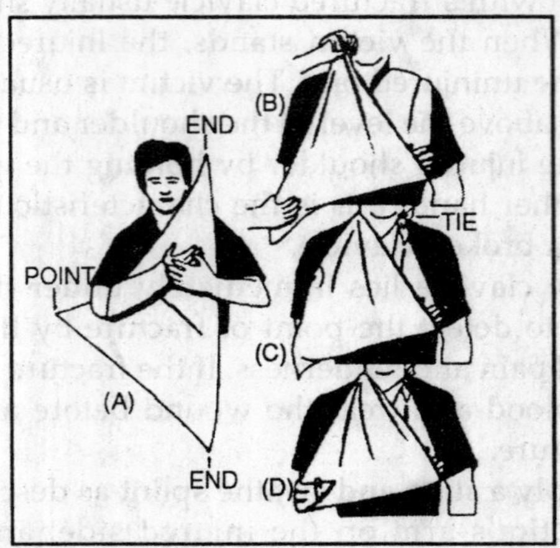

Fig. Sling for Immobilizing Fractured Clavicle.

Ordinarily, rib fractures are not bound, strapped, or taped

if the victim is reasonably comfortable. However, they may be splinted by the use of external support. If the patient is considerably more comfortable with the chest immobilized, the best method is to use a swathe in which the arm on the injured side is strapped to the chest to limit motion.

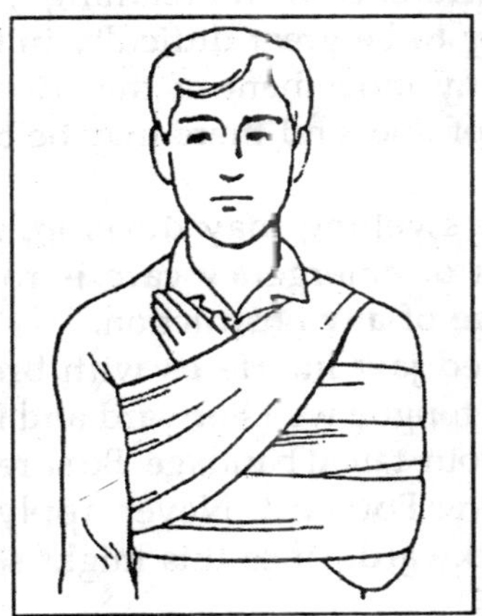

Fig. Swathe Bandage of Fractured Rib Victim.

Place the arm on the injured side against the chest, with the palm flat, thumb up, and the forearm raised to a 45° angle. Immobilize the chest, using wide strips of bandage to secure the arm to the chest.

Wide strips of adhesive plaster applied directly to the skin of the chest for immobilization should not be used since the adhesive tends to limit the ability of the chest to expand and this interferes with proper breathing. Treat the victim for shock and evacuate as soon as possible.

Fracture of the Nose

A fracture of the nose usually causes localized pain and swelling, a noticeable deformity of the nose, and extensive nosebleed. Stop the nosebleed. Have the victim sit quietly, with the head tipped slightly backward. Tell the victim to breathe through the mouth and not to blow the nose. If the bleeding does not stop within a few minutes, apply a cold compress or an ice bag over the nose.

Treat the victim for shock and see that he or she receives a medical officer's attention as soon as possible. Permanent deformity of the nose may result if the fracture is not treated promptly.

Fracture of the Jaw A person who has a fractured jaw may suffer serious interference with breathing.

There is likely to be great difficulty in talking, chewing, or swallowing. Any movement of the jaw causes pain. The teeth may be out of line, and there may be bleeding from the gums.

Considerable swelling may develop. One of the most important phases of emergency care is to clear the upper respiratory passage of any obstruction.

If the fractured jaw interferes with breathing, pull the lower jaw and the tongue well Forward and keep them in that position. Apply a four-tailed bandage. Be sure that the bandage pulls the lower jaw Forward. Never apply a bandage that forces the jaw backward, since this might seriously interfere with breathing.

The bandage must be firm so that it will support and immobilize the injured jaw, but it must not press against the victim's throat. Be sure that the victim has scissors or a knife to cut the bandage in case of vomiting. Treat the victim for shock and evacuate as soon as possible.

Fracture of the Skull

When a person suffers a head injury, the greatest danger is that the brain may be severely damaged; whether or not the skull is fractured is a matter of secondary importance.

In some cases, injuries that fracture the skull do not cause serious brain damage; but brain damage can, and frequently does, result from apparently slight injuries that do not cause damage to the skull itself.

It is often difficult to determine whether an injury has affected the brain because the symptoms of brain damage vary greatly.

A person suffering from a head injury must be handled very carefully and given immediate medical attention.

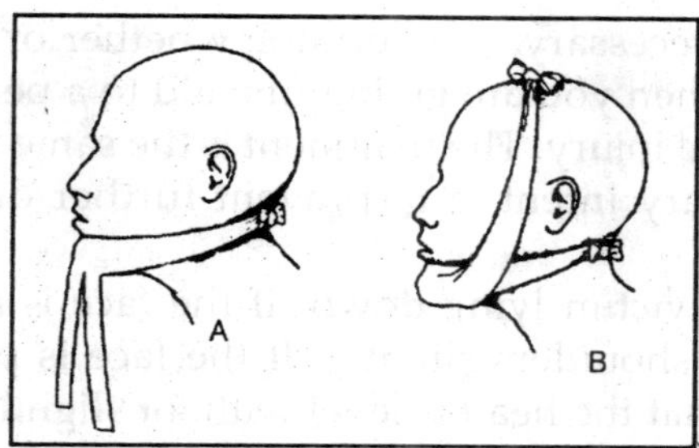

Fig. Four-tailed Bandage for the Jaw.

Some of the symptoms that may indicate brain damage are listed below. However, you must remember that all of these symptoms are not always present in any one case and that the symptoms that do occur may be greatly delayed.

- Bruises or wounds of the scalp may indicate that the victim has sustained a blow to the head. Sometimes the skull is depressed (caved in) at the point of impact. If the fracture is open, you may find glass, shrapnel, or other objects penetratingthe skull.
- The victim may be conscious or unconscious. If conscious, the victim may feel dizzy and weak, as though about to faint.
- Severe headache sometimes (but not always) accompanies head injuries.
- The pupils of the eyes maybe unequal in size and may not react normally to light.
- There may be bleeding from the ears, nose, or mouth.
- The victim may vomit.
- The victim may be restless and perhaps confused and disoriented.
- The arms, legs, face, or other parts of the body may be partially paralyzed.
- The victim's face may be very pale, or it may be unusually flushed.
- The victim is likely to be suffering from shock, but the symptoms of shock may be disguised by other symptoms.

It is not necessary to determine whether or not the skull is fractured when you are giving first aid to a person who has suffered a head injury. The treatment is the same in either case, and the primary intent is to prevent further damage to the brain.

Keep the victim lying down. If the face is flushed, raise the head and shoulders slightly. If the face is pale, have the victim lie so that the head is level with, or slightly lower than, the body. Watch carefully for vomiting. If the victim begins to vomit, position the head to prevent choking on the vomitus.

If there is serious bleeding from the wounds, try to control it by the application of direct pressure, using caution to avoid further injury to the skull or brain. Use a donut shaped bandage to gently surround protruding objects. Never manipulate those objects.

- Be very careful about moving or handling the victim. Move the victim no more than is necessary. If transportation is necessary, keep the victim lying down.
- In any significant head or facial injury, assume injury to the cervical spine. Immobilization of the cervical spine is indicated.
- Be sure that the victim is kept comfortably warm, but not too warm.
- Do Not give the victim anything to drink. Do not give any medicines. See that the victim receives a medical officer's attention as soon as possible.

Fracture of the Spine

If the spine is fractured at any point, the spinal cord may be crushed, cut, or otherwise damaged so severely that death or paralysis will result. However, if the fracture occurs in such a way that the spinal cord is not seriously damaged, there is a very good chance of complete recovery— Provided the victim is properly cared for. Any twisting or bending of the neck or back, whether due to the original injury or carelessness from handling later, is likely to cause irreparable damage to the spinal cord.

The primary symptoms of a fractured spine are pain, shock, and paralysis.

Pain is likely to be acute at the point of fracture. It may radiate to other parts of the body.

- Shock is usually severe, but (as in all injuries) the symptoms may be delayed for some time.
- Paralysis occurs if the spinal cord is seriously damaged. If the victim cannot move the legs, feet, or toes, the fracture is probably in the back; if the fingers will not move, the neck is probably broken.

Remember that a spinal fracture does not always injure the spinal cord, so the victim is not always paralyzed. Any person who has an acute pain in the back or the neck following an injury should be treated as though there is a fractured spine, even if there are no other symptoms.

First aid treatment for all spinal fractures, whether of the neck or of the back, has two primary purposes:

- To minimize shock.
- To prevent further injury to the spinal cord.

Keep the victim comfortably warm. Do not attempt to keep the victim in the position ordinarily used for the treatment of shock, because it might cause further damage to the spinal cord. Just keep the victim lying flat and do not attempt to lower the head.

To avoid further damage to the spinal cord, Do Not Move The Victim Unless It Is Absolutely Essential. If the victim's life is threatened in the present location or transportation is necessary to receive medical attention, then of course you must move the victim. However, if movement is necessary, be sure that you do it in a way that will cause the least possible damage.

Do not bend or twist the Victim's body, do not move The head forward, backward, or sideways, and do not under any Circumstances allow The Victim to sit up.

If it is necessary to transport a person who has suffered a fracture of the spine, follow these general rules:

- If the spine is broken at the Neck, the victim must be transported lying on the back, Face UP. Place pillows or sandbags beside the head so that it cannot turn to either side. Do Not put pillows or padding under the neck or head.

- If you suspect that the spine is fractured but do not know the location of the break, treat the victim as though the neck is broken—i.e., keep the victim supine. If both the neck and the back are broken, keep the victim supine.
- No matter where the spine is broken, Use A Firm Support In Transporting The Victim. Use a rigid stretcher, or a door, shutter, wide board, etc. Pad the support carefully and put blankets both under and over the victim. Use cravat bandages or strips of cloth to secure the vic-tim firmly to the support.

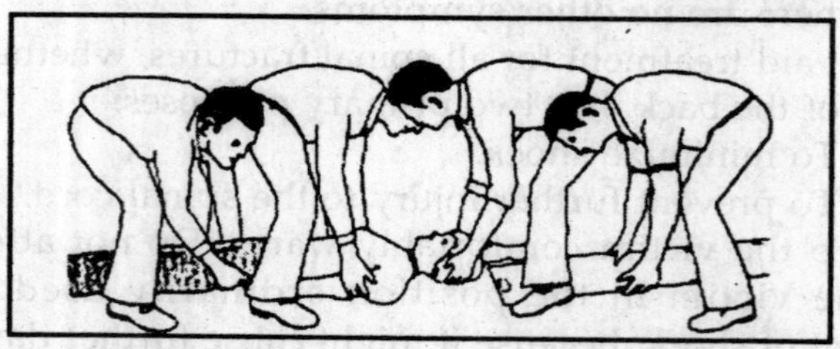

Fig. Moving Spinal Cord Injury Victim onto a Backboard.

- When placing the victim on a spine board, one of two acceptable methods may be used. However, do not attempt to lift the Victim unless you have adequate assistance. Remember, any bending or twisting of the body is almost sure to cause serious damage to the spinal cord. Figure shows the straddle-slide method. One person lifts and supports the head while a person at the shoulders and one at the hips lifts. A fourth person slides the spine board under the patient. Figure shows the logroll method. The victim is rolled as a single unit towards the rescuers, the spine board is positioned, and the victim is rolled back onto the spine board and secured in place. If there are at least four (preferable six) people present to help lift the victim, they can accomplish the job without too much movement of the victim's body, but a smaller number of people should Never attempt to lift the victim.

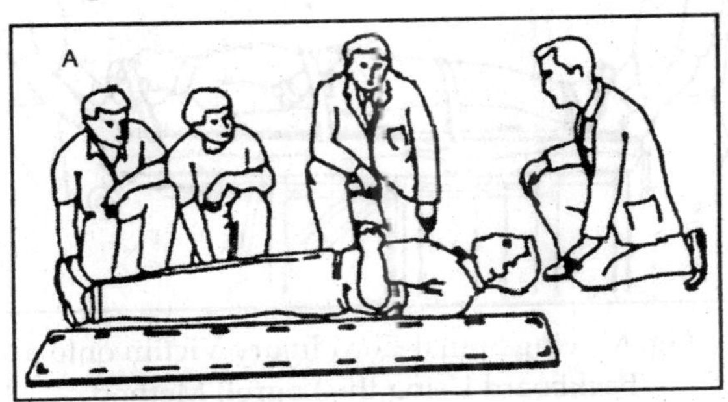

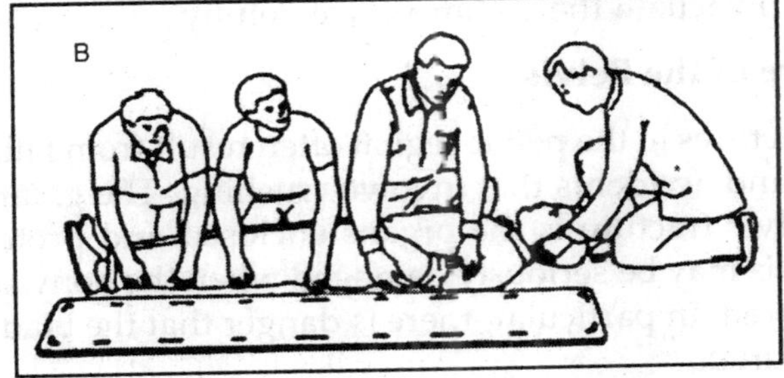

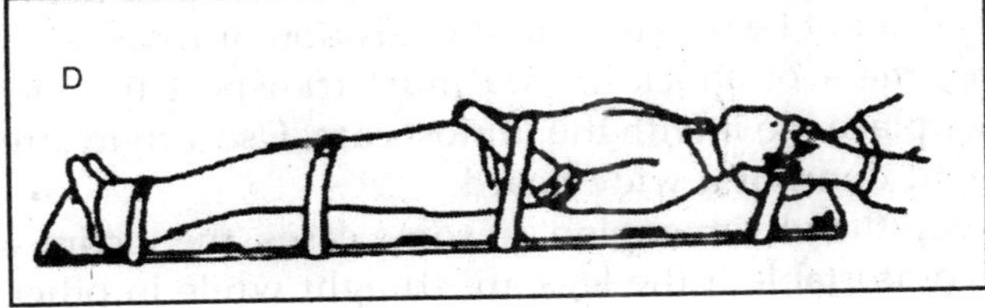

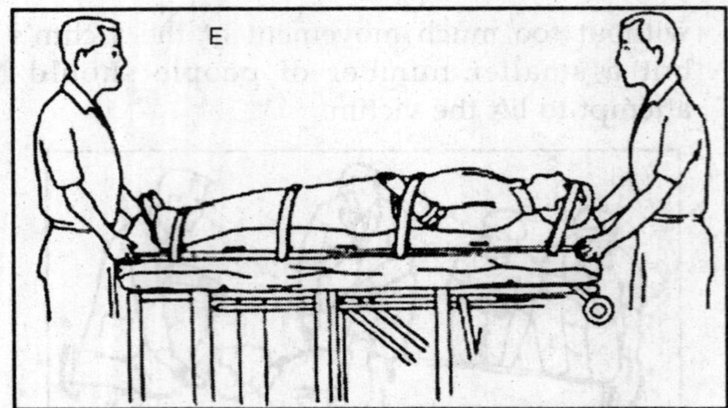

Fig. Moving Spinal Cord Injury Victim onto a Backboard Using the Logroll Method.

- Evacuate the victim very carefully.

Fracture of the Pelvis

Fractures in the pelvic region often result from falls, heavy blows, and accidents that involve crushing. The great danger in a pelvic fracture is the organs enclosed and protected by the pelvis may be seriously damaged when the bony structure is fractured. In particular, there is danger that the bladder will be ruptured.

There is also danger of severe internal bleeding; the large blood vessels in the pelvic region may be torn or cut by fragments of the broken bone. The primary symptoms of a fractured pelvis are severe pain, shock, and loss of ability to use the lower part of the body.

The victim is unable to sit or stand. If the victim is conscious, there may be a sensation of "coming apart. " If the bladder is injured, the victim's urine may be bloody. Do not move the victim unless Absolutely necessary.

The victim should be treated for shock and kept warm but should not be moved into the position ordinarily used for the treatment of shock. If you must transport the victim to another place, do it with the utmost care. Use a rigid stretcher, a padded door, or a wide board.

Keep the victim supine. In some cases, the victim will be more comfortable if the legs are straight while in other cases the victim will be more comfortable with the knees bent and the legs drawn up. When you have placed the victim in the most comfortable position, immobilization should be accomplished.

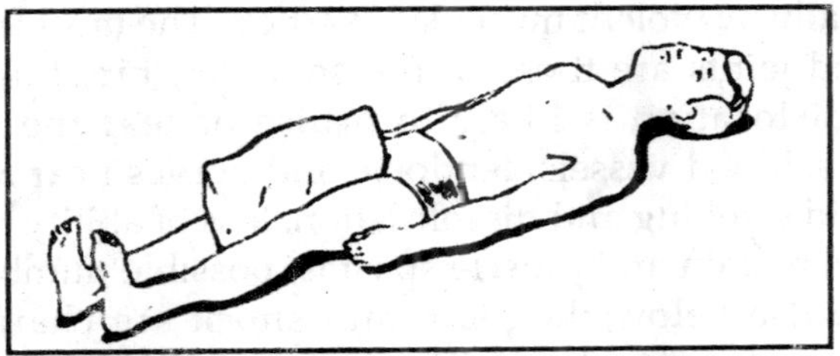

Fig. Immobilizing a Fractured Pelvis.

Fractures of the hip are best treated with traction splints. Adequate immobilization can also be obtained by placing pillows or folded blankets between the legs as shown in figure and using cravats, roller bandages, or straps to hold the legs together, or through the use of MAST garments. Fasten the victim securely to the stretcher or improvised support and evacuate very carefully.

INJURIES TO JOINTS AND MUSCLES

Injuries to joints and muscles often occur together, and sometimes it is difficult to tell whether the primary injury is to a joint or to the muscles, tendons, blood vessels, or nerves near the joint. Sometimes it is difficult to distinguish joint or muscle injuries from fractures. In case of doubt, Always treat any injury to a bone, joint, or muscle as though it were a fracture. In general, joint and muscle injuries may be classified under four headings:

(1) dislocations.
(2) sprains.
(3) strains.
(4) contusions (bruises).

Dislocations

When a bone is forcibly displaced from its joint, the injury is known as a Dislocation. In some cases, the bone slips back quickly into its normal position, but in other cases it becomes locked in the new position and remains dislocated until it is put back into place.

Dislocations are usually caused by falls or blows but occasionally by violent muscular exertion. The most frequently dislocated joints are those of the shoulder, hip, fingers, and jaw. A dislocation is likely to bruise or tear the muscles, ligaments, blood vessels, tendons, and nerves near a joint.

Rapid swelling and discoloration, loss of ability to use the joint, severe pain and muscle spasms, possible numbness and loss of pulse below the joint, and shock are characteristic symptoms of dislocations. The fact that the injured part is usually stiff and immobile, with marked deformation at the joint, will help you distinguish a dislocation from a fracture. In a fracture, there is deformity Between joints rather than at joints, and there is generally a wobbly motion of the broken bone at the point of fracture.

As a general rule, you should Not attempt to reduce a dislocation —that is, put a dislocated bone back into place— unless you know that a medical officer cannot be reached within 8 hours. Unskilled attempts at reduction may cause great damage to nerves and blood vessels or actually fracture the bone.

Therefore, except in great emergencies, you should leave this treatment to specially trained medical personnel and concentrate your efforts on making the victim as comfortable as possible under the circumstances.

The following first aid measures will be helpful:

- Loosen the clothing around the injured part.
- Place the victim in the most comfortable position possible.
- Support the injured part by means of a sling, pillows, bandages, splints, or any other device that will make the victim comfortable.
- Treat the victim for shock.
- Get medical help as soon as possible.

You should Never attempt to reduce the more serious dislocations, such as those of the hip. However, if it is probable that the victim cannot be treated by a medical officer within a Reasonable Time, you should make a careful effort to reduce certain dislocations, such as those of the jaw, finger, or shoulder IF there is no arterial or nerve involvement (pulse is palpable and there is no numbness below the joint). Treat all other dislocations as fractures, and evacuate the victim to a definitive care facility.

DISLOCATION OF THE JAW

When the lower jaw is dislocated, the victim cannot speak or close the mouth. Dislocation of the jaw is usually caused by a blow to the mouth; sometimes it is caused by yawning or laughing. This type of dislocation is not always easy to reduce, and there is considerable danger that the operator's thumbs will be bitten in the process.

For your own protection, wrap your thumbs with a handkerchief or bandage. While facing the victim, press your thumbs down just behind the last lower molars and, at the same time, lift the chin up with your fingers. The jaw should snap into place at once; you will have to remove your thumbs quickly in order to avoid being bitten.

No further treatment is required, but you should warn the victim to keep the mouth closed as much as possible during the next few hours. Figure shows the position you must assume to reduce a dislocated jaw.

DISLOCATION OF THE FINGER

The joints of the finger are particularly susceptible to injury, and even minor injuries may result in Figure—Position for reducing a dislocated jaw. prolonged loss of function. Great care must be used in treating any injury of the finger. To reduce a dislocation of the finger, grasp the finger firmly and apply a steady pull in the same line as the deformity.

If it does not slip into position, try it again, but if it does not go into position on the third attempt, do not try again. In any case, whether or not the dislocation is reduced, the finger should be strapped, slightly flexed, with an aluminum splint or with a roller gauze bandage over a tongue blade. Figur shows how a dislocated finger can be Immobilizing a dislocated finger.

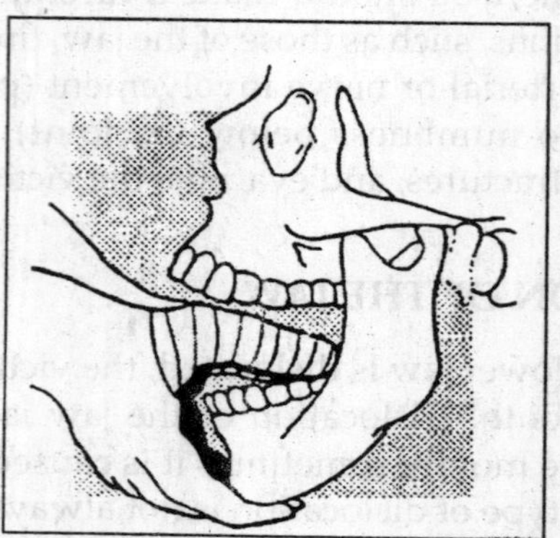

Fig. Position for Reducing a Dislocated Jaw

Prolonged loss of function. Great care must be used in treating any injury of the finger. To reduce a dislocation of the finger, grasp the finger firmly and apply a steady pull in the same line as the deformity.

If it does not slip into position, try it again, but if it does not go into position on the third attempt, Do Not Try Again. In any case, whether or not the dislocation is reduced, the finger should be strapped, slightly flexed, with an aluminum splint or with a roller gauze bandage over a tongue blade. Figure shows how a dislocated finger can be immobilized by strapping it to a flat, wooden stick, such as a tongue depressor.

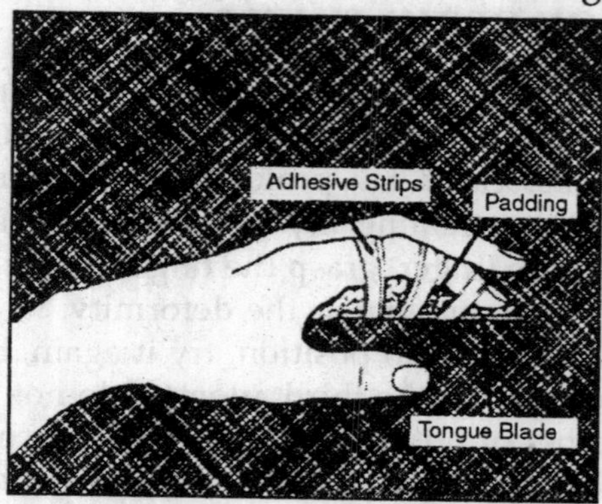

Fig. Immobilizing a Dislocated Finger.

DISLOCATION OF THE SHOULDER

Before reduction, place the victim in a supine position. After putting the heel of your foot in the victim's armpit, grasp the wrist and apply steady traction by pulling gently and increasing resistance gradually. Pull the arm in the same line as it is found. After several minutes of steady pull, flex the victim's elbow slightly. Grasp the arm below the elbow, apply traction from the point of the elbow, and gently rotate the arm into the external or outward position. If three reduction attempts fail, carry the forearm across the chest and apply a sling and swathe.

An alternate method involves having the patient lie face down on an examining table with the injured arm hanging over the side. Apply prolonged, firm, gentle traction at the wrist with gentle external rotation. A water bucket with a padded handle placed in the crook of the patient's elbow may be substituted. Gradually add sand or water to the bucket to increase traction. Grasping the wrist and using the elbow as a pivot point, gently rotate the arm into the external position.

Sprains

A Sprain is an injury to the ligaments and soft tissues that support a joint. A sprain is caused by the violent wrenching or twisting of the joint beyond its normal limits of movement and usually involves a momentary dislocation, with the bone slipping back into place of its own accord.

Although any joint may be sprained, sprains of the ankle, wrist, knee and finger are most common. Symptoms of a sprain include pain or pressure at the joint, pain upon movement, swelling and tenderness, possible loss of movement, and discoloration. Treat all sprains as fractures until ruled out by x-rays.

Emergency care for a sprain includes application of cold packs for the first 24 to 48 hours to reduce swelling and to control internal hemorrhage; elevation and rest of the affected area; application of a snug, smooth, figure-of-eight bandage to control swelling and to provide immobilization (basket weave adhesive bandages can be used on the ankle); a follow-up examination by a medical officer; and x-rays to rule out the presence of a fracture.

Note: Check bandaged areas regularly for swelling that might cause circulation impairment and loosen bandages if necessary.

After the swelling stops (24 to 48 hours) moist heat can be applied for short periods (15 to 30 minutes) to promote healing and to reduce swelling. Moist heat can be warm, wet compresses, warm whirlpool baths, etc.

Caution: Heat should not be applied until 24 hours after the last cold pack. Strains An injury caused by the forcible overstretching or tearing of a muscle or tendon is known as a

STRAIN

Strains may be caused by lifting excessively heavy loads, sudden or violent movements, or any other action that pulls the muscles beyond their normal limits. The chief symptoms of a strain are pain, lameness or stiffness (sometimes involving knotting of the muscles), moderate swelling at the place of injury, discoloration due to the escape of blood from injured blood vessels into the tissues, possible loss of power, and a distinct gap felt at the site.

Keep the affected area elevated and at rest; apply cold packs for the first 24 to 48 hours to control hemorrhage and swelling; after the swelling stops, apply mild heat to increase circulation and aid in healing.

As in sprains, heat should not be applied until 24 hours after the last cold pack. Muscle relaxants, adhesive straps, and complete immobilization of the area may be indicated. Evacuate the victim to a medical facility where x-rays can be taken to rule out the presence of a fracture.

Contusion

Contusions, commonly called Bruises, are responsible for the discoloration that almost always accompanies injuries to bones, joints, and muscles. Contusions are caused by blows that damage bones, muscles, tendons, blood vessels, nerves, and other body tissues, although they do not necessarily break the skin. The symptoms of a contusion or bruise are familiar to everyone. There is immediate pain when the blow is received. Swelling occurs because blood from the broken vessels oozes into the soft tissues under the skin.

At first the injured place is reddened due to local skin irritation from the blow; later the characteristic "black and blue" marks appear; and finally, perhaps several days later, the skin is yellowish or greenish. The bruised area is usually very tender. As a rule, slight bruises do not require treatment. However, if the victim has severe bruises, reat for shock.

Immobilize the injured part, keep it at rest, and protect it from further injury. Sometimes the victim will be more comfortable if the bruised area is bandaged firmly with an elastic or gauze bandage. If possible, elevate the injured part. A sling may be used for a bruised arm or hand. Pillows or folded blankets may be used to elevate a bruised leg.

Chapter 9

Poisons

A poison is a substance that, when taken into the body, produces a harmful effect on normal body structures or functions. Poisons come in solid, liquid, and gaseous forms and may be ingested, inhaled, absorbed, or injected into the system.

Children are most susceptible to toxic substances, but as a hospital corpsman you must also be prepared to respond to the accidental or intentional poisoning of adult victims. The handling of drug abuse cases will be covered at the end of this section.

OBTAINING INFORMATION

As a general rule, your first contact, whether on the phone or in person with a suspected poisoning victim or the victim's relatives or friends, will be complicated by excitement, especially if you are dealing with a parent. It is absolutely essential that you be calm, professional, and systematic if you are to be able to elicit all the essential information you will need.

After maintenance of life support systems, the first priority is to identify the poison. If the poisoning was not witnessed, and if the victim cannot or will not identify the agent, it becomes necessary to obtain the container that held the poison. A commercial label on the container should identify the name of the product, the ingredients, and the antidote to any toxic substance it may contain.

If there is no label or if you suspect that the container held an unidentified substance other than that listed on the side, send the container along with the victim to the hospital for laboratory analysis. The second priority is to determine the quantity of poison taken. Once again, if the victim cannot or will not provide the information, the container must be checked.

Whatever is not in the container is normally considered to be in the victim, unless someone familiar with the container can verify the quantity previously used. The third priority is to determine as closely as possible the time the poisoning occurred. If it was not witnessed, careful questioning of bystanders and the victim may be needed to approximate the time. The fourth priority is to establish as accurately as possible the victim's symptoms and medical history.

The symptoms will give you a good idea of the severity of the poisoning and its progression. They will also give you a clue as to whether the victim has taken any additional poisons. The medical history can establish if this is a repeat poisoning and if the victim has any illnesses or is using medications that may contraindicate certain methods of treatment.

Quick systematic questioning will give basic information about the poison and the victim's condition. Additional information about the toxic ingredients of almost every commercial product, along with recommended antidotes and treatments, is readily available through poison control centers at medical treatment facilities throughout the country.

Area centers are listed in the front of every telephone directory. Also, be familiar with your command's antidote locker and poison chart. With all this information in hand, a medical professional will be able to quickly assess the situation and plan and implement a course of treatment.

General Treatment

In most situations, the treatment of a poisoning victim will be under the direction of a medical officer. However, in isolated situations, a hospital corpsman must be ready to treat the victim. Poisoning should be suspected in all cases of sudden, severe, and unexpected illness. Once poisoning has been established, the general rule is to quickly remove as much of the toxic substance from the victim as possible. For most ingested poisons, there is a choice between emetics and gastric lavage, followed by absorbents and cathartics; for inhaled poisons, oxygen ventilation is the method of choice; for absorbed poisons, this primarily means cleansing the skin; and for injected poisons, antidotal medications are recommended.

INGESTED POISONS

Noncorrosives

The many different noncorrosive substances have the common characteristic of irritating the stomach. They produce nausea, vomiting, convulsions, and severe abdominal pain. The victim may complain of a strange taste, and the lips, tongue, and mouth may look different than normal. Shock occurs in severe cases. First aid for most forms of noncorrosive poisoning centers on quickly emptying the stomach of the irritating substance. *The following steps are suggested:*

- Maintain an open airway. Be prepared to give artificial ventilation.
- Dilute the poison by having the conscious victim drink one to two glasses of water or milk.
- Empty the stomach, using emetics or gastric lavage.
  - Giving an emetic is a preferred method for emptying the contents of the stomach. It is quick and can be used in almost every situation when the victim is conscious, except in cases of caustic or petroleum distillate poisoning, or when an antiemetic has been ingested. In most situations, a hospital corpsman will have access to syrup of Ipecac, which can be given in a 15 ml (3 tsp) oral dose, repeated in 20 minutes if the first dose is nonproductive. In an emergency room the medical officer can rapidly induce vomiting by the injection of various medications. If nothing else is available, tickle the back of the victim's throat with your finger or a blunt object to induce vomiting.

- Trained personnel may use gastric lavage by itself, or after 2 doses of Ipecac syrup have failed to induce vomiting. After passing a large caliber nasogastric tube, aspirate the stomach contents. Next, instill 100 ml of normal saline into the stomach, then aspirate it out again. Continue this flushing cycle until the returning fluid is clear. Gastric lavage is preferred when the victim is unconscious, or subject to seizures,as in strychnine poisoning.

- Collect the vomitus for laboratory analysis.
- Soothe the stomach with milk or milk of magnesia.
- Transport the victim to a definitive care facility if symptoms persist.

Corrosives

Acids and alkalies produce actual chemical burning and corrosion of the tissues of the lips, mouth, throat, and stomach. Acids do most of their damage in the acidic stomach environment, while alkalies primarily destroy tissues in the mouth, throat and esophagus. Stains and burns around the mouth and the presence of characteristic odors provide clues to corrosive poisoning.

Swallowing and breathing may be difficult, especially if any corrosive was aspirated into the lungs. The abdomen may be tender and swollen with gas. Examples of corrosive agents, and sources of contact are listed in table. When providing treatment for the above poisons, Do Not Induce Vomiting. The caustic damage to the mouth and esophagus will be compounded. In addition, the threat of aspiration during vomiting is too great. Gastric lavage could cause perforation of the esophagus or stomach, therefore, use it only on a doctor's order. First aid consists of diluting the corrosive and keeping alert for airway patency and shock. If spontaneous vomiting occurs, administer an antiemetic. Controversy exists over the value of attempting to neutralize corrosives because of the exothermic (heat producing) reaction when acids and alkalies are mixed.

Table. Examples of Common acids,Alkalies, Phenols with Possibles Source of Contact.

Agent	Sources of Contact
	Acids
Hydrochloric	Electroplating, metal cleaners, photoengraving.
Nitric	Sulfuric Industrial cleaners, laboratories, photoengraving, rocket fuels.
Oxalic	Cleaning solutions,paint and rust removers,photodeveloper.
Sulfuric	Auto batteries, detergents, dyes, laboratories, metal cleaners.
	Alkalies
Ammoni	Galvanizes,household cleaners, laboratories, pesticides, rocket fuels.
Lime	Brick masonry,cement, elec troplating, insecticides, soap, water treatment
Lye	Bleaches,degreasers,detergents, laboratories, paint and varnish removers.
	Phenols
Carbolic	Disinfectants, dry batteries, paint removers, photo materials, wood preservatives.
Creosol	Disinfectants, ink, paint and varnish removers, photo developer, stainers Creosote Asbestos, carpentry, diesel en gines, electrical shops, furnaces, lens grinders, painters, waterproofing,wood preservatives

Therefore, do not attempt to neutralize corrosives unless directed to do so by a physician. When neutralizing acids, use milk of magnesia following dilution.

Do Not use carbonates; they generate carbon dioxide gas which may cause perforation. When neutralizing alkalies, use a dilute solution of vinegar in water. Transport all poisoning patients to a medical treatment facility for evaluation and further treatment.

Petroleum Distillates

Volatile petroleum products such as kerosene, gasoline, turpentine, and related petroleum products, such as red furniture polish, usually cause severe chemical pneumonia as well as other toxic effects in the body. Symptoms include abdominal pain, choking, gasping, vomiting, and fever. Often these products may be identified by their characteristic odor. Mineral oil and motor oil are not as serious, since they usually do nothing more than cause diarrhea.

When providing treatment for the ingestion of petroleum distillates, Do Not Induce Vomiting unless told to do so by a physician or poison control centre. Vomiting may cause additional poison to enter the lungs. However, the quantity of poison swallowed or special petroleum additives may make gastric lavage or the use of cathartics advisable.

- If a physician or poison control centre cannot be reached, give the victim 30 to 60 ml of vegetable oil.
- Transport the victim immediately to a medical treatment facility.

Shellfish and Fish Poisoning

Mussels, clams, oysters, and other shellfish often become contaminated with bacteria during the warm months of March through November. Numerous varieties of shellfish should not be eaten at all, so wherever you serve in the world, learn which local seafoods are known to be safe.

Most fish poisoning occurs with fish that normally are considered safe to eat, but which become poisonous at different times of the year from eating poisonous algae and plankton (red tide) that appear in certain locations.

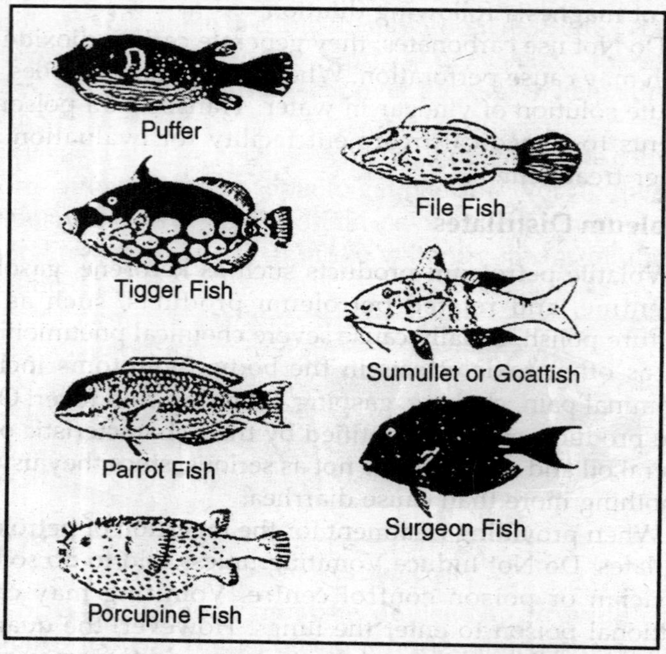

Fig. Poisonous Fish

Examples of fish that are always poisonous are shown in figure. The symptoms of shellfish and fish poisoning are tingling and numbness of the face and mouth, muscular weakness, nausea and vomiting, increased salivation, difficulty in swallowing, and respiratory failure.

Primary treatment is directed toward evacuating the stomach contents; if the victim has not vomited, cause him or her to do so. Use syrup of Ipecac, gastric lavage, or manual stimulation; then administer a cathartic. If respiratory failure develops, give artificial ventilation and treat for shock.

POISONS BY INHALATION

Many industrial processes are carried out. The problem of poisoning by inhalation is widespread. The handling of large quantities of petroleum products (fuel oil and gasoline, in particular) constitutes a special hazard, since all of these products give off hazardous vapors.

Other poisonous gases are by-products of certain operations or processes: exhaust gases from internal combustion engines; fumes or vapors from materials used in casting, molding, welding, or plating; gases associated with bacterial decomposition in closed spaces; and gases that accumulate in voids, double bottoms, empty fuel tanks, and similar places.

Carbon monoxide is the most common agent of gas poisoning. It is present in exhaust gases of internal combustion engines as well as in sewer gas, lanterns, charcoal grills, and in manufactured gas used for heating and cooking. It gives no warning of its presence since it is completely odorless and tasteless.

The victim may lose consciousness and suffer respiratory distress with no warning other than slight dizziness, weakness, and headache. The lips and skin of a victim of carbon monoxide poisoning are characteristically cherry red. Death may occur within a few minutes. Some sources of inhalation chemical poisoning are listed in table. Most inhalation poisoning causes shortness of breath and coughing.

The victim's skin will turn blue. If the respiratory problems are not corrected, cardiac arrest may follow. The first stage of treatment for an inhalation poisoning is to remove the victim from the toxic atmosphere immediately.

Warning: Never try to remove a victim from the toxic environment if you do not have the proper protective mask or breathing apparatus or if you are not trained in its use. Too often, well intentioned rescuers become victims. When in doubt, call for trained personnel. If help is not immediately available, and if you know you can reach and rescue the victim, take a deep breath, hold it, enter the area, and pull the victim out.

Next:

- Start basic life support as outlined in the first section of the chapter.

- Remove or decontaminate the clothing if chemical warfare agents or volatile fuels were the cause.
- Keep the victim quiet, treat for shock, and administer oxygen.
- Transport the victim to a medical treatment facility for further treatment.

Table. Sources of InhalationPoisoning.

Inhalant	Sources of Contact
Carbon dioxide	Wells and Sewers.
Carbon monooxide	Fires, lighting, heating and fuel exhausts.
Carbon Tetrachloride	Solvent in dry cleaning fluid Electrial equipment.
Trichloroethylene	Cleaners, decreasing agents, and Fire extinguishers.
Chemical warfare agents	Tear, nerve, blister and vomiting gases, screening Smokes, thermite and magnesium incendiary substance, hydrocyanic acid, and other systemic poisons.
Chlorine	Water Purification.
Ether, chloroform nitrous oxide, cyclopropane and freon.	Ice making and refrigeration units.

ABSORBED POISONS

Some substances may cause tissue irritation or destruction by contact with the skin, eyes, and lining of the nose, mouth, and throat. These substances include acids, alkalies, phenols, and some chemical warfare agents. Direct contact with these substances will cause inflammation or chemical burns in the affected areas.

Consult the "Chemical Burns" section of this chapter and the "Chemical Agents" section of chapter 12 of this manual for treatment.

INJECTED POISONS

Injection of venom by stings and bites from various insects, while not normally lifethreatening, can cause an acute allergic reaction that can be fatal. Poisons may also be injected by snakes and marine animals.

Bee, Wasp, and Fire Ant Stings

Stings from bees, wasps, and ants account for more poisonings than stings from any other insect group. Fortunately, they rarely result in death. The vast majority of stings cause a minor local reaction of pain, redness, itching, and swelling at the injection site.

These symptoms usually fade after a short time. A small per cent of these stings cause a severe anaphylactic reaction, presenting itching, swelling, weakness, headache, difficulty in breathing, and abdominal cramps. Shock may follow quickly and death may occur.

The following first aid measures are recommended:

- Closely monitor vital signs and remove all rings, bracelets, and watches.
- Remove stingers by scraping with a dull knife (pulling forces venom remaining in the sac into the wound).
- Place an ice cube or analgesic-corticosteroid lotion over the wound site to relieve pain.
- For severe reactions, apply a constricting band above the injured site at the edge of the swelling. Advance it as needed.
- For severe allergic reactions, immediately give the victim a subcutaneous injection of 1:1000 aqueous solution of epinephrine. Dosage ranges from 0.2 to 0.3 cc for children to 0.5 cc for adults.
- Patients with severe allergic reactions should be evacuated to a medical facility.

Scorpion Stings

The only North American scorpion of medical importance is the Centruroides sculturatus found in Mexico and certain areas of the American Southwest. Its sting causes severe pain and some weakness in the affected area.

It may also cause vomiting, visual disturbances, and circulatory and respiratory depression. In some cases, a state of excitability may occur, with muscle spasms, and in severe cases, progression to a comatose state. The following first aid treatment should be given for scorpion stings:

- Place ice over the sting site.
- Morphine and meperidine hydrochloride are contraindicated as they potentate the venom.
- Calcium gluconate 10 per cent may be given intravenously to relieve muscle spasms.
- Valium maybe used to control excitability and convulsions.
- An antivenin is available for Cenfruroides sculpturatus.
- Keep the victim under observation and be prepared to give symptomatic supportive care.

Spider Bites

Spiders in the United States are generally harmless, with several exceptions. The most notable are the black widow and brown recluse spiders.

Their bites are serious but rarely fatal. The female black widow spider is usually identified by the hourglass-shaped red spot on its belly.

Its bite causes a dull, numbing pain, which gradually spreads from the region of the bite to the muscles of the entire torso.

The pain becomes severe, and a board-like rigidity of the abdominal muscles is common. Nausea, vomiting, headache, dizziness, difficulty in breathing, edema, rash, hypertension, and anxiety are frequently present.

The bite site can be very hard to locate, since there is little or no swelling at the site, and the victim may not be immediately aware of having been bitten.

The buttocks and genitalia should be carefully examined for a bite site if the suspected victim has recently used an outside latrine.

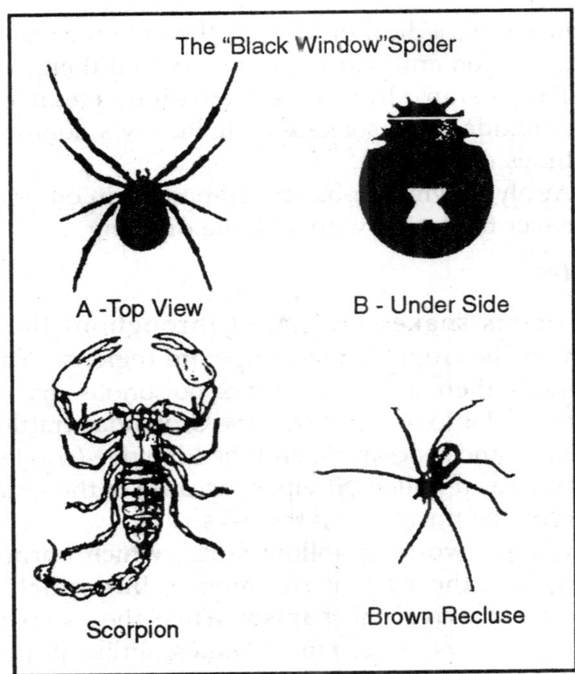

Fig. Black Widow and Brown Recluse Spiders and Scorpion.

The following first aid treatment steps are suggested:

- Place ice over the bite to reduce pain.
- Hospitalize victims who are under 16 or over 65 for observation.
- Be prepared to give antivenin in severe cases. The brown recluse spider is identified by its violin-shaped marking. Its bite may initially go unnoticed, but after several hours a bleb develops over the site, and rings of erythema begin to surround the bleb. Other symptoms include skin rash, fever and chills, nausea and vomiting, and pain. A progressively enlarging necrotic ulcerating lesion eventually develops. Treatment for brown recluse spider bites includes the following steps:
- Early diagnosis is important since, within the first 8

hours, a medical officer has the option of excising the lesion and starting corticosteroid therapy.

- The lesion should be debrided, cleansed with peroxide, and soaked with Burow's solution three times daily.
- Apply polymyxin-bacitracin-neomycin ointment, and cover the lesion with a sterile dressing.

Snakebites

Poisonous snakes are found throughout the world, primarily in the tropical and temperate regions. Within the United States, there are 20 species of poisonous snakes. They can be grouped into two families, the Crotalidae (rattlesnakes, copperheads, and moccasins) and the Elapidae (coral snakes). The Crotalidae are called pit vipers because of the small, deep pits between the nostrils and the eyes.

They have two long hollow fangs, which normally are folded against the roof of the mouth, but which can be extended by a swivel mechanism when they strike. Other identifying features include thick bodies, slitlike pupils of the eyes, and flat triangular heads.

Further identification is provided by examining the wound for signs of fang entry in the bite pattern shown in figure.

Individual identifying characteristics include audible rattles on the tails of most rattlesnakes, and the cotton white interior of the mouths of moccasins.

These snakes are found in every state except Maine, Alaska, and Hawaii.

Coral snakes are related to the cobra, kraits, and mamba snakes in other areas of the world. Corals, which are found in the 4-68.

Southeastern United States, are comparatively thin snakes with small bands of red, black, and yellow (or almost white). Some nonpoisonous snakes have the same coloring, but in the coral snake the red band always touches the yellow band. Its short, grooved fangs must chew into its victim before the poison can be introduced.

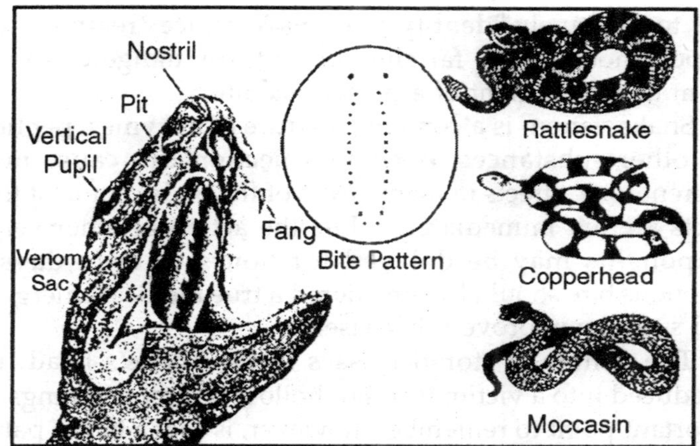

Fig. Merican Pit Vipers.

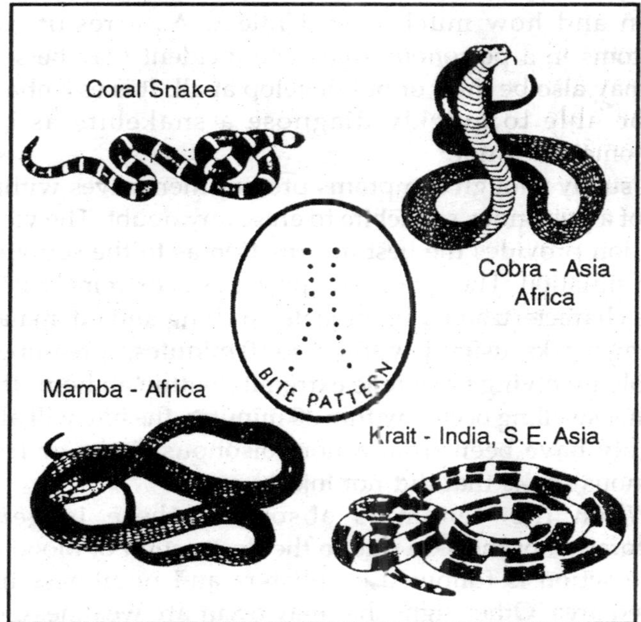

Fig. Corals, Cobras, Kraits and Mambas.

The bite pattern is shown in figure. In a snakebite situation, every reasonable effort should be made to kill or at least to positively identify the culprit, since treatment of a nonpoisonous bite is far simpler and less dangerous to the victim than treatment of a poisonous bite.

Snake venom is a complex mixture of enzymes, peptides, and other substances. A single injection can cause many different toxic effects in many areas of the body. Some of these effects are felt immediately while the action of other venom components may be delayed for hours or even days. A poisonous bite should be considered a true medical emergency until symptoms prove otherwise.

The venom is stored in sacs in the snake's head. It is introduced into a victim through hollow or grooved fangs. An important point to remember, however, is that a bitten patient has not necessarily received a dose of venom.

The snake can control whether or not it will release the poison and how much it will inject. As a result, while symptoms in a poisonous snakebite incident may be severe, they may also be mild or not develop at all. It is essential that you be able to quickly diagnose a snakebite as being envenomated or not.

Usually enough symptoms present themselves within an hour of a poisonous snakebite to erase any doubt. The victim's condition provides the best information as to the seriousness of the situation. The bite of the pit viper is extremely painful and is characterized by immediate swelling and edema about the fang marks, usually within 5 to 10 minutes, spreading and possibly involving the whole extremity within an hour. If only minimal swelling occurs within 30 minutes, the bite will almost certainly have been from a nonpoisonous snake or from a poisonous snake that did not inject venom.

When the venom is absorbed, there is general discoloration of the skin due to the destruction of blood cells. This reaction is followed by blisters and numbness in the affected area. Other signs that may occur are weakness, rapid pulse, nausea, shortness of breath, vomiting, shock, headache, fever, chills, drop in blood pressure, and blurred vision.

Severe poisoning can cause pulmonary edema and internal bleeding. The eastern diamondback rattler bite is further characterized by numbness and tingling of the mouth and possibly also of the face and scalp. A metallic taste on the tongue may be noted.

The aim of first aid for envenomated snakebites is to reduce the circulation of blood through the bite area, delay absorption of venom, prevent aggravation of the local wound, maintain vital signs, and transport the victim as soon as possible to a medical treatment facility. Other aid will be mainly supportive:

- Apply a constricting band (i.e., rubber tubing, belt, necktie, stocking) above and below the bite. Each band should be approximately 2 inches from the wound, but Never place the bands on each side of a joint. If only one constricting band is available, place it above the wound. It should be tight enough to stop the flow of blood in the veins, but not tight enough to shut off the arterial blood supply. The victim's pulse should be palpable below the band. Advance the constricting band to keep ahead of the swelling.
- If the victim cannot reach a medical treatment facility within 30 minutes of the time of the bite, and there are definite signs of poisoning, use a sterile knife blade to make an incision about 1/2 inch long and 1/4 inch deep over each fang mark on the long axis of the extremity. This technique is done only on the extremities, not on the head or trunk. Apply suction cups to help remove some of the injected venom. Suction by mouth is recommended only as a last resort, because the human mouth contains so many different bacteria that the bite could become infected. Incision and suction later than 30 minutes from the time of the bite is not recommended.
- Check the pulse and respiration frequently. Give artificial ventilation if necessary.
- Calm and reassure the victim, who will often be excited or hysterical. Keep the victimlying down, quiet, and warm. Do Not give alcohol or any other stimulant to drink.

- Treat for shock.
- Use a splint to immobilize the victim's affected extremity, keeping the involved area at or below the level of the heart.
- Cover the wound to prevent further contamination.
- Give aspirin for pain.
- Telephone the nearest medical facility so that the proper antivenin can be made available.
- Transport the victim (and the dead snake) to a medical treatment facility as soon as possible. All suspected snake bite victims should be taken to the hospital, whether they show signs of envenomation or not.

Treatment of a nonenvenomated snakebite is essentially the same as the treatment for puncture wounds. In most situation, the definitive care of the victim will be in the hands of a medical officer. This care will centre around the use of antivenin serum.

All western hemisphere snakes, with the exception of the eastern coral snake, can be treated with the same polyvalent antivenin. This is given in doses of 3 vials for small reactions; 5 to 8 vials for cases in which there is swelling of a hand or foot; and at least 8 vials for moderate or severe envenomation. Extra vials are kept at the ready.

Children will receive higher doses than adults since the poison has more effect on them because of their smaller size and lower weight. Because the antivenin is a horse serum base, the medical officer will order a sensitivity test before it is given.

Routine laboratory tests will also be run in preparation for the possible start of whole blood infusion. Additional medical facility care would include tetanus prophylaxis, wound cleansing and debridement, Burow's solution soaks, antiseptic ointment, and sterile dressing. Bites, Stings, and Punctures from Sea Animals A number of sea animals are capable of inflicting painful wounds by biting, stinging, or puncturing. Except under rare circumstances, these stings and puncture wounds are not fatal.

Major wounds from sharks, barracuda, moray eels, and alligators can be treated by controlling the bleeding, preventing shock, giving basic life support, splinting the injury, and transporting the victim to a medical treatment facility.

Minor injuries inflicted by turtles and stinging corals require only that the wound be thoroughly cleansed and the injury splinted. Other sea animals inflict injury by means of stinging cells located in tentacles. This group includes the jellyfish and Portuguese man-of-war. Contact with the tentacles produces burning pain, a rash with small hemorrhage in the skin, and, on occasion, shock, muscular cramping, nausea, vomiting, and respiratory distress.

Treatment consists of pouring sea water over the injured area and then removing the tentacles with a towel or gloves. Next, pour rubbing alcohol, formalin, vinegar, or diluted ammonia over the affected area to neutralize any remaining nematocysts (minute stinging structures).

Finally, cover the area with a dry powder, to which the last nematocysts will adhere, and then scrape them off with a dull knife. Spiny fish, stingrays, urchins, and cone shells inject their venom by puncturing with spines General signs and symptoms include swelling, nausea, vomiting, generalized cramps, diarrhea, muscular paralysis, and shock.

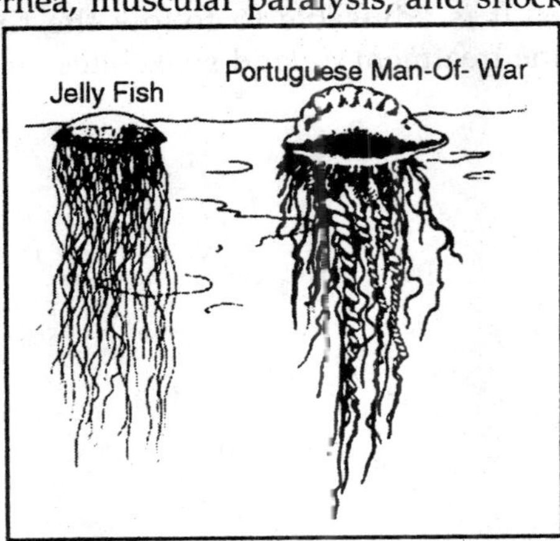

Fig. Jellyfish and Portuguese Man-of-war.

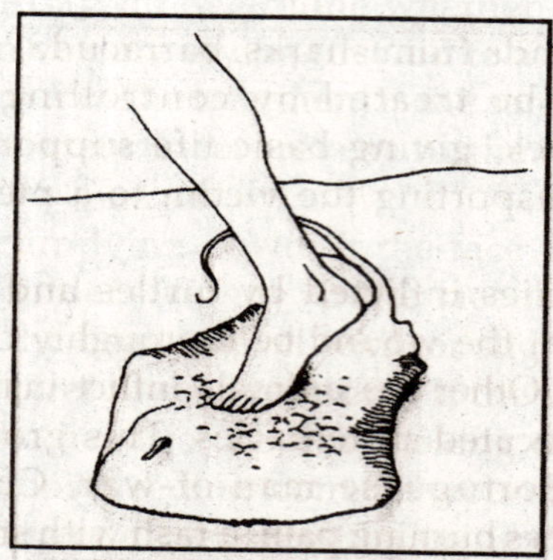

Fig. Stingray Sting

Emergency care consists of prompt flushing with cold sea water to remove the venom and to constrict hemorrhaging blood vessels. Next, debride the wound of any remaining pieces of the spine's venom-containing integumentary sheath.

Soak the wound area in very hot water for 30 to 60 minutes to neutralize the venom. Finally, completely debride the wound, control hemorrhage, suture, provide tetanus prophylaxis and a broad-spectrum antibiotic, and elevate the extremity. Sea snakes are found in the warm water areas of the Pacific and Indian Oceans.

Their venom is very poisonous, but their fangs are only 1/4 inch long. It is advisable to follow the first aid steps outlined for the treatment of land snakebites.

Chapter 10

Drug Abuse

Drug abuse is the habitual or excessive use of drugs for purposes or in quantities for which they were not intended. Drugs are chemical compounds or biological substances that, when introduced into the body, affect its mental or physical functions. When abused, drugs become a source of "poison" to the body.

They can lead to serious illness, dependency, and death. Death is usually due to acute intoxication or overdose. The group classification used in this manual is intended to categorize drugs most commonly abused into useful clusters. For our purposes, it is considered the most appropriate of several methods of classification.

The drugs with their recognized trade names, some commonly used street names, and observable symptoms of abuse. The following sections contain specific information about commonly abused drugs including availability and methods of administration.

Narcotic Intoxication

Unfortunately, abuse of narcotic drugs is common. This group of drugs includes the most effective and widely used pain killers in existence. Continual use of narcotic drugs, even under medical supervision, inevitably leads to physical and psychological dependence.

The more commonly known drugs within this group are opium, morphine, heroin, codeine, and methadone (a synthetic narcotic). In addition, Darvon and Talwin are included in this group because of their narcotic-like action. Next to cocaine (discussed later), heroin is the most popular narcotic drug because of its intense euphoria and long-lasting effect. It is far more potent than morphine but has no legitimate use in the United States. Heroin appears as a white, gray, or tan, fluffy powder.

The most common method of using heroin is by injection directly into the vein, although it can be sniffed. Codeine, although milder than heroin and morphine, is sometimes abused as an ingredient in cough syrup preparations.

Symptoms of narcotic drug abuse include slow shallow breathing, possible unconsciousness, constriction (narrowing) of the pupils of the eyes to pinpoint size, drowsiness, confusion, and slurred speech. The narcotic drug abuser, suddenly withdrawn from drugs, may appear as a wildly disturbed person who is agitated, restless, and possibly hallucinating.

Barbiturate Intoxication

The legitimate use of barbiturates is primarily to induce sleep and to relieve tension. They are depressants (downers), and statistically they are the most lethal of the abused drugs because of the depth of coma that can result from respiratory depression and circulatory collapse. The commonly known drugs within this group include phenobarbital, amobarbital, pentobarbital, and secobarbital. They may appear in the form of capsules, tablets, and liquids.

Overdose potential is extremely high, and can occur accidentally, especially if the barbiturate is taken in conjunction with alcohol, which tends to multiply the effects of depressant drugs.

The physical symptoms of barbiturate abuse include slurred speech, faulty judgment, poor memory, staggering, tremors, rapid movement of the eyeballs with the pupils appearing normal, rapid shallow breathing, and possible shock and coma.

Nonbarbiturate Tranquilizer Intoxication

This group of drugs exhibits the same depressant

(downer) action as the barbiturates. The more commonly known drugs within this group include Librium, Valium, Doriden, Miltown, Equanil, and Quaalude.

Although there is a possibility of overdose and physical addiction, it is not nearly as great as with the barbiturate drugs and requires larger doses taken over a longer period of time. These drugs are widely used in clinical practice because they are considered to have a wide margin of safety.

Stimulant Intoxication

The stimulants (uppers) directly affect the central nervous system by increasing mental alertness and combating drowsiness and fatigue. One group of stimulants, called amphetamines, is legitimately used in the treatment of conditions such as mild depression, obesity, and narcolepsy (sleeping sickness).

The amphetamines, known as "speed" by the abuser, are the most commonly abused stimulants and include such drugs as Benzedrine, Dexedrine, Dexamyl, Desoxyn, Methedrine, and Syndrox. Stimulants may be abused by taking them orally as capsules or tablets, "snorting" them through the nose, or injecting them into the veins for an immediate and more intense effect.

Physical symptoms of amphetamine abuse include hyperactivity, increased respiration, dilated pupils, increased alertness, sweating, elevated temperature, depressed appetite, and convulsions. The "comedown" from amphetamine abuse is so unpleasant that the temptation to take repeated doses is overwhelming and sometimes results in the abuser going on "speed runs, " which can last up to a week. Then the abuser may sleep several days before awaking depressed, lethargic, and extremely hungry.

Large quantities of amphetamines are physically addicting, and even small amounts can result in psychological dependence. Tolerance to high doses develops, and withdrawal symptoms occur. During the depression state associated with withdrawal, suicide attempts are not uncommon. Cocaine, although classified as a narcotic, acts as a stimulant and is commonly abused. It is relatively ineffective when taken orally; therefore the abuser either injects it into the vein or "snorts" it through the nose.

Its effect is much shorter than that of amphetamines, and occasionally the abuser may inject or snort cocaine every few minutes in an attempt to maintain a constant stimulation and prevent depression experienced during withdrawal (comedown).

Overdose is very possible, often resulting in convulsion and death. The physical symptoms observed in the cocaine abuser will be the same as those observed in the amphetamine abuser.

Hallucinogen Intoxication

The group of drugs that affect the central nervous system by altering the user's perception of self and environment are commonly known as hallucinogens. Included within this group are lysergic acid diethylamide (LSD), mescaline, dimethoxymethylamphetamine (STP), phenicyclidine (PCP), and psilocybin. They appear in several forms: crystals, powders, and liquids.

The symptoms of hallucinogenic drugs include dilated pupils, flushed face, increased heartbeat, and a chilled feeling. In addition, the person may display a distorted sense of time and self, show emotions ranging from ecstasy to horror, and experience changes in visual depth perception.

Although no known deaths have resulted from the drugs directly, hallucinogen-intoxicated persons have been known to jump from windows, walk in front of automobiles, or injure themselves in other ways because of the vivid but unreal perception of their environment.

Even though no longer under the direct influence of a hallucinogenic drug, a person who has formerly used one of the drugs may experience a spontaneous recurrence (flashback) of some aspect of the drug experience.

The most common type of flashback is the recurrence of perceptual distortion, but disturbing emotion or panic have also occurred. Flashback may be experienced by heavy or occasional users of the hallucinogenic drugs, and its frequency is unpredictable and its cause unknown.

Cannabis Intoxication

Cannabis sativa, commonly known as marijuana, is widely abused and can best be classified as a mild hallucinogen. The most common physical appearance of marijuana is as ground dried leaves, and the most common method of consumption is by smoking. After a single inhaled dose of marijuana, measurable physical effects reach a maximum within 1/2 hour and disappear in 3 to 5 hours.

The physical symptoms of Cannabis (marijuana) abuse include dryness of the mouth, irritation of the throat, bloodshot eyes, increased appetite, dizziness or sleepiness, and, in heavy smokers, a cough.

Adverse reactions to the drug include anxiety, fear, drying, depression, suspicion, delusions, and, in rare cases, hallucinations. Although marijuana can produce psychological dependence, there is no evidence of physical dependence; therefore, there are usually no withdrawal symptoms following its discontinuance.

Handling Drug-Intoxicated

Persons As in any emergency medical situation, priorities of care must be established. Conditions involving respiratory or cardiac failure must receive immediate attention before specific action is directed to the drug abuse symptom. General priorities of care are outlined below.

- Check for adequacy of airway, breathing, and circulation, and for shock. Give appropriate treatment.
- Keep the victim awake
- If the victim is sleepy or poorly responding to pain, stimulate by using cold wet towels, gentle shaking, conversation, and moving about. If the victim cannot be aroused, place him or her on his or her side so secretions and vomitus will drain from the mouth and not be aspirated into the lungs.

- Induce vomiting if the victim is conscious and the drug was taken orally.
- Prevent the victim from self-injury while highly excited or lacking coordination. Use physical restraints only if absolutely necessary.
- Calm and reassure the excited victim by "talking him or her down" in a quiet, relaxed, and sympathetic manner.
- Gather materials and information to assist in identifying and treating the suspected drug problem. Spoons, paper sacks, eye droppers, hypodermic needles, vials, or collapsible tubes are excellent identification clues.
- The presence of capsules, pills, drug containers, or needle marks (tracks) on the victim's body are also significant.
- A personal history of drug use from the victim or those accompanying the victim is very important and may reveal how long the victim has been abusing drugs, approximate amounts taken, and time between doses. Also, knowledge of past medical problems, including history of convulsion (with or without drugs) is important.
- Transport the victim and the materials collected to a medical treatment facility.
- Brief medical facility personnel and present the materials collected at the scene upon arrival at the medical treatment facility.

Chapter 11

Burns

A burn is a type of injury that may be caused by heat, electricity, chemicals, light, radiation, or friction. Burns can be highly variable in terms of the tissue affected, the severity, and resultant complications. Muscle, bone, blood vessel, dermal and epidermal tissue can all be damaged with subsequent pain due to profound injury to nerves.

Depending on the location affected and the degree of severity, a burn victim may experience a wide number of potentially fatal complications including shock, infection, electrolyte imbalance and respiratory distress. Beyond physical complications, burns can also result in severe psychological and emotional distress due to scarring and deformity.

CLASSIFICATION

A number of different classification systems exist. The traditional system divided burns in first-, second-, or third-degree This system is however being replaced by one reflecting the need for surgical intervention. The burn depths are described as either superficial, superficial partial-thickness, deep partial-thickness, or full-thickness.

By degree

- First-degree burns are usually limited to redness (erythema), a white plaque and minor pain at the site of injury. These burns involve only the epidermis. Most sunburns can be included as first-degree burns.
- Second-degree burns manifest as erythema with superficial blistering of the skin, and can involve

more or less pain depending on the level of nerve involvement. Second-degree burns involve the superficial (papillary) dermis and may also involve the deep (reticular) dermis layer.

- Third-degree burns occur when the epidermis is lost with damage to the subcutaneous tissue. Burn victims will exhibit charring and extreme damage of the epidermis, and sometimes hard eschar will be present. Third-degree burns result in scarring and victims will also exhibit the loss of hair shafts and keratin. These burns may require grafting.
- Fourth-degree burns damage muscle, tendon, and ligament tissue, thus result in charring and catastrophic damage of the hypodermis. In some instances the hypodermis tissue may be partially or completely burned away as well as this may result in a condition called compartment syndrome, which threatens both the life and the limb of the patient. Grafting is required if the burn does not prove to be fatal.

ENVIRONMENTAL INJURIES

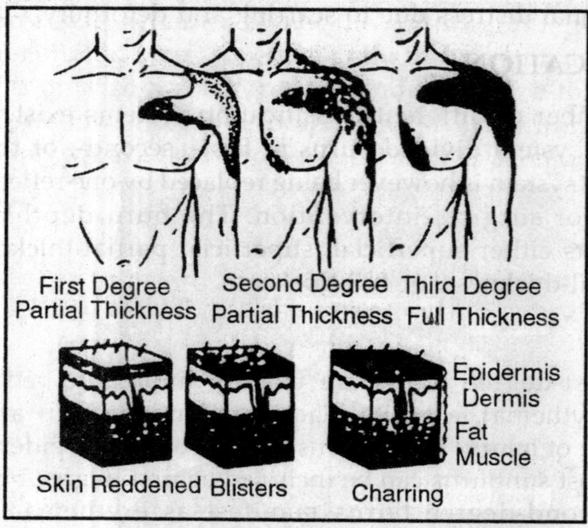

Fig. Classification of Burns.

Under the broad category of environmental injuries, we will consider a number of first aid problems. Exposure to extremes of temperature,whether heat or cold, causes injury to skin, tissues, blood vessels, vital organs, and, in some cases, the whole body.

In addition, contact with the sun's rays, electrical current, or certain chemicals cause injuries similar in character to burns.

THERMAL BURNS

True burns are generated by exposure to extreme heat that overwhelms the body's defensive mechanisms. Burns and scalds are essentially the same injury, burns being caused by dry heat, and scalds by moist heat.

The seriousness of the injury can be estimated by the depth, extent, and location of the burn, the age and health of the victim, and other medical complications. Burns can be classified according to their depth as first-, second-, and third-degree burns. With a first-degree burn, the epidermal layer is irritated, reddened, and tingling. The skin is sensitive to touch and blanches with pressure. Pain is mild to severe. Edema is minimal. Healing usually occurs naturally within a week. A second-degree burn is characterized by epidermal blisters, mottled appearance, and a red base.

Damage extends into, but not through, the dermis. Recovery usually takes 2 to 3 weeks, with some scarring and depigmentation. This condition is painful. Body fluids may be drawn into the injured tissue, causing edema and possible a "weeping" fluid (plasma) loss at the surface.

Third-degree burns are full-thickness injuries penetrating into muscle and fatty connective tissues or even down to the bone. Tissues and nerves are destroyed. Shock with blood in the urine is likely to be present. Pain will be absent at the burn site if all the area nerve endings are destroyed and the surrounding tissue, which is less damaged, will be painful.

Tissue colour will range from white (scalds) to black (charring burns). Although the wound is usually dry, body fluids will collect in the underlying tissue and if the area has not been completely cauterized, significant amounts of fluids will be lost by plasma "weeping" or by hemorrhage, thus reducing circulation volume.

There is considerable scarring and possible loss of function. Skin grafts may be necessary.Of greater importance than the depth of the burn in evaluating the seriousness of the condition is the extent of the burned area. A first-degree burn over 50 per cent of the body surface area (BSA) may be more serious than a third-degree burn over 3 per cent. The "Rule of Nines" is used to give a rough estimate of the surface area affected.

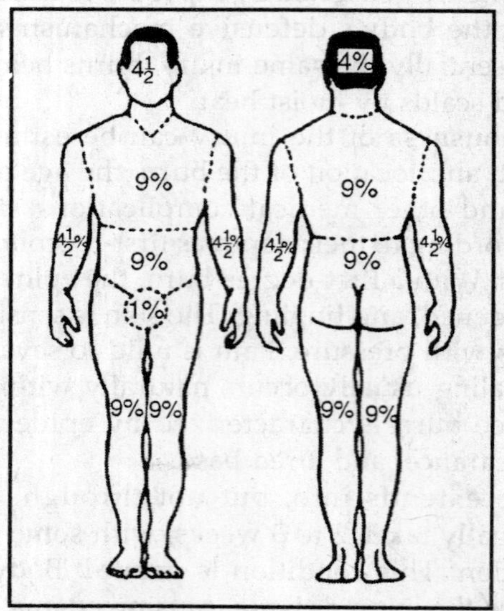

Fig. Rule of Nines.

Figure shows how the rule is applied to adults. A third factor in burn evaluation is the location of the burn. Serious burns of the head, hands, feet, or genitals will require hospitalization.

The fourth factor is the presence of any other complications, especially respiratory tract injuries or other major injuries or factors.

The corpsman must take all these factors into consideration when evaluating the condition of the burn victim, especially in a triage situation.

First Aid

After the victim has been removed from the source of the thermal injury, first aid should be kept to a minimum.

- Maintain an open airway.
- Control hemorrhage, and treat for shock.
- Remove constricting jewelry and articles of clothing.
- Protect the burn area from contamination by covering it with clean sheets or dry dressings. Do Not remove clothing adhering to a wound.
- Splint fractures.
- For all serious and extensive burns (over 20 per cent BSA), and in the presence of shock, start intravenous therapy with an electrolyte solution (Ringer's lactate) in an unburned area.
- Maintain intravenous treatment during transportation.
- Relieve mild pain with aspirin. Relieve moderate pain with cool wet compresses or ice water immersion (for burns of less than 20 per cent BSA). Severe pain may be relieved with morphine or demerol injections. Pain resulting from small burns may be relieved with an anesthetic ointment if the skin is not broken

Aid Station Care

- Continue to observe for airway patency, hemorrhage, and shock.
- Continue intravenous therapy that is in place, or start a new one under a medical officer's supervision to control shock and replace fluid loss.
- Monitor urine output.
- Shave body hair well back from the burned area and then cleanse the area gently with disinfectant soap and warm water. Remove dirt, grease, and nonviable tissue. Apply a sterile dressing of dry gauze. Place bulky dressings around the burned parts to absorb serous exudate.
- All major burn victims should be given a booster dose of tetanus toxoid to guard against infection.

Administration of antibiotics may be directed by a medical officer.

- If evacuation to a definitive care facility will be delayed for 2 to 3 days, start topical antibiotic chemotherapy after the patient stabilizes and following debridement and wound care. Gently spread a 1/16-inch thickness of Sulfamylon or Silvadene over the burn area. Repeat the application after 12 hours, and then after daily debridement. Treat minor skin reactions with antihistamines.

SUNBURN

Sunburn results from prolonged exposure to the ultraviolet rays of the sun. Firstand seconddegree burns similar to thermal burns result. Treatment is essentially the same as that outlined for thermal burns.

Unless a major percentage of the body surface is affected, the victim will not require more than first aid attention. Commercially prepared sunburn lotions and ointments may be used.

Prevention through education and the proper use of sun screens is the best way to avoid this condition.

ELECTRICAL BURNS

Electrical burns may be far more serious than a preliminary examination may indicate. The entrance and exit wounds may be small, but as electricity penetrates the skin it burns a large area below the surface.

A corpsman can do little for these victims other than monitoring the basic life functions, delivering CPR, treating for shock if necessary, covering the entrance and exit wounds with a dry, sterile dressing, and transporting the victim to a medical treatment facility.

Before treatment is started, ensure that the victim is no longer in contact with a live electrical source.

Shut the power off or use a nonconducting rope or stick to move the victim away from the line or the line away from the victim.

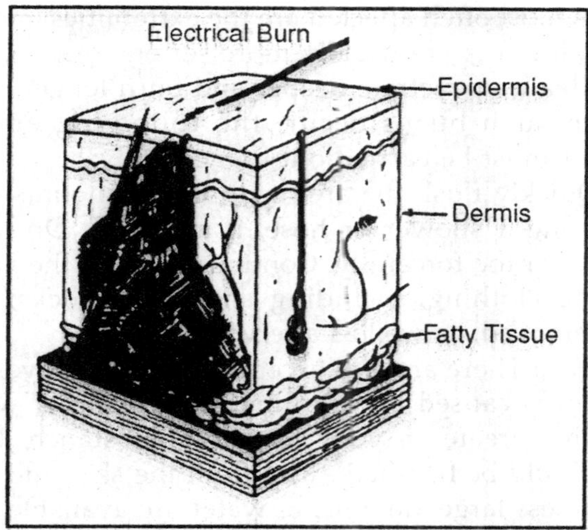

Fig. Electrical Burns.

Fig. Moving a Victim away from an Electrical Line.

CHEMICAL BURNS

When acids, alkalies, or other chemicals come in contact with the skin or other body membranes, they may cause injuries that are generally referred to as chemical burns. For the most part, these injuries are not caused by heat but by direct chemical destruction of body tissues.

Areas most often affected are the extremities, mouth, and eyes. Alkali burns are usually more serious than acid burns, because alkalies penetrate deeper and burn longer.

When such burns occur, the following emergency procedures must be carried out immediately:

- Quickly flush the area with large amounts of water, using a shower or hose, if available. Do not apply water too forcefully. Continue to flood the area while the clothing, including shoes and socks, is being removed, as well as afterwards.

  Note: There are two exceptions to the above. In alkali burns caused by dry lime, the mixing of water and lime creates a very corrosive substance. Dry lime should be brushed away from the skin and clothing, unless large amounts of water are available for rapid and complete flushing. In acid burns caused by phenol (carbolic acid), wash the affected area with alcohol because phenol is not water soluble; then wash with water. If alcohol is not available, flushing with water is better than no treatment at all.
- After thorough washing, neutralize any chemical remaining on the affected area.

  Warning: Do Not attempt to neutralize a chemical unless you know exactly what it is and what substance will neutralize it. Further damage may be done by a neutralizing agent that is too strong or incorrect. For acid burns make a solution of 1 teaspoon of baking soda in a pint of water and flush it over the affected area. For alkali burns mix 1 or 2 teaspoons of vinegar in a pintof water and flush it over the affected area.
- Flush the area again with water and gently pat dry with a sterile gauze. Do not rub the area.
- Transport the victim to a medical treatment facility.

Chemical Burns

The one and the victim to a medical treatment to the Eye only emergency treatment is to flush the eye(s) immediately with large amounts of water or a sterile saline solution. Acid burns to the eyes should be irrigated for at least 5 to 10 minutes with at least 2000 ml of water. Alkali burns should be irrigated for at least 20 minutes.

Because of the intense pain, the victim may be unable to open the eyes. If this occurs, hold the eyelids apart so that water can flow across the eye. A drinking fountain or field "water buffalo" may be used to supply a steady stream of water.

Hold the victim's head in a position that allows water to flow from the inside corner of the eye toward the outside. Do not allow the water to fall directly on the eye, not use greater force than is necessary to keep the water flowing across the eye.

Caution: Never use any chemical antidotes such as baking soda or alcohol in treating burns of the eye and do not try to neutralize chemical agents.

After thorough irrigation loosely cover both eyes with a clean dressing. This prevents further damage by decreasing eye movement. The aftercare for all chemical burns is similar to that for thermal burns: cover the affected area and get the victim to a medical treatment facility as soon as possible.

WHITE PHOSPHORUS BURNS

A special category of burns that may affect military personnel in a wartime or training situation is that caused by exposure of white phosphorus (WP or Willy Peter). First aid for this type of burn is complicated by the fact that white phosphorus particles ignite upon contact with air.

Superficial burns caused by simple skin contact or burning clothes should be flushed with water and treated like thermal burns. Partially embedded white phosphorus particles must be continuously flushed with water while the first aid provider removes them with whatever tools are available (i.e., tweezers, pliers, forceps). Do this quickly but gently.

Firmly or deeply embedded particles that cannot be removed by the first aid provider must be covered with a saline soaked dressing, which must be kept wet until the victim reaches a medical treatment facility. The wounds containing embedded phosphorus particles may then be rinsed with a dilute, one per cent freshly mixed solution of copper sulfate.

This solution combines with phosphorus on the surface of the particles to form a blue-black cupric phosphite covering, which both impedes further oxidation and facilitates identification of retained particles. Under no circumstances should the copper sulfate solution be applied as a wet dressing.

Wounds must be flushed thoroughly with a saline solution following the copper sulfate rinse to prevent absorption of excessive amounts of copper, since copper has been associated with extensive intravascular hemolysis. An adjunct to the management of phosphorus burn injuries is the identification of the retained phosphorescent particles in a darkened room during debridement.

Note: Combustion of white phosphorus results in the formation of a severe pulmonary irritant.

The ignition of phosphorus in a closed space such as the BAS tent or sickbay may result in the development of irritant concentrations sufficient to cause acute inflammatory changes in the tracheobronchial tree. The effects of this gas, especially during debridement, can be minimized 4-80 by placing a moist cloth over the nose and mouth to inactivate the gas and by ventilating the tent.

HEAT EXPOSURE INJURY

Excessive heat affects the body in a variety of ways. When a person exercises or works in a hot environment, heat builds up inside the body. The body automatically reacts to get rid of this heat through the sweating mechanism. This depletes water and electrolytes from the circulating volume. If they are not adequately replaced, body functions are affected, and initially, heat cramps and heat exhaustion develop.

If the body becomes too overheated, or water or electrolytes too depleted, the sweat control mechanism of the body malfunctions and shuts down. The result is heat stroke (sunstroke). Heat exposure injuries are a threat in any hot environment, but especially in desert or tropical areas and in the boiler rooms of ships. Under normal conditions it is a preventable injury. Individual and command awareness of the causes of heat stress problems should help eliminate heat exposure injuries.

Heat Cramps

Excessive sweating may result in painful cramps in the muscles of the abdomen, legs, and arms. Heat cramps may also result from drinking ice water or other cold drinks either too quickly or in too large a quantity after exercise.

Muscle cramps are often an early sign of approaching heat exhaustion. To provide first aid treatment for heat cramps, move the victim to a cool place. Since heat cramps are caused by loss of salt and water, give the victim plenty of cool (not cold) water to drink, adding about one teaspoon of salt to a liter or quart of water. Apply manual pressure to the cramped muscle, or gently massage it to relieve the spasm. If there are indications of anything more serious, transport the victim immediately to a medical treatment facility.

Heat Exhaustion

Heat exhaustion (heat prostration or heat collapse) is the most common condition caused by working or exercising in hot environments. In heat exhaustion there is a serious disturbance of blood flow to the brain, heart, and lungs.

This causes the victim to experience weakness, dizziness, headache, loss of appetite, and nausea. The victim may faint, but he or she will probably regain consciousness as the head is lowered, which improves the blood supply to the brain. Signs and symptoms of heat exhaustion are similar to those of shock; the victim will appear ashen gray, the skin cool, moist, and clammy and the pupils may be dilated.

The vital signs usually are normal; however, the victim may have a weak pulse, together with rapid and shallow breathing. Body temperature may be below normal. Treat heat exhaustion as if the victim were in shock. Move the victim to a cool or airconditioned area. Loosen the clothing, apply cool wet cloths to the head, axilla, groin, and ankles, and fan the victim. Do not allow the victim to become chilled (if this does occur, then cover with a light blanket and move into a warmer area). If the victim is conscious, give a solution of 1 teaspoon of salt dissolved in a liter of cool water. If the victim vomits, do not give any more fluids. Transport the victim to a medical treatment facilit y as soon as possible. Intravenous fluid infusion may be necessary for effective fluid and electrolyte replacement to combat shock.

Heat Stroke

Sunstroke is more accurately called heat stroke since it is not necessary to be exposed to the sun for this condition to develop. It is a less common but far more serious condition than heat exhaustion, since it carries a 20 per cent mortality rate.

The most important feature of heat stroke is the extremely high body temperature (105°F, 41°C, or higher) accompanying it. In heat stroke the victim suffers a mechanism and breakdown of the sweating is unable to eliminate excessive body heat build up while exercising.

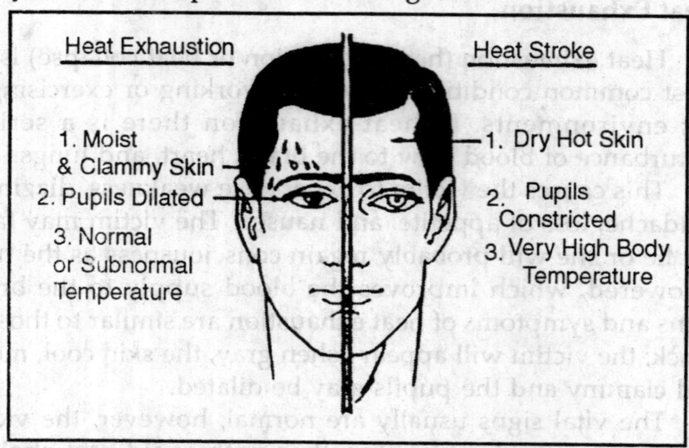

Fig. Heat Exhaustion and Heat Stroke.

If the body temperature rises too high, the brain, kidneys, and liver may be permanently damaged. Sometimes the victim may have preliminary symptoms such as headache, nausea, dizziness, or weakness. Breathing will be deep and rapid at first, later shallow and almost absent. Usually the victim will be flushed, very dry, and very hot.

The pupils will be constricted (pinpoint) and the pulse fast and strong. Compare these symptoms with those of heat exhaustion. When providing first aid for heat stroke, remember that this is a true life-and-death emergency. The longer the victim remains overheated, the more likely irreversible brain damage or death will occur.

First aid is designed to reduce body heat fast. Reduce heat immediately by dousing the body with cold water or by applying wet, cold towels to the whole body. Move the victim to the coolest possible place and remove as much clothing as possible. Maintain an open airway.

Place the victim on his or her back, with the head and shoulders slightly raised. If cold packs are available, place them under the arms, around the neck, at the ankles, and in the groin. Expose the victim to a fan or air conditioner, since drafts will promote cooling. Immersing the victim in a cold water bath is also very effective. If the victim is conscious, give cool water to drink.

Do not give any hot drinks or stimulants. Discontinue cooling when the rectal temperature reaches 102°F; watch for recurrence of temperature rise by checking every 10 minutes. Repeat cooling if temperature reaches 103 rectally. Get the victim to a medical facility as soon as possible. Cooling measures must be continued while the victim is being transported. Intravenous fluid infusion may be necessary for effective fluid and electrolyte replacement to combat shock.

Prevention of Heat Exposure Injuries

The prevention of heat exposure injuries is a command responsibility, but the medical department plays a role in it by educating all hands about the medical dangers, monitoring environmental health, and advising the commanding officer. On the individual level, prevention centers on water and salt replacement. Sweat must be replaced ounce for ounce; in a hot environment, water consumption must be drastically increased. Salt should be replaced by eating well-balanced meals, three times a day, salted to taste.

In the field, "C" rations contain enough salt to sustain a person in most situations. Do Not use salt tablets unless specified by a physician, Do Not consume alcoholic beverages. At the command level, prevention centers on an awareness of the environment.

The Wet Bulb Globe Temperature (WGBT) must be monitored regularly, and the results interfaced with the Physiological Heat Exposure Limits (PHEL) chart and the work/rest chart before work assignments are made. In addition, unnecessary heat sources, especially steam leaks, must be eliminated, and vents and exhaust blowers must be checked for adequate circulation. The results will be a happier, healthier, and more productive crew.

Chapter 12

Cold Exposure Injury

When the body is subjected to extremely cold temperatures, blood vessels constrict, and body heat is gradually lost. As the body temperature drops, tissues are easily damaged or destroyed. The cold injuries resulting from inadequate response to the cold in military situations have spelled disaster for many armies; for example, those of Napoleon and Hitler in their Russian campaigns.

The weather (i.e., temperature, humidity, precipitation, and wind) is the predominant influence in the development of cold injuries. Falling temperature interacting with high humidity, a wet environment, and rising wind accelerates the loss of body heat. The other major causative factor is the type of mission.

For example, riflemen involved in static defence or pinned down by enemy fire suffer from greater exposure to the elements and lack the opportunity to properly warm their bodies, change clothes, keep clean, or eat balanced meals. They may also suffer from fatigue and fear, which contribute to apathy and neglect.

Other factors that influence the development of cold injuries are dehydration, the presence of other injuries (especially those causing a reduction in circulatory flow), and a previous cold injury (which increases susceptibility by lowering resistance). In addition, the use of any drug, including alcohol, that modifies autonomic nervous system response or alters judgment ability can drastically reduce an individual's chance for survival.

Like heat exposure injuries, cold exposure injuries are

preventable. Acclimatization, the availability y of warm, layered clothing, and maintenance of good discipline and training standards are important factors.

These are command, not medical, responsibilities, but the corpsman will have a crucial role as a monitor of 4-82 nutritional intake and personal hygiene (with emphasis on foot care) and as an advisor to the commanding officer.

A corpsman will also be responsible for acquainting the troops with the dangers of cold exposure and with prevention measures. Two major points must be stressed in the management of all cold injuries: Rapid rewarming is of primary importance, and all unnecessary manipulations of affected areas must be avoided.

More will be said about these points later. In military operations the treatment of cold injuries is influenced by:

- The tactical situation,
- The facilities available for the evacuation of casualties,
- The fact that most cold injuries are encountered in large numbers during periods of intense combat when many other wounded casualties appear.

Highly individualized treatment under these circumstances may be impossible because examination and treatment of more lifeendangering wounds must be given priority. In a high casualty situation, shelter cold injury victims, and try to protect them from further injury until there is sufficient time to treat them.

All cold injuries are similar, varying only in the degree of tissue damage. In general, the effects of cold are broken down into two types: general cooling of the entire body and local cooling of parts of the body, but cold injuries will seldom be totally of one type.

General Cooling (Hypothermia)

General cooling of the whole body is caused by continued exposure to low or rapidly falling temperatures, cold moisture, snow, or ice. Those exposed to low temperatures for extended periods may suffer ill effects, even if they are well protected by clothing, because cold affects the body systems slowly, almost without notice.

As the body cools, there are several stages of progressive discomfort and disability. The first symptom is shivering, which is an attempt to generate heat by repeated contractions of surface muscles.

This is followed by a feeling of listlessness, indifference, and drowsiness. Unconsciousness can follow quickly. Shock becomes evident as the victim's eyes assume a glassy stare, respiration becomes slow and shallow, and the pulse is weak or absent.

As the body temperature drops even lower, peripheral circulation decreases and the extremities become susceptible to freezing. Finally, death results as the core temperature of the body approaches 80°F.

Treatment for hypothermia is enumerated as follows:

- Local Carefully observe respiratory effort and heart beat; CPR may be required while the warming process is underway.
- Rewarm the victim as soon as possible. It may be necessary to treat other injuries before the victim can be moved to a warmer place. Severe bleeding must be controlled and fractures splinted over clothing before the victim is moved.
- Replace wet or frozen clothing and remove anything that constricts the victim's arms, legs, or fingers, interfering with circulation.
- If the victim is inside a warm place and is conscious, the most effective method of warming is immersion in a tub of warm (100° to 105°F or 38° to 41°C) water. The water should be warm to the elbow—never hot. Observe closely for signs of respiratory failure and cardiac arrest (rewarming shock). Rewarming shock can be minimized by warming the body trunk before the limbs to prevent vasodilation in the extremities with subsequent shock due to blood volume shifts.
- If a tub is not available, apply external heat to both sides of the victim. Natural body heat (skin to skin)

from two rescuers is the best method. This is called "buddy warming." If this is not practical, use hot water bottles or an electric rewarming blanket, but do not place them next to bare skin, and be careful to monitor the temperature of the artificial heat source, since the victim is very susceptible to burn injury. Because the victim is unable to generate adequate body heat, placement under a blanket or in a sleeping bag is not sufficient treatment.

- If the victim is conscious, give warm liquids to drink. Never give alcoholic beverages or allow the victim to smoke.
- Dry the victim thoroughly if water is used for rewarming.
- As soon as possible, transfer the victim to a definitive care facility. Be alert for the signs of respiratory and cardiac arrest during transfer, and keep the victim warm. Cooling

Local Cooling

Local cooling injuries, affecting parts of the body, fall into two categories: freezing and nonfreezing injuries. In the order of increasing seriousness, they include chilblain, immersion foot, superficial frostbite, and deep frostbite. The areas most commonly affected are the face and extremities.

CHILBLAIN

Chilblain is a mild cold injury caused by prolonged and repeated exposure for several hours to air temperatures from above freezing (32°F/0°C) to as high as 60°F (16°C). Chilblain is characterized by redness, swelling, tingling, and pain to the affected skin area. Injuries of this nature require no specific treatment except warming of the affected part (if possible use a water bath of 90° to 105°F), keeping it dry, and preventing further exposure.

IMMERSION FOOT

Immersion foot, which also may occur in the hands, results

from prolonged exposure to wet cold at temperatures ranging from just above freezing to 50°F (10°C) and usually in connection with limited motion of the extremities and water-soaked protective clothing. Signs and symptoms of immersion foot are tingling and numbness of the affected areas; swelling of the legs, feet, or hands; bluish discoloration of the skin; and painful blisters. Gangrene may occur. General treatment for immersion foot is as follows:

- Get the victim off his or her feet as soon as possible.
- Remove wet shoes, socks, and gloves to improve circulation.
- Expose the affected area to warm dry air.
- Keep the victim warm.
- Do not rupture blisters or apply salves and ointments.
- If the skin is not broken or loose, the injured part may be left exposed; however, if it is necessary to transport the victim, cover the injured area with loosely wrapped fluff bandages of sterile gauze.
- If the skin is broken, place a sterile sheet under the extremity and gently wrap it to protect the sensitive tissue from pressure and additional injury.
- Transport the victim as soon as possible to a medical treatment facility as a litter patient.

FROSTBITE

Frostbite occurs when ice crystals form in the skin or deeper tissues after exposure to a temperature of 32°F (0°C) or lower. Depending upon the temperature, altitude, and wind speed, the exposure time necessary to produce frostbite varies from a few minutes to several hours. The areas commonly affected are the face and extremities. The symptoms of frostbite are progressive.

Victims generally incur this injury without being acutely aware of it. Initially, the affected skin reddens and there is an uncomfortable coldness. With continued heat loss, there is a numbness of the affected area due to reduced circulation. As ice crystals form, the frozen extremity appears white, yellow-white, or mottled blue-white, and is cold, hard, and insensitive to touch or pressure. Frostbite is classified as superficial or deep, depending on the extent of tissue involvement.

Superficial Frostbite: In superficial frostbite the surface of the skin will feel hard, but the underlying tissue will be soft, allowing it to move over bony ridges. This is evidence that only the skin and the region just below it are involved. General treatment for superficial frostbite is as follows:

- Take the victim indoors.
- Rewarm hands by placing them under the armpits, against the abdomen, or between the legs.
- Rewarm feet by placing them in the armpit or against the abdomen of the buddy.
- Gradually rewarm the affected area by warm water immersion, skin to skin contact, or hot water bottles.
- Never rub a frostbite area.

Deep Frostbite

In deep frostbite the freezing reaches into the deep tissue layers. There are ice crystals in the entire thickness of the extremity. The skin will not move over bony ridges and feels hard and solid. The objectives of treatment are to protect the frozen areas from further injury, to rapidly thaw the affected area, and to be prepared to respond to circulatory or respiratory difficulties.

- Carefully assess and treat any other injuries first. Constantly monitor the victim's pulse and breathing since respiratory and heart problems can develop rapidly. Be prepared to administer CPR if necessary.
- Do not attempt to thaw the frostbitten area if there is a possibility of refreezing. It is better to leave the part frozen until the victim arrives at a medical treatment facility equipped for long term care. Refreezing of a thawed extremity causes severe and disabling damage.
- Treat all victims with injuries to the feet or legs as litter patients. When this is not possible, the victim may walk on the frozen limb, since it has been

proven that walking will not lessen the chances of successful treatment as long as the limb has not thawed out.

- When adequate protection from further cold exposure is available, prepare the victim for rewarming by removing all constricting clothing such as gloves, boots, and socks. Boots and clothing frozen on the body should be thawed by warm water immersion before removal.
- Rapidly rewarm frozen areas by immersion in water at 100° to 105°F (38° to 41°C). Keep the water warm by adding fresh hot water, but do not pour it directly on the injured area. Ensure that the frozen area is completely surrounded by water; do not let it rest on the side or bottom of the tub.
- After rewarming has been completed, pat the area dry with a soft towel. Later it will swell, sting, and burn. Blisters may develop. These should be protected from breaking. Avoid pressure, rubbing, or constriction of the injured area. Keep the skin dry with sterile dressings and place cotton between the toes and fingers to prevent their sticking together.
- Protect the tissue from additional injury and keep it as clean as possible (use sterile dressings and linen).
- Try to improve the general morale and comfort of the victim by giving hot, stimulating fluids such as tea or coffee. Do not allow the victim to smoke or use alcoholic beverages while being treated.
- Transfer to a medical treatment facility as soon as possible. During transportation, slightly elevate the frostbitten area and keep the victim and the injured area warm. Do not allow the injured area to be exposed to the cold.

Later Management of Cold Injury

When the patient reaches a hospital or a facility for definitive care, the following treatment should be employed:

- Maintain continued vigilance to avoid further

damage to the injured tissue. In general, this is accomplished by keeping the patient at bed rest with the injured part elevated, on surgically clean sheets, and with sterile pieces of cotton separating the toes or fingers. Expose all lesions to the air at normal room temperature. Weight bearing on injured tissue must be avoided.

- Whirlpool baths, twice daily at 98.6°F (37°C) with surgical soap added, assist in superficial debridement, reduce superficial bacterial contamination, and make range of motion exercises more tolerable.
- Analgesics may be required in the early post-thaw days but will soon become unnecessary in uncomplicated cases.
- Encourage the patient to take a nutritious diet with adequate fluid intake to maintain hydration.
- Perform superficial debridement of ruptured blebs, and remove suppurative scabs and partially detached nails.

COMMON MEDICAL EMERGENCIES

This section of the chapter deals with some other relatively common medical problems a corpsman may face in a first aid situation.

Generally speaking, these particular problems are the result of previously diagnosed medical conditions, so at least for the victim they do not come as a complete surprise.

Many of these victims will be wearing a Medic Alert necklace or bracelet, or carrying a Medic Alert identification card that specifies the nature of the medical condition or the type of medications being taken.

In all cases of sudden illness, search the victim for a Medic Alert symbol. It may help you diagnose the victim's problem and start appropriate first aid procedures immediately.

After checking the vital signs, you must carefully assess all the signs and symptoms before making a preliminary diagnosis.

- Determine the victim's level of consciousness,

including orientation to surroundings and reaction to pain stimulus.

- Check the limbs for weakness or paralysis.
- Check pupil size and reaction to light for signs of brain injury. Continuously monitor respiration depth and rate..
- Log all observations tion by a physician.

FAINTING (SYNCOPE)

Uncomplicated fainting carefully for evaluais the result of blood pooling in dilated veins, which reduces the amount of blood being pumped to the brain. Causes include getting up too quickly, standing for long periods with little movement, and stressful situations. Signs and symptoms that may be present are dizziness, nausea, visual disturbance from pupillary dilation, sweating, pallor, and a weak, rapid pulse.

As the body collapses, blood returns to the head and consciousness is quickly regained. Revival can be promoted by carefully placing the victim in the shock position or in a sitting position with the head between the knees. Placing a cool wet cloth on the face and loosening the — clothing can also help. Syncope may also result from an underlying medical problem such as diabetes, cerebrovascular accident (stroke), heart condition, or epilepsy.

DIABETIC CONDITIONS

Diabetes mellitus is an inherited condition in which the pancreas secretes an insufficient amount of the protein hormone insulin. Insulin regulates carbohydrate metabolism by enabling glucose to enter cells for use as an energy source. Diabetics almost always wear a Medic Alert identification symbol.

Diabetic Ketoacidosis

Diabetics may suffer from rising levels of glucose in the blood stream (hyperglycemia). The rising levels of glucose result in osmotic diuresis, and increase renal excretion of urine. A serious dehydration (hypovolemia) may result. Concurrently, lack of glucose in the cells leads to an increase in metabolic acids in the blood (acidosis) as other substances, such as fats, are metabolized as energy sources.

The result is gradual central nervous system depression, starting with symptoms of confusion and disorientation and leading to stupor and coma. Blood pressure falls and the pulse rate becomes rapid and weak. Respirations are deep, and a sickly sweet acetone odor is present on the breath. The skin is warm and dry.

Note: Too often a diabetic victim is treated as if intoxicated; the signs and symptoms presented are similar to those of alcohol intoxication.

The diabetic under treatment tries to balance the use of insulin against glucose intake to avoid the above problems. Diabetic ketoacidosis most often results either from forgetting to take insulin or from taking too little insulin to maintain a balanced condition. The victim or the victim's family may be able to answer two key questions:.

- Has the victim eaten today?.
- Has he or she taken the prescribed insulin?

If the answer is yes to the first and no to the second question, the victim is probably in a diabetic coma. Emergency first aid centers around ABC support, administration of oral or intravenous fluids to counter shock, and rapid evacuation to a medical officer's supervision.

Insulin Shock

Insulin shock results from too little sugar in the blood (hypoglycemia). It develops when a diabetic exercises too much or eats too little after taking insulin. This is a very serious condition, because glucose is driven into the cells to be metabolized, leaving too little in circulation to support the brain. Brain damage develops quickly. Signs and symptoms include:.

- Pale, moist skin.
- Dizziness and headache.
- Strong, rapid pulse.
- Fainting, seizures, and coma.

- Normal respiration and blood pressure.

Treatment is centered on getting glucose into the system quickly to prevent brain damage. Placing sugar cubes under the tongue is most beneficial. Transport the victim to a medical treatment facility as soon as possible.

Note: If you are in doubt as to whether the victim is in insulin shock or a ketoacidotic state, give sugar. Brain damage develops very quickly in insulin shock and must be reversed immediately. If the victim turns out to be ketoacidotic, the extra sugar will do no appreciable harm since this condition progresses slowly.

CEREBROVASCULAR ACCIDENT

A cerebrovascular accident, also known as a stroke or apoplexy, is caused by an interruption of the arterial blood supply to a portion of the brain. This interruption may be caused by arteriosclerosis or by a clot forming in the brain. Tissue damage and loss of function result. Onset is sudden, with little or no warning.

The first signs include weakness or paralysis on the side of the body opposite the side of the brain that has been injured. Muscles of the face on the affected side may be involved. The level of consciousness varies from alert to nonresponsive. Motor functions on the affected side are disturbed, including vision and speech, and the throat may be paralyzed.

First aid is mainly supportive. Special attention must be paid to the airway, since the victim may not be able to keep it clear. Place the victim in a semireclining position or on the paralyzed side.

- Be prepared to use suction if the victim vomits.
- Act in a calm, reassuring manner, and keep onlookers quiet since the victim may be able to hear what is going on.
- Administer oxygen to combat cerebral hypoxia.
- Carefully monitor vital signs and keep a log. Pay special attention to respirations, pulse strength and rate, and the presence or absence of the bilateral carotid pulse.

- Transport the victim to a medical treatment facility as soon as possible.

ANAPHYLACTIC REACTIONS

This condition, also called anaphylaxis or anaphylactic shock, is a severe allergic reaction to foreign material. Penicillin and the toxin from bee stings are probably the most common causative agents, although foods, inhalants, and contact substances can also cause a reaction. Anaphylaxis can happen at any time, even to people who have taken penicillin many times before without experiencing any problems.

This condition produces severe shock and cardiopullmonary failure of a very rapid onset. Because of this, immediate intervention is necessary. The general treatment for severe anaphylaxis is the subcutaneous injection of 0.3cc of epinephrine and supportive care.

The most characteristic and serious symptoms of an anaphylactic reaction are loss of voice and difficulty breathing. Other typical signs are giant hives, coughing, and wheezing. As the condition progresses, signs and symptoms of shock develop, followed by respiratory failure. Emergency management consists of maintaining vital life functions. The medical officer must be summoned immediately.

HEART CONDITIONS

A number of heart conditions are commonly refereed to as heart attacks. These include angina pectoris, acute myocardial infarction, and congestive heart failure. Together they are the cause of at least half a million deaths per year in our country.

They occur more commonly in men in the 50 to 60 year age group. Predisposing factors are lack of physical conditioning, high blood pressure and blood cholesterol levels, smoking, diabetes, and a family history of heart disease.

Angina Pectoris

This condition is caused by insufficient oxygen being circulated to the heart muscle. It results from a partial occlusion of the coronary artery, which allows the heart to function adequately at rest, but it does not allow enough oxygen enriched blood through to support sustained exercise.

When the body exerts itself, the heart muscle becomes starved for oxygen, resulting in a squeezing substernal pain that may radiate to the left arm and to the jaw.

Angina is differentiated from other forms of heart problems since the pain results from exertion and subsides with rest. Many people who suffer from angina pectoris carry nitroglycerin tablets.

If the victim of a suspected angina attack is carrying a bottle of these pills, place one pill under the tongue. Relief will be almost instantaneous. Other first aid procedures include reassurance, comfort, monitoring vital signs, and transporting the victim to a medical treatment facility.

Acute Myocardial Infarction

This condition results when a coronary artery is severely occluded by arteriosclerosis or completely blocked by a clot. The pain is similar to that of angina pectoris, but is longer in duration, not related to exertion or relieved by nitroglycerin, and leads to death of heart muscle tissue.

Other symptoms are sweating, weakness, and nausea. The pulse rate increases and may be irregular; blood pressure falls; respirations are usually normal. The victim may have an overwhelming feeling of doom. Quick or lingering death may result.

First aid for an acute myocardial infarction includes:.

- Reassurance and comfort while placing the victim in a semi-sitting position.
- Loosening of all clothing.
- Carefully maintaining a log of vital signs, and recording the history and general observations..
- Continuously monitoring vital signs and being prepared to start CPR.
- Starting a slow intravenous infusion of 5 per cent dextrose solution in water.
- Administering oxygen.

- Quickly transporting the victim to a medical treatment facility.

Congestive Heart Failure

A heart suffering from prolonged hypertension, valve disease, or heart disease will try to compensate for decreased function by increasing the size of the left ventricular pumping chamber and increasing the heart rate. As blood pressure increases, fluid is forced out of the blood vessels and into the lungs, causing pulmonary edema.

This leads to rapid shallow respirations, the appearance of pink frothy bubbles at the nose and mouth and a distinctive "rales" sound in the chest. Increased blood pressure may also cause body fluids to pool in the extremities. Emergency treatment for congestive heart failure is essentially the same as that for acute myocardial infarction.

Do not start CPR unless heart function ceases. A sitting position promotes blood pooling in the lower extremities. If an intravenous line is started, it should be maintained at the slowest rate possible to keep the vein open; an increase in the circulatory volume will worsen the condition. Immediate transport to a medical treatment facility is indicated.

CONVULSIONS

Convulsions, or seizures, are a startling and often frightening phenomenon. They are characterized by severe muscle spasms or muscle rigidity of an uncontrolled nature. Convulsive episodes occur in 1 to 2 per cent of the general population.

Although epilepsy is the most widely known form of seizure activity, there are numerous causes that are classified as either central nervous system (CNS) or non-CNS in origin. It is especially important to determine the cause in patients who have no previous history of seizure activity. This may require an extensive medical workup in the hospital. Since epilepsy is the most widely known, this section will highlight epileptic seizure disorders.

Epilepsy, also known as seizures or fits, is a condition

characterized by an abnormal focus of activity in the brain that produces severe motor responses or changes in consciousness. It may result from head trauma, scarred brain tissue, brain tumors, cerebral arterial occlusion, fever, or a number of other factors.

Fortunately, it can often be controlled by medications. Grand mal seizure is the more serious type of epilepsy. It may be, but is not always preceded by an aura that its victim soon comes to recognize, allowing time to lie down and prepare for the onset of the seizure.

A burst of nerve impulses from the brain causes unconsciousness and generalized muscular contractions, often with loss of bladder and bowel control. The primary dangers are tongue biting and injuries resulting from falls. A period of sleep or mental confusion follows.

When full consciousness returns, the victim will have little or no recollection of the attack. Petit mal seizure is of short duration and is characterized by an altered state of awareness or partial loss of consciousness and localized muscular contractions.

There is no warning and little or no memory of the attack after it is over. Although first aid treatment consists of protecting the victim from self injury and placing a padded bite stick between the jaws to prevent tongue biting, additional methods of control may be employed under a medical officer's supervision. In all cases, be prepared to provide suction since the risk of aspiration is significant.

Medications

Unless hypoglycemia can be ruled out, an intravenous infusion of 50cc of a 50 per cent dextrose solution in water may be used. For immediate control of severe convulsions, Diazepam (Valium) may be used, administered 5 to 10 mg intravenously at 5 mg/min. Watch for respiratory depression and hypotension.

Diphenylhydantoin (Dilantin) can also be used, but it takes approximately 20 minutes to achieve therapeutic levels. Administration is 50 mg/min up to the 1000 mg maximum dose. Phenobarbital is an alternate to Diphenylhydantoin but is not preferred due to its hypnotic effects. Dosage is 150 to 250 mg intravenously at 25 mg/min. This may be repeated in 15 minutes up to a maximum dosage of 400 mg in the first 2 hours.

Drowning

Drowning is a suffocating condition in a water environment. Water seldom enters the lungs in appreciable quantities because, upon contact with fluid, laryngeal spasms occur which seals the airway from the mouth and nose passages. To avoid serious damage from the resulting hypoxia, quickly bring the victim to the surface and start artificial ventilation, even before the victim is pulled to shore.

Do not interrupt artificial ventilation until the rescuer and victim are on dry ground, then quickly administer an abdominal thrust to empty the lungs and immediately restart the ventilation until spontaneous breathing returns. Oxygen enrichment is desirable if a mask is available. Remember that an apparently lifeless person who has been immersed in cold water for a long period may be revived if artificial ventilation is started immediately.

Psychiatric Emergencies

A psychiatric emergency is defined as a sudden onset of behavioral or emotional responses that, if not responded to, will result in a lifethreatening situation. Probably the most common psychiatric emergency is the suicide attempt. This may range from verbal threats and suicide gestures to successful suicide.

Always assume that a suicide threat is real; do not leave the patient alone. In all cases, the prime consideration is to keep patients from inflicting harm to themselves and getting them under the care of a trained psychiatric professional. In the case of gestures or attempts, treat self-inflicted wounds as any other wound. In the case of ingested substances, do not induce vomiting in the patient who is not awake and alert.

For specific treatment of ingested substances, refer to the

section on poisons. There are numerous other psychiatric conditions that would require volumes to expound upon. In almost all cases, first aid treatment is a calm, professional understanding demeanor without aggravating or agitating the patient.

With the assaultive or hostile patient, a "show of force" may be all that is required. Almost all cases of psychiatric emergencies will present with a third party, either the family or friend of the patient, who has recognized a distinct change in the behaviour pattern of the patient and who is seeking help for them.

Dermatologic Emergencies

Most dermatologic cases that present as emergencies are not really emergencies. The patient perceives them as such because of the sudden presentation and/or repulsive appearance or excessive discomfort.

Most dermatologic conditions are treated symptomatically. The major exception to this is toxic epidermal necrolysis (TEN). Toxic epidermal necrolysis is a condition of sudden onset characterized by excessive skin irritation, painful erythema, bullae, and exfoliation of the skin in sheets.

It is also known as the scalded skin syndrome because of its appearance. It is thought to be caused by a staphylococcal infection in children and a toxic reaction to medications in adults.

Since skin is the largest single organ of the body and serves as a barrier to infection, prevention of secondary infection is of utmost concern. Treatment consists of isolation techniques, silver nitrate compresses, aggressive skin care, intravenous antibiotic therapy (Nafcillin or Methicillin) and, in drug induced cases, systemic steroids.

Emergency Childbirth

Every corpsman must be prepared to handle the unexpected arrival of a new life into the world. If the corpsman is fortunate, a prepackaged sterile delivery pack will be available. This will contain all the equipment needed to deliver a normal baby. If the pack is not available, imaginative improvisation of clean alternatives will be needed.

When the corpsman is faced with an imminent childbirth, the first determination to be made is whether there will be time to transport the expectant mother to a hospital. To help make this determination, the corpsman should try to find out whether or not this will be the woman's first delivery (first deliveries usually take much longer than subsequent deliveries); how far apart the contractions are (if less than 3 minutes, delivery is approaching); whether or not a mother senses that she has to move her bowels (if so then the baby's head is well advanced down the birth canal); whether or not there is crowning (bulging) of the orifice (crowning indicates that the baby is ready to present itself); and how long it will take to get to the hospital.

The corpsman must weigh the answers to these questions to decide if it will be safe to transport the patient to the hospital. Prior to childbirth a corpsman must quickly "set the stage" to aid the event. The mother must not be allowed to go to the bathroom since the straining may precipitate the delivery in the worst possible location.

Do not try to inhibit the natural process of childbirth by having the mother cross her legs. The mother should be lying back on a sturdy table, bed, or stretcher. A folded sheet or blanket should be placed under her buttocks for absorption and comfort. Remove all clothing below the waist, bend the knees and move the thighs apart, and drape the woman with clean towels or sheets. The corpsman should then don sterile gloves or, if these are not available, rewash his or her hands.

In a normal delivery, your calm professional manner and sincere reassurance to the mother will go a long way towards alleviating her anxiety and making the delivery easier for everyone. Help the woman rest and relax as much as possible between contraction. During contraction, deep, open mouth breathing will relieve some pain and straining.

As the child's head reaches the area of the rectum, its pressure will cause the mother to feel an urgent need to defecate. Reassurance that this is a natural feeling and a sign that the baby will soon be born will alleviate her apprehension. Watch for the presentation of the top of the head. Once it appears, take up your station at the foot of the bed and gently push against the head to keep it from popping out in a rush. Allow it to come out slowly.

As more of the head appears, check to be sure that the umbilical cord is not wrapped around the neck. If it is, gently try to untangle it, or move one section over the baby's shoulder. If this is impossible, clamp in two places, 2 inches apart, and cut it.

Once the chin emerges, use the bulb syringe from the pack to suction the nostrils and mouth while you support the head with one hand. Compress the bulb prior to placing it in the mouth or nose; otherwise, there will be a forceful aspiration into the lungs. The baby will now start a natural rotation to the left or right, away from the face down position. As this is occurring, keep the head in a natural relationship with the back.

The shoulders appear next, usually one at a time. From this point on, it is essential to remember that the baby is VERY slippery, and great care must be taken so that you do not drop it. The surface beneath the mother should extend at least 2 feet out from the buttocks so that the baby would not be hurt if it did slip out of your hands.

Keep one hand beneath the baby's head, and use the other to support its emerging body. Once the baby has been born, suction the nose and mouth again if breathing has not started. Wipe the face, nose, and mouth clean with sterile gauze. Your reward will be the baby's hearty greeting to the world. Clamp the umbilical cord as the pulsations cease.

Use two clamps from the prepackaged sterile delivery pack, 2 inches apart, with the first clamp 6 to 8 inches from the navel. Cut between the clamps. For safety, use gauze tape to tie the cord 1 inch from the clamp toward the navel. Secure the tie with a square knot. Wrap the child in a warm, sterile blanket and log the time of the child's arrival.

The placenta (afterbirth) will deliver itself in 10 to 20 minutes. This can be aided by massaging the mother's lower abdomen. Do not pull on the placenta. Log the time of its delivery, and wrap it up for hospital analysis. Place a small strip of tape (1/2 inch wide), folded and inscribed with the date, time of delivery, and mother's name, around the baby's wrist.

COMPLICATIONS IN CHILDBIRTH

Breech Delivery

If the baby's legs and buttocks emerge first, follow the steps for a normal delivery, supporting the lower extremities with one hand. If the head does not emerge within 3 minutes, try to maintain an airway by gently pushing fingers into the vagina, pushing the vagina away from the face and opening the baby's mouth with one finger. Get medical aid immediately.

Prolapsed Cord

If the cord precedes the baby, protect it with moist, sterile wraps. If a physician cannot be reached soon, place the mother in an extreme shock position, give her oxygen if available, and gently move your gloved hand into the vagina to keep its walls and the baby from compressing the cord. Get medical aid immediately.

Excessive Bleeding

If bleeding is severe, treat the mother for shock and give her oxygen. Place sanitary napkins over the vaginal entrance and rush her to a hospital.

Limb Presentation

If a single limb presents itself first, get the mother immediately to a hospital.

Chapter 13

Rescue and Transportation Procedures

It is a basic principle of first aid that an injured person must be given essential treatment before being moved. However, it is impossible to treat an injured person who is in a position of immediate danger. If the victim is drowning, or if his or her life is endangered by fire, steam, electricity, poisonous or explosive gases, or other hazards, rescue must take place before first aid treatment can be given. The life of an injured person may well depend upon the manner in which rescue and transportation to a medical treatment facility are accomplished.

Rescue operations must be accomplished quickly, but unnecessary haste is both futile and dangerous. After rescue and essential first aid treatment have been given, further transportation must be accomplished in a manner that will not aggravate the injuries. As a corpsman it may be your responsibility to direct, and be the primary rescuer in, these operations. The life and safety of the victim and the members of the rescue team may rest on your decisions. In this section, we will consider the use of common types of protective equipment, phases of rescue operations, ways of effecting rescue from dangerous situations, emergency methods of moving injured persons to safety, and procedures for transporting them after first aid has been given.

PROTECTIVE EQUIPMENT

The use of appropriate items of protective equipment will

increase your ability to effect rescue from life-threatening situations. Protective equipment that is generally available on naval vessels and some shore activities include the oxygen breathing apparatus (OBA); hose (air line) masks; protective (gas) masks; asbestos suits; steel-wire life lines; and devices for detecting oxygen insufficiency, explosive vapors, and some poisonous gases.

Oxygen Breathing Apparatus

An oxygen breathing apparatus (OBA) is provided for emergency use in compartments containing toxic gases and lacking sufficient oxygen to support life. The apparatus is particularly valuable for rescue purposes because it is a self-contained unit. The wearer is not dependent upon outside air or any type of air line within the effective life of the canister. There are several types of oxygen breathing apparati, but they are all similar in operation. Independence of the outside atmosphere is achieved by having air within the apparatus circulated through a canister.

Within the canister, oxygen is continuously generated. The effective life of the canister varies from 20 to 45 minutes, depending on the particular apparatus and the type of work being done. One of the newer types of oxygen breathing apparatus is designed so that you can change canisters without leaving the toxic atmosphere.

If you are to enter an extremely hazardous area, you should also wear a life-line. The life-line should be tended by two persons, one of whom is also wearing a breathing apparatus. Never allow oil or grease to come in contact with any part of an oxygen breathing apparatus.

Oxygen is violently explosive in the presence of oil or grease. If any part oft he apparatus becomes contaminated with oil or grease smudges, clean it before it is stowed. Care should be taken to prevent oil or oily water from entering the canister between the time it is opened and the time of disposal.

Hose (Air Line) Masks

Hose masks are part of the allowance of all ships having

repair party lockers. They are smaller than the oxygen breathing outfits and can therefore be used by persons who must enter voids or other spaces that have very small access hatches. The hose or air line mask consists essentially of a gas mask facepiece with an adjustable head harness and a length of airhose.

Note that the air line mask uses air rather than pure oxygen. It must never be connected to an oxygen bottle, oxygen cylinder, or other source of oxygen; even a small amount of oil or grease in the air line could combine rapidly with the oxygen and cause an explosion.

When properly connected to a suitable source of air, such as the low-pressure ship's service air line, the hose mask can be worn safely, even in spaces containing a high concentration of oil or gasoline vapors; for this service, the air line mask is superior to the oxygen breathing apparatus.

Safety belts are furnished with each air line mask and must be worn. A life-line must be fastened to the safety belt; and the life-line should be loosely lashed to the airhose to reduce the possibility of fouling. The airhose and life-line must be carefully tended at all times, so that they will not become fouled or cut. The person wearing the airline mask and the person tending the lines should maintain communication by means of standard divers' signals.

Protective (Gas) Masks

Protective masks provide respiratory protection against chemical, biological, and radiological warfare agents. They do not provide protection from the effects of carbon monoxide, carbon dioxide, and a number of industrial gases.

Protection from these gases is discussed in the section "Rescue from Unventilated Compartments." In emergencies, protective masks may be used for passage through a smoke-filled compartment or for entry into such a compartment to perform a job that can be done quickly, such as close a valve, secure a fan, or de-energize a circuit.

However, they provide only limited protection against smoke. The length of time you can remain in a smoke-filled compartment depends on the type of smoke and it concentration. The most important thing to remember about protective masks is that they do not manufacture or supply oxygen.

They merely filter the air as it passes through the canister. Therefore, the protective mask should not be used in air containing less than 16 per cent oxygen, or having a heavy concentration of smoke from oil fires excepts for very short periods of time.

Asbestos Suits

The Navy asbestos suit is made in a single unit, is easy to get into, and provides complete cover for the wearer. With it on, a firefighter can move quickly through flame to effect a rescue or to perform some other job that can be done quickly. While asbestos will not burn, it will char and conduct heat.

Therefore, the suit provides protection against flame only for short periods of time. The length of time the suit can be worn depends upon the conditions under which it is used.

The person wearing the suit should return immediately to a safe, cool area if he or she experiences severe discomfort such as difficulty in breathing or extreme heat. Heavy clothing should be worn under the suit to give additional protection from heat.

If the asbestos suit becomes wet, as is more than likely in firefighting, the wearer might be scalded unless withdrawal from the heated area is accomplished before the water turns to steam. Continued wetting will keep the wearer cool, but the suit will become water soaked and reduce freedom of movement, already restricted by the cumbersome suit.

Life-lines

The life-line is a steel-wire cable, 50 feet long. Each end is equipped with a strong hook that closes with a snap catch. The line is very pliable and will slide freely around obstructions. Life-lines are used as a precautionary measure to aid in the rescue of persons wearing rescue breathing apparatus, hose masks, or similar equipment.

Rescue, if necessary, should be accomplished by having another person equipped with a breathing apparatus follow the life-line to the person being rescued, rather than by attempting to drag the person out. Attempts to drag a person from a space may result in fouling the life-line on some obstruction or in parting the harness, in which case it would still be necessary to send a rescue person into the space.

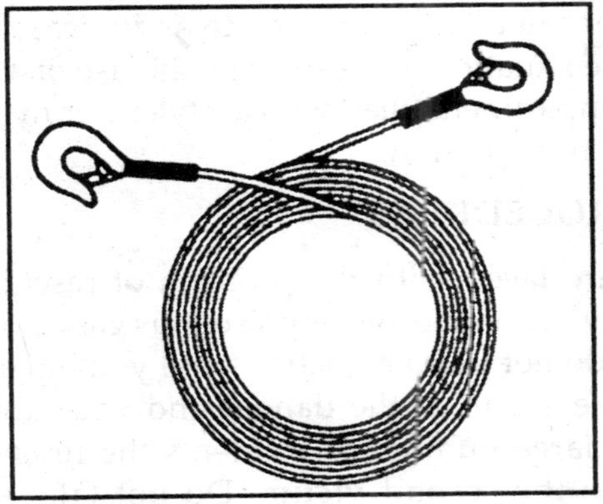

Fig. Steel Wire Life-line.

An important point to remember is that a stricken person must never be hauled by a life-line attached to the waist. The victim may be dragged along the deck a short distance, but his or her weight must never be suspended on a line attached to the waist.

If not wearing a harness of some kind, pass the line around the chest under the armpits and fasten it in front or in back. When tending a life-line, you must wear gloves to be able to handle the line properly. Play out the line carefully, so that it will not foul. Try to keep the life-line in contact with grounded metal; do not allow it to come in contact with any energized electrical equipment.

Detection Devices

The detection devices used to test the atmosphere in closed or poorly ventilated spaces include the Oxygen Indicator, for detecting oxygen deficiency; Combustible-gas

Indicators, for determining the concentration of explosive vapors; and Toxic-gas Indicators, such as the Carbon Monoxide Indicator for finding the concentration of certain poisonous gases.

The devices are extremely valuable and should be used whenever necessary; however, they Must Be Used Only As Directed. Improper operation of these devices may lead to false assurances of safety or, worse yet, to an increase in the actual danger of the situation. For example, the use of a flame safety lamp in a compartment filled with acetylene or hydrogen could cause a violent explosion.

RESCUE PROCEDURES

If you are faced with the problem of rescuing a person threatened by fire, explosive or poisonous gases, or some other emergency, do not take any action until you have had time to determine the extent of the danger and your ability to cope with it. In a large number of accidents the rescuer rushes in and becomes the second victim. Do not take unnecessary chances! Do not attempt any rescue that needlessly endangers your own life!

Phases of Rescue Operations

In disasters where there are multiple patients (as in explosions or ship collisions), rescue operations should be performed in phases. These rescue phases apply only to extrication operations.

The first phase is to remove lightly pinned casualties, such as those who can be freed by lifting boxes or removing a small amount of debris. In the second phase remove those casualties who are trapped in more difficult circumstances but who can be rescued by use of the equipment at hand and in a minimum amount of time.

In the third phase remove casualties where extrication is extremely difficult and time consuming. This type of rescue may involve cutting through decks, breaching bulkheads, removing large amounts of debris, or cutting through an expanse of metal. An example would be rescuing a worker from beneath a large, heavy piece of machinery. The last phase is the removal of dead bodies.

Stages of Extrication

The first stage of extrication within each of the rescue phases outlined above is gaining access to the victim. Much will depend on the location of the accident, damage within the accident site, and the position of the victim. The means of gaining access must also take into account the possibility of causing further injury to the victim since force may be needed. Further injury must be minimized. The second stage involves giving lifesaving emergency care.

If necessary, establish and maintain an open airway, start artificial respiration, and control hemorrhage. The third stage is disentanglement. The careful removal of debris and other impediments from the victim will prevent further injury to both the victim and the rescuer.

The fourth stage is preparing the victim for removal, with special emphasis on the protection of possible fractures. The final stage, removing the victim from the trapped area and transporting to an ambulance or sickbay, may be as simple as helping the victim walk out of the area or as difficult as a blanket dragged out of a burning space.

Rescue from Fire

If you must go to the aid of a person whose clothing is on fire, try to smother the flames by wrapping the victim in a coat, blanket, or rug. Leave the head Uncovered. If you have no material with which to smother the fire, roll the victim over—Slowly—and beat out the flames with your hands. Beat out the flames around the head and shoulders, and then work downward toward the feet.

If the victim tries to run, throw him or her down. Remember that the victim Must lie down while you are trying to extinguish the fire. Running will cause the clothing to burn rapidly. Sitting or standing may cause the victim to be killed instantly by inhaling flames or hot air.

Caution: Inhaling flame or hot air can kill you, too. Do

not get your face directly over the flames. Turn your face away from the flame when you inhale. If your own clothing catches fire, roll yourself up in a blanket, coat, or rug.

Keep Your Head Uncovered: If material to smother the fire is not available, lie down, roll over slowly, and beat at the flames with your hands. If you are trying to escape from an upper floor of a burning building, be very cautious about opening doors into hallways or stairways. Always feel a door before you open it; if it feels hot, do not open it if there is any other possible way out.

Remember, also, that opening doors or windows will create a draft and make the fire worse; so do not open any door or window until you are actually ready to get out. If you are faced with the problem of removing an injured person from an upper story of a burning building, you may be able to improvise a life-line by tying sheets, blankets, curtains, or other materials together, using square knots.

Secure one end around some heavy object inside the building, and fasten the other end around the casualty under the arms. You can lower the victim to safety and then let yourself down the line.

Do not jump from an upper floor of a burning building except as a last resort. It is often said the the "best" air in a burning room or compartment is near the floor, but this is true only to a limited extent. There is less smoke and flame down low, near the floor, and the air may be cooler; but carbon monoxide and other deadly gases are just as likely to be present near the floor as near the ceiling.

If possible, use an oxygen breathing apparatus or other protective breathing equipment when you go into a burning compartment. If protective equipment is not available, cover your mouth and nose with a wet cloth to reduce the danger of inhaling smoke, flame, or hot air.

Remember, However, that a wet cloth gives you no Protection Against Poisonous gases or lack of Oxygen!

Rescue from Steam-filled Spaces

It is sometimes possible to rescue a person from a space

in which there is a steam leak. Since steam rises, escape upward may not be possible, If the normal exit is blocked by escaping steam, move the casualty to the escape trunk or, if there is none, to the lowest level in the compartment.

The equipment that offers protection against fire does not protect you against steam. In particular, it should be mentioned that the asbestos suit absorbs water and is therefore of no value in a steam-filled space. Steam would penetrate the asbestos very quickly, and the person wearing the suit would be scalded.

Rescue from Electrical Contact

Rescuing a person who has received an electrical shock is likely to be difficult and dangerous. Extreme caution must be used, or you may be electrocuted yourself. You must not touch the Victim's Body, the wire, or any other object that may be conducting electricity. Look for the switch first of all; if you find it, turn off the current immediately.

Do not waste too much time hunting for the switch; every second is important. If you cannot find the switch, try to remove the wire from the victim with a DRY broom handle, branch, pole, oar, board, or similar Nonconducting object.

It may be possible to use a dry rope or dry clothing to pull the wire away from the victim. You can also break the contact by cutting the wire with a Woodenhandled axe, but this is extremely dangerous because the cut ends of the wire are likely to curl and lash back at you before you have time to get out of the way. When you are trying to break an electrical contact, always stand on some nonconducting material such as a Dry board, Dry newspapers, or Dry clothing.

Rescue from Unventilated Compartments

Rescuing a person from a void, double bottom, gasoline or oil tank, or any closed compartment or unventilated space is generally a very hazardous operation. Aboard naval vessels and at naval shore activities, no person is permitted to enter any such space or compartment until a damage control officer (DCO), or some person designated by the DCO, has indicated that the likelihood of suffocation, poisoning, and fire or explosion have been eliminated as far as possible.

The rescue of a person from any closed space should therefore be performed under the supervision of the DCO or in accordance with the DCO's instructions. In general, it is necessary to observe the following precautions when attempting to rescue a person from any closed or poorly ventilated space:

- If possible, test the air for oxygen deficiency, poisonous gases, and explosive vapors.
- Wear a hose (air line) mask or oxygen breathing apparatus. The air line mask is preferred for use in spaces that may contain high concentrations of oil or gasoline vapors. Do not depend upon a protective mask or a wet cloth held over your face to protect you from oxygen deficiency or poisonous gases.
- Before going into a compartment that may contain explosive vapors, be sure that people are stationed nearby with fireextinguishing equipment.
- When going into any space that may be deficient in oxygen or contain poisonous or explosive vapors, be sure to maintain communication with someone outside. Wear a life-line, and be sure that it is tended by a competent person.
- Do not use, wear, or carry any object or material that might cause a spark. Matches, cigarette lighters, flashlights, candles or other open flames, and ordinary electrical lights must Never be taken into a compartment that may contain explosive vapors. The kind of portable light used by cleaning parties in boilers, fuel tanks, and similar places may be taken into a suspect compartment; this is a steam-tight, glovetype light whose exposed metal parts are either made of nonsparking alloy or protected in some way so they will not strike a spark.

Electrical apparatus or tools that might spark must never be taken into a compartment until a DCO has indicated that it is safe to do so. When electrical equipment is used (e.g., an electric blower might be used to vent a compartment of explosive vapors) it must be explosion proof and properly grounded. If you go into a space that may contain explosive vapors, do not wear clothing that has any exposed spark producing metal. For example, do not wear boots or shoes that have exposed nailheads or rivets, and do not wear coveralls or other garments that might scrape against metal and cause a spark.

A particular caution must be made concerning the use of the steelwire life-line in compartments that may contain explosive vapors. If you use the line, be sure that it is carefully tended and properly grounded at all times. When other considerations permit, you should use a rope line instead of the steel-wire life-line when entering compartments that may contain explosive vapors.

Rescue from the Water

You should never attempt to swim to the rescue of a drowning person unless you have been trained in lifesaving methods—and then only if there is no better way of reaching the victim. A drowning person may panic and fight against you so violently that you will be unable either to carry out the rescue or to save yourself.

Even if you are not a trained lifesaver, however, you can help a drowning person by holding out a pole, oar, branch, or stick for the victim to catch hold of or by throwing a life-line or some buoyant object that will support the victim in the water. Various methods are used aboard ship to pick up survivors from the water.

The methods used in any particular instance will depend upon weather conditions, the type of equipment available aboard the rescue vessel, the number of people available for rescue operations, the physical condition of the people requiring rescue, and other factors. In many cases it has been found that the best way to rescue a person from the water is to send out a properly trained and properly equipped swimmer with a life-line.

It is frequently difficult to get survivors up to the deck of the rescuing vessel, even after they have been brought alongside the vessel. Cargo nets are often used, but many survivors are unable to climb them without assistance. Persons equipped with life-lines (and, if necessary, dressed in antiexposure suits) can be sent over the side to help survivors up the nets.

If survivors are covered with oil, it may take the combined efforts of four or five people to get one survivor up the net. A seriously injured person should never, except in an extreme emergency, be hauled out of the water by means of a rope or life-line.

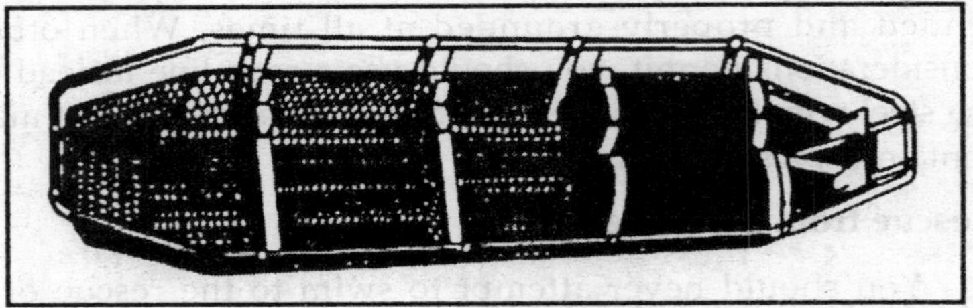

Fig. Stokes Stretcher

Special methods must be devised to provide proper support, to keep the victim in a horizontal position, and to provide protection from any kind of jerking, bending, or twisting motion. The Stokes stretcher can often be used to rescue an injured survivor.

The stretcher is lowered into the water, and the survivor is floated into position over it. People on the deck of the ship can then bring the stretcher up by means of handlines. Life preservers, balsa wood, unicellular material, or other flotation gear can be used if necessary to keep the stretcher afloat.

Moving the victim to Safety

In an emergency, there are many ways to move a victim to safety, ranging from one-person carries to stretchers and spineboards. The vicitim's conditions and the immediacy of danger will dictate the appropriate methods, but remember to give all necessary first aid before moving the victim.

Stretchers

The military uses a number of standard stretchers.The following discussion will familiarize you with the most common types. When using a stretcher, you should consider a few general rules:

- Use standard stretchers when available, but be ready to improvise safe alternatives.
- When possible, bring the stretcher to the casualty.
- Always fasten the victim securely to the stretcher.
- Always move the victim feet first so the rear bearer can watch for signs of breathing difficulty.

STOKES STRETCHER.

The Navy service litter most commonly need for transporting sick or injured persons is called the stokes stretcher. The Stokes stretcher is essentially a wire basket supported by iron rods but a new version is made of molded plastic. It is adaptable to a variety of uses, since the casualty can be held securely in place even if the stretcher is tipped or turned. The Stokes stretcher is particularly valuable for transferring injured persons to and from boats. As mentioned before, it can be used with flotation devices to rescue injured survivors from the water. It is also used for direct ship-to-ship transfer of injured persons. Fifteenfoot handling lines are attached to each end for shipboard use in moving the victim.

The Stokes stretcher should be padded with three blankets: two of them should be placed lengthwise, so that one will be under each of the casualties legs, and the third should be folded in half and placed in the upper part of the stretcher to protect the head and shoulders. The casualty should be lowered gently into the stretcher and made as comfortable as possible.

The feet must be fastened to the end of the stretcher so that the casualty will not slide down. Another blanket (or more, if necessary) should be used to cover the casualty. The casualty must be fastened to the stretcher by means of straps that go over the chest, hips, and knees. Note that the straps go over the blanket or other covering, thus holding it in place.

Army Litter

The Army litter is a collapsible stretcher made of canvas and supported by wooden or aluminum poles. It is very useful for transporting battle casualties in the field.

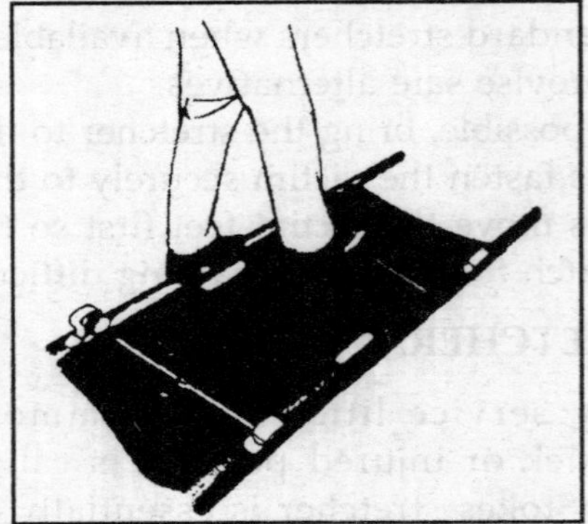

Fig. Opening an Army Litter.

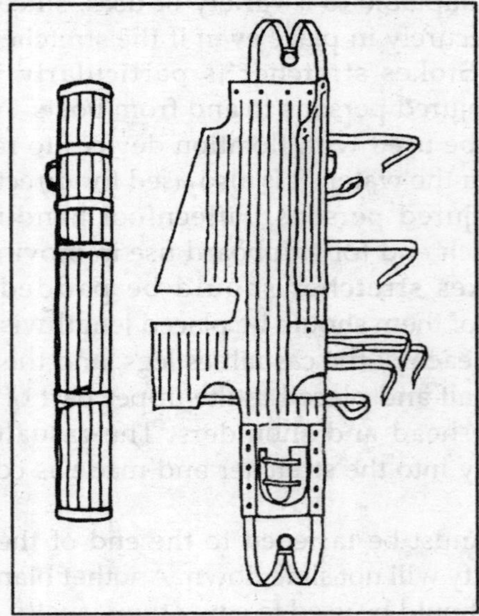

Fig. Neil Robertson Stretcher

However, it is sometimes difficult to fasten the casualty onto the Army litter, and for this reason its use is somewhat limited aboard ship. The litter legs keep the patient off the ground and fit it into the restraining tracks of a jeep or field ambulance to hold the litter in place during transport.

Neil Robertson Stretcher

The Neil Robertson stretcher is especially designed for removing an injured person from engine rooms, holds, and other compartments where access hatches are too small to permit the use of regular stretchers. You can also use it to hoist a casualty aboard a hovering helicopter by attaching a rescue line. The Neil Robertson stretcher is made of semirigid canvas with sewn-in wooden slats sewn the length of the stretcher.

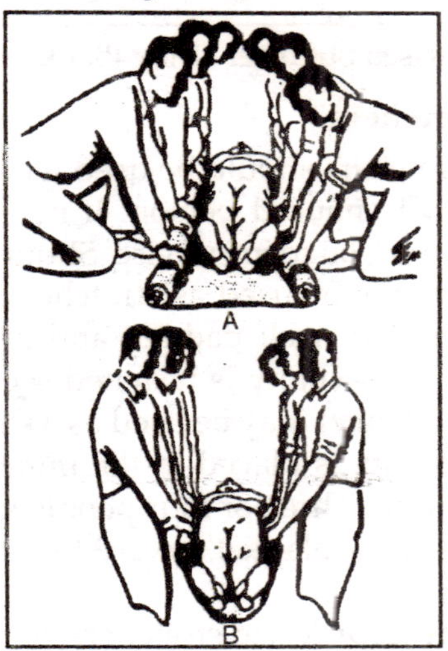

Fig. Blanket used as an Improvised Stretcher.

When firmly wrapped around the casualty mummy-fashion, it gives sufficient support for a vertical lift. A guideline is tied to the bottom ring to keep the casualty from swaying against bulkheads and hatchways while being lifted.

Stretchers of this type can be made on board ship and kept in appropriate places ready for use. If a Neil Robertson stretcher is not available when needed, a piece of heavy canvas, wrapped firmly around the casualty, will serve somewhat the same purpose. Periodically check your ship's Neil Robertson stretchers for dry rot or other damaged caused by humidity, sea water, or handling.

Fig. Improvised Stretcher Using Blankets and Poles.

Improvised Stretchers

Standard stretchers should be used whenever possible to transport a seriously injured person. If none are available, it may be necessary for you to improvise. Shutters, doors, boards, and even ladders may be used as stretchers. All stretchers of this kind must be very well padded and great care must be taken to see that the casualty is fastened securely in place.

Sometimes a blanket may be used as a stretcher, as shown in figure. The casualty is placed in the middle of the blanket in the supine position. Three or four people kneel on each side and roll the edges of the blanket toward the casualty, as shown in figure.

Caution: Many improvised stretchers do not give sufficient support in cases where there are fractures or extensive wounds of the body. They should be used only when the casualty is able to stand some sagging, bending, or twisting without serious consequences. An example of this type of improvised stretcher would be one made of 40 to 50 feet of rope or 1 1/2-inch firehose.

Spineboards

Spineboards are essential equipment in the immobilization of suspected or real fractures of the spinal column. Made of fiberglass or exterior plywood, they come in two sizes, short (18" x 32") and long (18" x 72"), and are provided with handholds and straps, and have a runner on the bottom to allow clearance to lift. A short spineboard is primarily used in extrication of sitting victims, especially in automobile wrecks, where it would be difficult to maneuver the victim out of position. Improvised stretcher using rope or firehose damage to the spine.

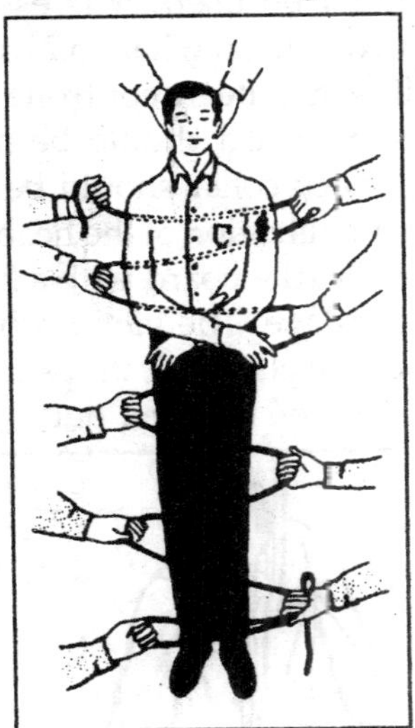

Fig. Improvised Stretcher Using Rope or Firehose

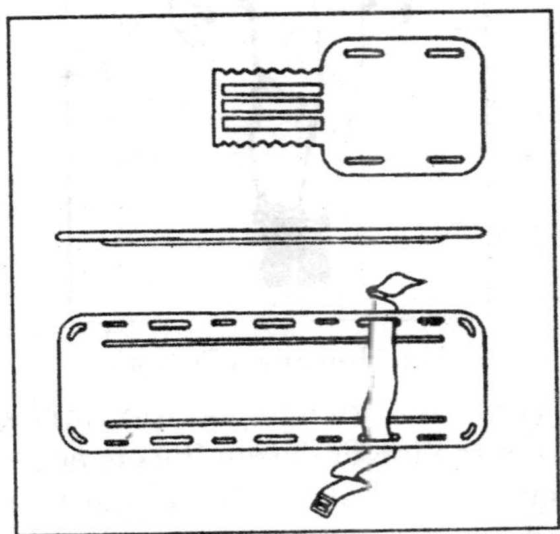

Fig. Spineboards.

The long board makes a firm litter, protecting the back and neck, and providing a good surface for CPR and a good sliding surface for difficult extrications. The short and long boards are often used together. For example, at an automobile accident site, the corpsman's first task is to assess the whole situation and to plan the rescue.

If bystanders must be used, it is essential that they be thoroughly briefed, in detail, on what you want them to do. After all accessible bleeding has been controlled and the fractures splinted, the short spineboard should be moved into position behind the victim. A neck collar should be applied in all cases and will aid in the immobilization of the head and neck. The head should then be secured to the board with a headband or a 6-inch self-adhering roller bandage. The victim's body is then secured to the board by use of the supplied straps around the chest and thighs. The victim may then be lifted out.

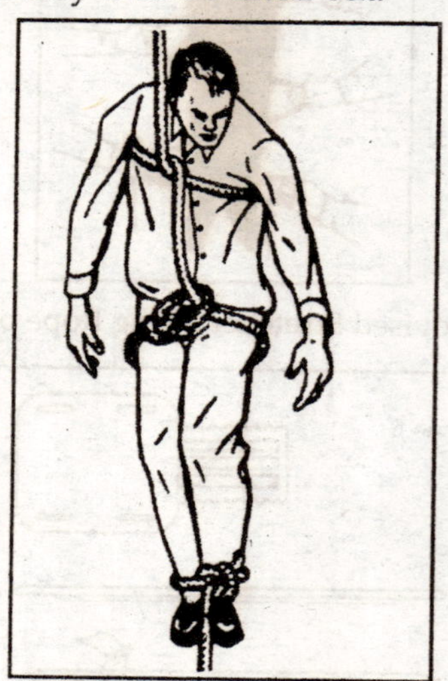

Fig. Hoisting a Person.

If, however, the victim is too large, or further immobilization of the lower extremities is necessary, the long spineboard may be slid at a right angle behind the short spineboard, and the victim is maneuvered onto his or her side and secured to the long board. The possible uses of the spineboard in an emergency situation are limited only by the imagination of the rescuers.

LIFTS, DRAGS, AND CARRIES

Emergency Rescue Lines

A s previously mentioned, the steel-wire life-line can often be used to haul a person to safety. An emergency rescue line can also be made from any strong fibre line. Both should be used only in extreme emergencies, when an injured person must be moved and no other means is available.

An emergency rescue line that could be used to hoist a person from a void or small compartment. Notice that a running bowline is passed around the body, just below the hips, and a half hitch is placed just under the arms. Notice also that a guideline is tied to the casualty's ankles to prevent banging against bulkheads and hatchways.

Fireman's Carry

One of the easiest ways to carry an unconscious person is by means of the fireman's carry.

- Place the casualty in the prone position. Face the victim, and kneel on one knee at his or her head.

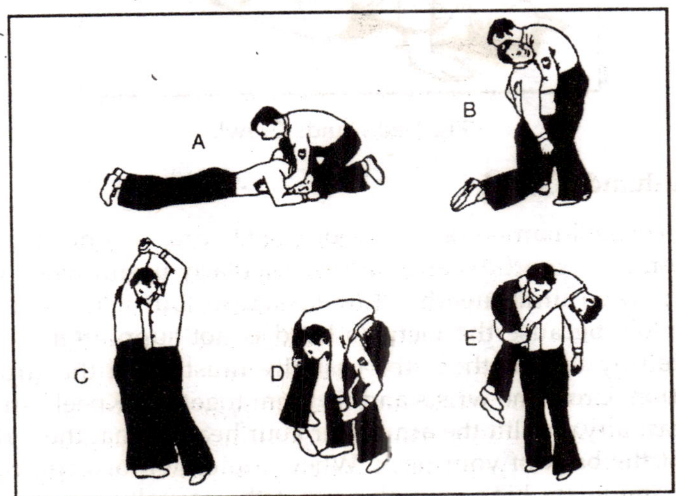

Fig. Fireman's

Pass your hands under the armpits; then slide your hands down the sides and clasp them across the back.

- Raise the casualty to the kneeling position. Take a better hold across the back.
- Raise the casualty to a standing position and place your right leg between the legs. Grasp the right wrist in your left hand and swing the arm around the back of your neck and down your left shoulder.
- Stoop quickly and pull the casualty across your shoulders and, at the same time, put your right arm between the legs.
- Grasp the right wrist with your right hand an straighten up.

Fig. Tied Hands Crawl.

Tied-hands Crawl

The tied-hands crawl, may be used to drag an unconscious person for a short distance. It is particularly useful when you must crawl underneath a low structure, but it is the least desirable because the victim's head is not supported. To be carried by this method, the casualty must be in the supine position. Cross the wrists and tie them together. Kneel astride the casualty and lift the arms over your head so that the wrists are at the back of your neck. When you crawl forward, raise your shoulders high enough so that the casualty's head will not bump against the deck.

Blanket Drag

The blanket drag can be used to move a person who, due to the severity of the injury, should not be lifted or carried by one person alone. Place the casualty in the supine position on a blanket and pull the blanket along the floor or deck.

Always pull the casualty head first, with the head and shoulders slightly raised, so that the head will not bump against the deck.

Pack-strap Carry

With the packstrap carry it is possible to carry a heavy person for some distance. Use the following procedure:

- Place the casualty in a supine position.
- Lie down on your side along the casualty's uninjured or less injured side. Your shoulder should be next to the casualty's armpit.

Fig. Blanket Drag.

Fig. Packstrap Carry.

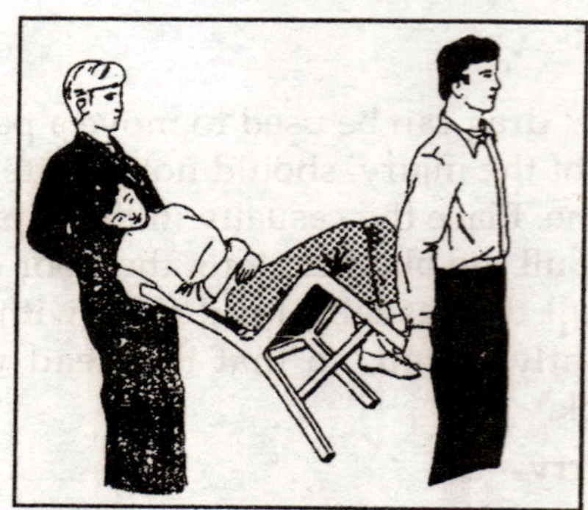

Fig. Chair Carry.

- Pull the casualty's far leg over your own, holding it there if necessary.
- Grasp the casualty's far arm at the wrist and bring it over your upper shoulder as you roll and pull the casualty onto your back.
- Raise up on your knees, using your free arm for balance and support. Hold both the casualty's wrists close against your chest with your other hand.
- Lean forward as you rise to your feet, and keep both of your shoulders under the casualty's armpits. Do not attempt to carry a seriously injured person by means of the pack-strap carry, especially if the arms, spine, neck, or ribs are fractured.

Chair Carry

The chair carry can often by used to move a sick or injured person away from a position of danger. The casualty is seated on a chair and the chair is carried by two rescuers.

This is a particularly good method to use when you must carry a person up or down stairs or through narrow, winding passageways. It must never be used to move a person who has an injured neck, back, or pelvis.

Arm Carries

There are several kinds of arm carries that can be used in emergency situations to move an injured person to safety.

Fig. One-person Arm Carry.

Figure shows how one person can carry the casualty alone. However, you should never try to carry a person this way who is seriously injured. Unless considerably smaller than you are, you will not be able to carry the casualty very far by this method

The two-person arm carry can be used in some cases to move an injured person. However, it should not be used to carry a person who has serious wounds or broken bones. Another two-person carry that can be used in emergencies. Two rescuers position themselves beside the casualty, on the same side, one at the level of the chest and the other at the thighs.

The rescuers interlock their adjacent arms as shown, while they support the victim at the shoulders and knees. In unison they lift the victim and roll his or her front toward theirs. This carry must not be used to move seriously injured persons.

TRANSPORTATION OF THE INJURED

Thus far in this chapter we have dealt with Emergency methods used to move an injured person out of danger and into a position where first aid can be administered. As we have seen, these emergency rescue procedures often involve substantial risk to the casualty and should be used Only when clearly necessary. Once you have rescued the casualty from the immediate danger, Slow Down! From this point on, handle and transport the casualty with every regard for the injuries that have been sustained. In the excitement and confusion that almost always accompany an accident, you are likely to feel rushed, wanting to do everything rapidly.

Fig. Two-person Arm Carry.

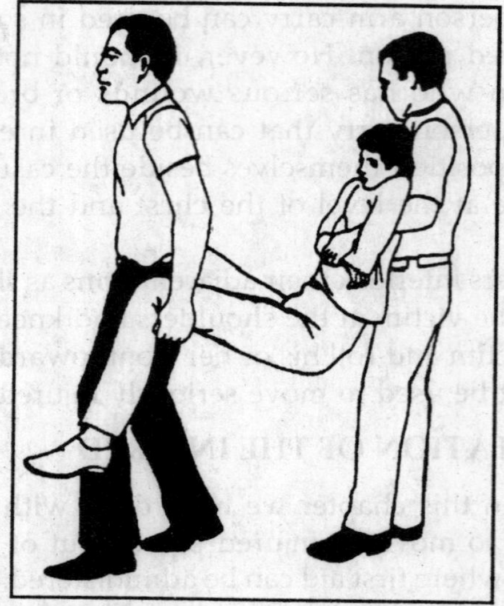

Fig. Two-person Arm Carry (Alternate).

To a certain extent this is a reasonable feeling. Speed is essential in treating many injuries and in getting the casualty to a medical treatment facility, However, it is not reasonable to let yourself feel so hurried that you become careless and transport the victim in a way that will aggravate the injuries.

Emergency Vehicles, Equipment, and Supplies

In most peacetime emergency situations, some form of ambulance will be available to transport the victim to a medical treatment facility. Navy ambulances vary in size and shape from the old "gray ghost" to modern van and modular units. Although there are many differences in design and storage capacity, most Navy ambulances are equipped to meet the same basic emergency requirements.

They contain equipment and supplies for emergency airway care, artificial ventilation, suction, oxygenation, hemorrhage control, fracture immobilization, shock control, blood pressure monitoring, and poisoning.

Fig. Two-person Arm Carry (Alternate)

They will also contain a wheeled litter, an Army litter, and both long and short spineboards. Supplies you may find include the following:

- *Airways:* Oropharyngeal airways come in sizes for adults, children, and infants. In addition, padded tongue blades or bite sticks for convulsive seizures, and tracheotomy tubes for victims with a tracheotomy will be provided.

- *Artificial Ventilation Devices:* Ambu-Bag (1 or 2) with masks of different sizes and oxygen enrichment capability.
- *Suction Equipment:* Portable and/or installed suction equipment for pharyngeal and tracheotomy suction, with tubes, tips, and collection bottles.
- *Oxygen Supply:* A portable unit with an extra cylinder and masks of different sizes.
- *Hemorrhage Control*: Sterile gauze pads, battle dressings, soft self-adhering roller bandages, adhesive tape, safety pins, and bandage scissors.
- *Splinting Supplies:* Various materials for upper and lower extremity splints, and triangular bandages.
- *Shock Control:* Intravenous fluids in unbreakable containers, and administration kits, as determined by local directives.
- *Blood Pressure Monitoring:* Blood pressure cuff and stethoscope.
- Poison Response: Lpecac syrup in measured doses.

SPINEBOARD

Long and short for spinal immobilization, extrication, and as a CPR surface. Deployed units at sea and in the field and certain commands near air stations will also have access to helicopter Medevac support.

Helicopters are ideal for use in isolated areas but are of limited practical use at night, in adverse weather, under certain tactical conditions, or in developed areas where building and power lines interfere. In addition to taking these factors into consideration, the corpsman must decide if the victim's condition is serious enough, or too serious, to justify a call for the helicopter.

Some injuries require very smooth transportation or are affected by the pressure changes incurred in flight. The final decision will be made by the unit commander, who is responsible for requesting the helicopter support. Field operational units will have access to field ambulances, jeeps, and "gamma-goats" for casualty transportation. They have room for two to four Army litters and are used for behind the lines movement.

Care en Route

The emergency care a corpsman can offer patients en route is limited only by the availability of supplies, the level of external noise and vibrations, and the degree of skill and ingenuity the corpsman possesses.

Care at the Medical Treatment Facility do not turn the victim over to anyone without giving a complete account of the situation, especially if a tourniquet was used or medications administered.

If possible, while en route, write down the circumstances of the accident, the treatment given, and keep a log of vital signs. After turning the patient over to the medical treatment facility, ensure that depleted ambulance supplies are replaced so that the vehicle is in every way ready to handle another emergency.

Index

A

Abdominal 27, 40, 42, 48, 51, 60, 80, 81, 82, 84, 91, 115, 137, 138, 149, 169, 199, 216, 217, 218, 229, 236, 238, 268, 270, 277, 278, 280
Abrasions 134, 177
Accident 95, 103, 264, 266, 282, 293, 299, 302
Acute Myocardial Infarction 267, 268, 269
Adrenal Glands 57, 74
Adrenal Medulla 74, 75
Airway Obstruction 100, 109, 110, 111, 112, 113, 115, 117, 129, 168
Amputations 134, 135, 141, 181
Anaphylactic 181, 185, 226, 267
Angina Pectoris 267, 268
Appendicular Skeleton 13, 16
Artificial Ventilation 112, 113, 117, 118, 120, 122, 123, 124, 128, 219, 223, 232, 271, 300
Asbestos Suits 277, 279
Avulsions 134, 135
Axial Skeleton 13

B

Bandages 97, 106, 132, 143, 144, 145, 146, 149, 150, 151, 192, 195, 207, 210, 211, 214, 215, 260, 301
Barbiturate 237, 238
Battle Dressings 106, 107, 160,
Bladder 9, 25, 40, 61, 62, 80, 82, 86, 88, 209, 270
Blanket Drag 282, 296
Blood 5, 7, 8, 10, 23, 24, 25, 2 31, 38, , 48, 74, 75, 96, 99, 117, 133, 134, 142, 143, 162, 163, 164, 167, 185, , 195, 197, 198, 200, 209, 210, 211, 215, 216, 231, 232, 268, 269, 300, 301
Bones 1, 6, 10, 12, 13, 15, 16, 17, 18, 19, 20, 21, 22, 25, 29, 48, 68, 73, 74, 100, 139, 140, 191, 192, 195, 198, 199, 215, 298
Brain 8, 13, 31, 39, 42, 49, 52, 53, 58, 60, 61, 65, 68, 69, 70, 72, 96, 117, 133, 205, 252, 253, 254, 264, 265, 266, 270
Breech Delivery 275
Bulbourethral Glands 89
Burns 97, 101, 134, 181, 189, 190, 220, 225, 242, 243, 244, 245, 246, 247, 248, 249, 250

C

Cannabis Intoxication 240

Cardiogenic Shock 181, 185, 186, 188
Casualty 107, 108, 109, 176, 190, 257, 283, 284, 288, 289, 290, 291, 294, 295, 296, 297, 298, 299, 300, 301
Cell 3, 4, 5, 6, 8, 9, 10, 24, 30, 31, 32, 33, 34, 35, 37, 42, 43, 44, 89, 94, 163, 164, 174, 175, 186, 231, 234, 241, 264
Central Nervous System 23, 31, 52, 102, 184, 238, 239, 265, 269
Chemical Burns 190, 225, 248, 249, 250
Chest Thrusts 115,116, 128
Chest Wounds 168, 181
Childbirth 92, 272, 273,275
Circulatory System 32, 122, 136, 184, 185
Clavicle 17, 27, 39, 101, 138, 200, 201
Contusion 99, 142, 191, 201, 210, 215, 216
Convulsions 74, 219, 227, 238, 269, 270
Corrosives 219, 220, 222
Cranial Nerves 57, 61
Cravat Bandage 156, 157, 158, 159, 196, 207
Cricothyroidotomy 125, 127

D

Deep Frostbite 259, 261
Diabetic 264, 265
Digestive System 45, 77, 81
Dislocations 191, 210, 211, 212

E

Electrical Burns 247,248
Emergency Childbirth 272
Endocrine System 51, 70, 71
Esophageal Obturator Airway 124
Esophagus 48, 58, 77, 78, 79, 125, 220
Evacuation 107, 109, 184, 247, 257, 265
Excessive Bleeding 275
Extrication 281, 282, 292, 293, 301

F

Facial Wounds 167
Fainting 184, 185, 264
Fallopian Tubes 92, 93, 94
First aid 95, 96, 105, 107, 121, 127, 132, 133, 136, 138, 145, 160, 163, 167, 168, 169, 171, 185, 226, 227, 228, 232, 235, 244, 246, 247, 250, 276, 287, 298
Fish Poisoning 222, 223
Fracture 129, 140, 187, 192, 193, 196, 197, 198, 199, 203, 204, 205, 206, 209, 211, 300
Frostbite 259, 260, 261

G

Gallbladder 40, 80, 82
Gastric Distention 120
Genitalia 90, 227
Gonads 72, 75, 92

H

Hallucinogen Intoxication 239
Hearing 13, 53, 58, 67, 68
Heart 8, 9, 26, 32, 33, 34, 35, 36, 37, 38, 40, 43, 48, 54, 57, 60, 103, 108, 110, 120, 121, 127,

128, 137, 138, 177, 187, 201, 233, 239, 252, 258, 267, 268, 269, 274
Heat Stroke 253
Heel 20, 114, 117, 118, 119, 129, 131, 138, 148, 150, 199, 214
Hemorrhage 35, 38, 96, 99, 129, 132, 136, 137, 138, 139, 140, 142, 167, 181, 183, 188, 190, 234, 235, 245, 246, 282, 300
Hypothermia 257, 258
Hypovolemic Shock 181, 183, 184

I

Improvised Stretchers 291
Impulse 51, 52, 56, 57
Incisions 134, 162
Infection 34, 68, 90, 132, 133, 134, 135, 136, 137, 161, 162, 163, 164, 173, 174, 178, 180, 181, 185, 242, 246, 272
Inflammation 48, 54, 81, 163, 164, 225
Ingested Poisons 219
Inhalation 48, 105, 186, 223, 224, 225
Insulin Shock 265, 266
Integumentary System 29
Intoxication 79, 236, 237, 238, 239, 240, 265

J

Jaw 13, 26, 72, 78, 113, 117, 118, 123, 124, 125, 128, 131, 138, 150, 157, 190, 203, 204, 211, 212, 213, 268, 270
Jaw Thrust 113, 117, 128, 131
Joints 6, 20, 21, 69, 180, 191, 210, 211, 212, 215

K

Ketoacidosis 264, 265
Kidneys 5, 7, 9, 40, 74, 75, 82, 85, 86, 133, 181, 183, 253
Kneecap 197, 199

L

Lacerations 100, 101, 102, 134
Large Intestine 80, 81
Limb Presentation 275
Liver 5, 9, 33, 35, 40, 41, 74, 75, 77, 80, 81, 82, 93, 105, 120, 121, 122, 123, 128, 129, 133, 253, 272, 273, 274, 275
Lymph 5, 7, 8, 32, 43, 44, 68, 69, 71, 88

M

Mask-to-Mask 119
Medications 97, 105, 176, 186, 218, 219, 263, 270, 272, 302
Middle Ear 67, 68, 69
Morphine 106, 182, 188, 189, 190, 227, 237, 246
Mouth-to-mouth 117, 118, 128
Mouth-to-nose 118, 128
Muscles 1, 6, 8, 10, 15, 19, 22, 23, 24, 25, 26, 27, 28, 29, 31, 37, 62, 64, 69, 73, 74, 75, 169, 195, 197, 198, 210, 211, 215, 258, 266

N

Narcotic 236, 237
Nasopharyngeal 121
Nervous System 23, 31, 51, 52, 55, 57, 59, 60, 70, 102, 181,

184, 238, 239, 256, 265, 269
Neuron 9, 11, 50, 51, 52, 53, 57

O

Organs 1, 3, 6, 7, 9, 10, 13, 31, 41, 42, 47, 51, 60, 75, 77, 78, 79, 80, 82, 87, 90, 91, 133, 169, 187, 191, 209, 244
Oropharyngeal 121, 122, 123, 300
Ovaries 72, 75, 90, 92
Oxygen Breathing Apparatus 277
Oxygen Breathing Apparatus 277, 278, 283, 285

P

Pack-strap Carry 296,297
Pancreas 40, 72, 75, 77, 80, 81, 264
Parasympathetic 58, 60, 61, 62
Parathyroid Glands 73, 74
Pelvis 15, 16, 19, 79, 83, 84, 85, 187, 197, 198, 209, 210, 297
Penis 87, 88, 89, 90, 91
Pharynx 45, 46, 47, 58, 68, 77, 78, 79, 100, 110, 121, 122, 127
Pituitary Gland 72, 92
Prolapsed Cord 275
Prostate Gland 87, 89
Psychiatric 271, 272

R

Reproductive System 72, 86, 87,90, 91
Respiration 23, 27, 44, 48, 49, 50, 70, 129, 190, 232, 238, 258, 264, 265, 266, 268, 269, 282
Roller Bandage 144, 145, 147, 149, 201, 210, 293, 301

S

Scorpion Stings 226, 227
Semen 89, 90
Septic Shock 181, 185
Shock 49, 96, 108, 121, 132, 133, , 186, 187, 188, 189, 190, 193, 203, 204, 206, 209, 211, 216, 253, 254, 258, 264, 265, 266, 267, 275, 284, 300, 301
Sight 53, 58, 62, 165
Skeletal System 10
Skeleton 10, 13, 16, 74
Skin 5, 30, 31, 32, 39, 41, 57, 58, 62, 69, 87, 89, 91, 111, 126, 178, 179, 180, 182, 190, 202, 246, 247, 248, 249, 250, 252, 261, 262, 265, 272
Skull 12, 13, 21, 53, 96, 99, 133, 138, 167, 203, 204, 205
Small Intestine 43, 79, 80, 82, 175
Smell 58, 61, 62
Snakebites 229, 232, 235
Soft Tissue 132, 136, 142, 143, 167
Spider Bites 227, 228
Spinal Cord 8, 13, 15, 52, 53, 54, 55, 56, 57, 59, 60, 205, 206, 207
Spinal Nerves 55, 57, 59, 60
Splints 105, 137, 191, 192, 194, 195, 197, 198, 199, 210, 211, 301
Sprains 191, 210, 214, 215
Stokes Stretcher 287, 288
Stomach 8, 25, 40, 70, 77, 79, 81, 120, 219, 220, 223
Syncope 143, 184, 264

T

Tactical 107, 108, 109, 172, 257, 301
Taste 58, 61, 62, 78, 219, 224, 232, 255
Thigh 18, 19, 20, 28, 29, 40, 42, 139, 154, 159, 197, 198, 200, 273, 293, 298
Thorax 13, 15, 16, 27, 38, 100, 101, 102, 103
Thyroid Gland 72, 73, 74
Tourniquet 106, 107, 135, 137, 140, 141, 142, 195, 302
Tranquilizer Intoxication 237
Transmission 51, 68
Trauma 97, 98, 99, 104, 135, 140, 142, 164, 176, 181, 185, 270
Triage 107, 108, 109, 245
Triangular Bandage 144, 151, 152, 153, 154, 155, 156

U

Ureters 9, 82, 86
Urethra 9, 82, 86, 87, 88, 89, 90, 91
Urinary System 9, 82, 86
Uterus 73, 75, 89, 90, 92, 93, 94

V

Vagina 86, 89, 90, 91, 93, 94, 142, 275
Venous Circulation 40,42
Vertebral 13, 14, 15, 16, 53, 54, 59, 101
Vision 32, 54, 58, 65, 66, 109, 165, 177, 185, 187, 246, 266, 285
Vital Signs 97, 98, 129, 131, 187, 188, 226, 232, 252, 263, 266, 268, 302

W

Wounds 97, 108, 132, 133, 134, 135, 142, 144, 145, 149, 156, 161, 162, 163, 165, 167, 168, 187, 190, 191, 195, 204, 205, 233, 234, 247, 251, 257, 271